Essays in Technology, Security and Strategy

Essays in Technology, Security and Strategy

Stephen D. Bryen

With Rebecca Abrahams and Shoshana Bryen

Cover Page Credit

Photo

"Japanese Special Naval Landing Forces in Battle of Shanghai 1937" by Unknown photographer, Ministry of the Navy (Masao Hiratsuka), ed. (1995) (Shoeisha) ISBN: 4881352652. p.38 Photograph enhanced and remastered by Brent Jones: Rising Sun in the East 1937. Licensed under Public Domain via Wikimedia Commons - http://commons.wikimedia.org/wiki/File:Japanese_Special_Naval_Landing_Forces_in_Battle_of_Shanghai_1937.jpg#/media/File:Japanese_Special_Naval_Landing_Forces_in_Battle_of_Shanghai_1937.jpg

© Copyright 2015, All Rights Reserved, Stephen D. Bryen
ISBN: 1511957425
ISBN 13: 9781511957427

Table of Contents

	Introduction · xiii
April 08 2015	The Fish in Peace and War* · · · · · · · · · · · · · · · 3
February 23 2015	America's Retreat and Japan · · · · · · · · · · · · · · · 8
Feb 09 2015	Lenin is in Poland · 13
Jan 27 2015	Greece Will Need a New Currency · · · · · · · · · · 17
Jan 12 2015	Now it is Centcom: But it is Just the Tip of the Iceberg · · · · · · · · · · 19
Spring 2014	The Real Realpolitik · 23
Oct 30 2014	The Obama Administration is Failing the Reliability Test · · · · · · · · · · · · · · · 31
Sep 24 2014	What Dura Europos Means to Jews and Christians · · · · · · · · · · · · · · 34
Jun 13 2014	Iraq– A National Security Disaster · · · · · · · · · · 38

June 02 2014	Bergdahl and Alan Gross, The One Who Did Not Walk Away	42
Fall 2014	Will Nato Fight, Talk or Trade?	47
Mar 10 2014	The Klos-C Missiles --Target Israel or Egypt?	55
Feb 03 2014	The Sodastream Factory and Peace in the Middle East	58
Jan 27 2014	Chemical Weapons: Iraq and a History of Abuse	62
Jan 14 2014	The Israeli Defense Minister Speaks Out	68
Dec 13 2013	What Really Happened in North Korea?	71
Dec 01 2013	Pre-Payment on the Iran Deal	77
Nov 08 2013	Saudi and Israeli Options After the Us-Iran Deal	81
Oct 21 2013	What's Behind the Spying?	85
Sep 30 2013	The Nuclear Tide Comes In	88
Sep 16 2013	The Un Report on Syrian Chemicals is Out –No Evil Doers	92
Sep 12 2013	Putin's Speech (Well, Putin's Op Ed)	96
Sep 09 2013	Cutting Off Supplies of Nerve Gas and WMD Equipment	99
Sep 01 2013	When they Wake from the Dead	103

Aug 23 2013	Reacting to Chemical Weapons & What to Do About Syria	107
Jun 15 2013	Perilous Syria	111
Jun 7 2013	All Shook Up –National Security, the Patriot Act and Prism	114
Jun 6 2013	Will China Stop Cyber-Espionage? Absolutely Not	117
Apr 27 2013	A Question About the Bomb Making Magazine	120
Apr 11 2013	What is the North Korean Game? it May be Unification	124
Apr 07 2013	Is Kim Jong Un Working for the Cia?	127
Mar 08 2013	The Coming War and Chemical Weapons	130
Jan 31 2013	Russia, Iran and Syria Take a Big Risk and Cover it With the Big Lie	138
Jan 20 2013	"Incapacitating" Agents and Hostage Taking Raids	144
Jan 06 2013	An E-Z Pass for Guns?	148
Dec 05 2012	Syria and Gas Warfare	151
	Oil and the Changing Shape of American Security	154
Apr 09 2012	Exporting Spy Technology to Iran	157

Feb 12 2012	The Swarming Boat Problem – What Does it Mean?	160
February 7 2012	Can the Us Navy Cope With Iranian Mines?	162
Dec 22 2011	Patriots for Tehran	166
Summer 2012	Iran Gets Spy and Nuclear Technology Despite Embargo	168
November 12 2012	Why Did Al-Qaeda Target Ambassador Stevens?	175
Dec 16 2011	America's Shift in International Security Strategy	178
Jul 27 2011	Sharing our Defense Budget with China	185
March 2015	Encryption is Only Half the Story	191
Jan 06 2015	Will the Stringray End Up at the Supreme Court?	193
Dec 18 2014	When There is No Price to Be Paid the Hackers Win	196
Dec 05 2014	The Day the Critical Infrastructure Goes Up in Smoke	199
Dec 01 2014	Is Hollywood Going Back to Flip Phones?	205
Nov 21 2014	Saving the Critical Infrastructure	209
Nov 06 2014	Us Policy and Cyber Attacks: A Byte for a Byte	212

Oct 25 2014	Time to Dump Microsoft and Google	215
Oct 10 2014	Hacking Back and the Cyber Balance of Power	219
Sep 15 2014	Losing the Cyber War: How to Get Out of the Box and Win	222
Sep 05 2014	Give Me $46 Billion and I Will Build a Safe Computer System	227
Aug 31 2014	Is China's New Computer Operating System a Threat?	231
Jul 08 2014	Deep Panda: Chinese Leaders Want to Reap the Benefits of Cyber Spying But They Will End Up Depressed	234
Jun 26 2014	Is the Supreme Court Cellphone Decision a Bad Decision?	238
May 26 2014	Your Camera is on, Beware!	242
Apr 24 2014	Verizon Blockbuster Data Breach Report is Bad News for Organizations	247
Apr 19 2014	Facebook's "Nearby Friends" is A Really, Really Bad Idea	250
Apr 11 2014	Intelligence Agencies are Happy as Clams Thanks to Heartbleed "Bug"	253
Apr 03 2014	Sometime Privacy Rules Lead to Murder -The Fort Hood Case	256

Jan 09 2014	Have You Been Guccifer'd? Better Give it Some Thought	259
Dec 24 2013	Is Knox the Answer to Android Security?	262
Dec 07 2013	Bitcoins, Privacy and Democracy	266
Oct 29 2013	Gifts From Moscow Turn Out to Be Spy Devices	269
Oct 24 2013	How Did They Hack Merkel's Phone?	272
Oct 07 2013	Was the NSA Backdoor Worth It?	276
Aug 20 2013	Destroying the Fourth Amendment	279
Aug 01 2013	Suppose Bradley Manning and Edward Snowden Were Crooks?	283
Jul 20 2013	Smartphones and Tablets: Two Suggestions that May Help You Stay Secure	286
Jun 30 2013	Don't Blame Nsa Only –It is Bad Government Decision Making	290
	On the Rise of Cyber Anarchism	293
Jun 6 2013	Will China Stop Cyber-Espionage? Absolutely Not	297
May 28 2013	Finding A Cure for China's Technology Theft	300
May 19 2013	The Spy & the Mobile Phone	303
May 10 2013	Atm Heist — Who Is Behind It?	305

Aug 13 2012	Who Is Behind the Gauss Virus?	308
Jun 07 2012	On Vacation Consider a Qr Code for Your Kids	311
November 2011	It is Time for R-Toos™	313
May 15 2012	The Spy on Your Cell Phone is a Professional	315
May 07 2012	The National Security Risk of Mobile Phones	320
Mar 25 2012	King David and the Supercomputers	324
Feb 07 2012	The Revolution in Transportation Affairs	330
July 05 2012	Gps Hijacking: Team of Us Faculty, Students Take Control of Drone	334
Nov 28 2011	Our Fault: China, Supercomputers and National Security	336
Mar 26 2014	Noah -Hollywood Missed the Big Story	343
Mar 18 2014	My Theory of What Happened to Mh-370	349
Nov 23 2013	American Football: Helmets, Cracked Eggs, and a Red Card	354
Oct 14 2013	What Asteroid 1950 Da May Mean	358
Sep 23 2013	Life Out Of Comets and our Future	362
May 14 2013	The 3-D Plastic Gun and Airport Screening	366
Feb 20 2014	A Nice Story in a Sea of Pain and Distress	371

Oct 28 2011	A Tribute to an American Hero	376
Feb 22 2012	A War Memory - The Band Plays On	380
Apr 23 2012	The Tim Tebow of the Army: A Memorial Salute to Maj. Gen. Orde Wingate	384
Dec 07 2011	Remembering Bernie	388
	Authors	393

Introduction

Over the past three years I have been publishing short essays on my blog Technology Security. The blog has over 2,500 followers and circulates around the world. In addition I have published articles on my own, sometimes teamed with my wife Shoshana Bryen, and sometimes with Rebecca Abrahams. Our articles have been published in The American Thinker, PJ Media, inFocus Quarterly, the Technology Security Blog and the Huffington Post. This book pulls together some of the articles into a single volume.

Why publish a book of essays? In part these essays presage my forthcoming book, Technology Security and National Power: Winners and Losers that will be published in 2016 by Transaction Press. Thus this book of essays can be seen as a fore spice, perhaps not manna from heaven but at least some insight into how I approach today's critical issues that relate to technology and security. In my opinion national power grows out of and is linked to technology. Control of technology is a critical ingredient in national security.

My professional history starts as a graduate student where I began to consider the importance of computer technology to understanding international affairs. My dissertation and my first book, The Application of Cybernetic Analysis to the Study of International Politics (Martinus Nijhoff, 1971 and Springer, 2012) started me in a direction that led me to Lehigh University where I devised computer-aided applications in the social sciences. From there I served on Capitol Hill first as Executive Assistant to Senator Clifford P. Case and later as the Director of the Near East Subcommittee of the US Senate Committee on Foreign Relations. From there I became Deputy under Secretary of Defense and the founder and first Director of the Defense Technology Security Administration, with responsibility to stop the hemorrhaging of American technology to the Soviet Union and China. After retiring from government service, I headed my own high technology companies and then became the President of Finmeccanica North America, the US part of the Italian aerospace, defense and high technology conglomerate. After ten years I again started my own consultancy and have been working on advanced solutions to computer and mobile platform security.

To add just one more item to the above list, I also served as a Commissioner on the US China Economic and Security Review Commission. China poses a major long term challenge to the United States.

My professional experience now covers 48 years (not counting time in undergraduate and graduate education). Putting in that amount of time does not make anyone an expert of any kind. But I have been blessed with assignments and responsibilities that have helped me understand some of the dynamics that are shaping events today and will surely affect future outcomes. On that basis, offering creative ideas based on experience I take as a kind of calling, a mission I need to fulfill.

We live in a time of exponential technology expansion. That is good in some cases, creates social and political problems in others, and in the wrong hands can wreak havoc. The GPS is a great example of a terrific tool that can be misused in many ways. In the hands of First Responders, the GPS can help medics get to the scene of an accident and give life saving help. But in the hands of a predator, you can be tracked if the GPS in your smartphone is giving away your location. Similarly, the GPS can be used to guide weapons accurately to a target; but as the GPS becomes globally available it can be used by terrorists against our soldiers.

In like manner social media such as Facebook makes it possible for families and friends to stay in touch and to enjoy each other from afar. But it also makes it possible for more sinister people to exploit relationships or cause harm to users of social media. It is exactly this that helped Islamic terrorists in France target leaders in the Paris and Toulouse Jewish communities.

Problems like the above are multiplying. If they are left unaddressed or supposedly "fixed" because some anonymous corporate public relations agency says they have tightened security, than we all we lose. The level of leadership in security at the national level is appallingly bad. There is almost no initiative taken to protect citizens from harm, and there are few ideas on what to do in any case. Our government is more concerned about freedom to spy, then the need to protect freedom.

I hope some of the ideas tabled in these essays can contribute to changing attitudes and practices and make our lives more peaceful and predictable today and tomorrow.

--Stephen Bryen

NATIONAL SECURITY
PART 1

April 08 2015

The Fish in Peace and War*

The British learned about it from a spy working in a New York Congressman's office who informed the British governor of New York by sending a coded message. The message said that the colonists would launch a new weapon in Boston Harbor where the British fleet was then based in 1775. Thus warned the British tried to take precautions, but at that point nothing happened.

The secret weapon was a near-underwater vehicle equipped with a drill screw and a barrel bomb. The purpose of the screw was to drill a hole into the submerged side of a British warship. Then, using a timing mechanism designed by a New Haven watchmaker named Isaac Doolittle; a flint-lock trigger would set off gunpowder packed into a barrel. On September 6, 1776 the semi-submersible, dubbed The Turtle, was taken out into New York harbor near Governor's island where the British fleet flagship HMS Eagle was moored. The drill could not penetrate the Eagle's hull because, while it was wooden, it was covered with copper sheathing. When British soldiers caught on to the attempt to attack the Eagle, the barrel bomb, which was then called a Torpedo, was released and floated down-river where it exploded. The Turtle managed to escape.

The Turtle, designed by Yale student David Bushnell, was the first submersible system used in combat. That it failed was rather an intelligence failure more than anything else, since the copper sheathing of the

Eagle and other British vessels had only recently been introduced. While the presence of copper sheathing was new for the British fleet, other historians claim that the HMS Eagle didn't have it, but that the crewman manning the Turtle either hit an iron bolt or some other iron plate and not the copper.

Bushnell was a creative inventor. While he used the Turtle to go after the British flagship, he went on to set off a floating keg mine aside the HMS Cerberus in 1777. It killed four sailors but the ship survived until it was captured by the French in 1778 and burned. Bushnell's adventures with floating keg bombs not only earned him the admiration of many colonists, but a popular ditty was written to cheer the troops and encourage the public to keep the revolutionary faith. (Listen to the song Battle of the Kegs here)

The Turtle was one of a number of early submarines built in the United States and Europe from the mid-1600's until the latter part of the 19th century. All of them followed an important principal learned from fish: the ability to raise and lower themselves in water by adjusting ballast.

A fish does this by use of its bladder, called a swim bladder. Not all fish have swim bladders, but those that do can use them to raise or lower themselves in water.

The swim bladder has had value to humans for many centuries.** Today the collagen derived from the fish bladder from cooking is used to produce Isinglass that is used to clarify beer (and making Isinglass-cleared beers problematic for vegetarians). More recently Isinglass is being used to treat wounds without the need for additional dressing. Thus an ancient material is playing a new role in the rapid treatment of wounded soldiers.

The same material was used centuries back for condoms. It was also used in court plaster because of its glue like character. But most importantly it was used to produce much strong weapons in ancient times.

The bow and arrow is a very ancient weapon, known for more than 10,000 years. It was essential for hunting as well as for war. But, as archers surely knew, there were problems that plagued this weapon. The bow was subject to breakage, either snapping or cracking which made it worthless. So too was the bow string, made of animal gut, likely to fail at the most inopportune moment. Fighting range was limited and accuracy was poor because of the shock to the structure when the bow string was pulled back hard and released. The "snap" was moderated by transversal forces on the string, creating twist in the released arrow that would throw it off course unless compensated by an experienced archer.

The invention of the composite bow improved archery and was a key to giving the chariot archers greater range, better accuracy, and more killing power since an arrow launched from a composite bow at a target could penetrate a hard target up to three inches.

There is debate about the origin of the composite bow; whether it initially was a Sumerian or Akkadian invention, or whether it was Canaanite. It was surely a vital weapon for the Hyksos who, along with their chariots, overpowered Egypt's military forces around 1650 BC.

The composite bow is made from wood, horn sinew and fish bladder. The secret is the fish bladder which, when prepared and cooked down, forms durable glue, the epoxy of the ancient war fighter.

The bladder itself is primarily a collagen material, and the best fish bladders for the collagen glue are found in carp, sturgeon, catfish and cod.

The advantage of glue based on the fish bladder is that it is stronger and can stand more torsion effects than glue made from beef sinew scrapings either from an animal's gut or from the surface of leather. We don't know whether bow makers in the Middle East produced their own Isinglass, or if it was imported. Certainly, for chariot and composite bow making, many of the woods needed to manufacture the bow had to be imported. The production of a composite bow was a slow process. Wealthy property owners paid by tribal chiefs managed bow and arrow production and used slave labor to do the manufacturing. Some believe that the production of a good composite bow could take a year's work. This suggests there were many hands involved in bow and arrow making and that production was a vital part of a well organized and disciplined community that was hierarchically organized. The system provided everything for the foot soldier; uniforms, food, weapons, transportation and medical care.

If fish bladders could be used to help produce more accurate, more lethal and longer range bows for warfare, other parts of the fish can also serve in peace and war.

At the Tokyo Institute of Technology Junzo Tanaka and Toshiyuki Ikoma are using collagen derived from fish scales to help elderly people regenerate bones that have been weakened by tumors. They chose Tilapia for their experimentation and found that bone regeneration can be accomplished in as little as three months using this "new" fish technology.

At the Massachusetts Institute of Technology and the Technion in Israel fish scales are the inspiration for a new generation of body armor. The Technion team has "created a composite material that consists of stiff, overlapping outer 'scales,' combined with a layer of soft and flexible material underneath. The addition of the scales boosts the softer material's penetration resistance by a factor of 40, while reducing its flexibility by a factor of only five."

Of course Samurai warriors' armor also took advantage of the design of fish scales in the form of overlapping curved enameled iron plates sewn into their armor garments. So the latest from MIT and the Technion inventions owe a lot not only to the fish, but also to the skilled artisans in Japan in the Sengoku period who fashioned the Samurai's protective gear.

While we all know that fish are an important source of protein and nutrients for mankind, the fish is also an inspiration for inventors and for innovations that stretch over countless centuries, uniting our past with our future.

---

*part of this essay is derived from my forthcoming book, **Technology Security and National Power: Winners and Losers** (Transaction Publishers: 2016)
**fish bladders are also tasty and used in Chinese and Asian cooking where they are known as Fish Maws. For a recipe click here.

FEBRUARY 23 2015

America's Retreat and Japan

Japan is not much of a military power today, a mere shadow of what it was before World War II. Since her defeat in 1945, Japan has relied on the United States for security. The US keeps a large number of bases on Japan and Okinawa, and also shares facilities with Japan. The United States has more than 50,000 military personnel stationed in Japan and Okinawa and employs around 5,500 civilians. There are over 40,000 military family members associated with America's presence.

Japan is the home base at Yokosuka for the US Seventh fleet and also the home of the 3rd Marine Expeditionary Force. Along with troops, helicopters, ships and submarines the US Air Force has 130 fighters based in Japan.

The American presence is the successor to the US occupation of Japan at the end of World War II. While the number of bases, facilities, training centers and storage facilities is large, the US also closed down close to the same number of facilities and bases over the years.

Japan pays the United States around $2 billion as compensation for America's presence. While this seems like a large number, the actual cost to the United States for the deployment is many billions more than the Japanese contribution. Japan therefore benefits from the American presence because it can keep a small defense budget even where potential threats in the region are growing.

And they are. North Korea is already a nascent nuclear power and is likely in future years to use its missiles as a means of getting concessions from Japan. The Japanese have had a rocky relationship with Korea. In 1905 Japan forced Korea to become a protectorate. In 1910 Japan annexed Korea (then a unified peninsula). Under this annexation Japan dealt harshly with the Korean people and exploited its resources. Before and during World War II the northern part of Korea was an industrial center supplying Japan with armaments and ammunition. It is also one of the places where Japan worked on building an atomic bomb.

Along with roughly treating Koreans, using them as conscripts and forced labor, thousands were transferred to Japan and use as laborers there. When Hiroshima and Nagasaki were hit by atom bombs, thousands of Koreans working in those cities were killed. Adding to the misery of the Korean people was the use of young Korean ladies as "comfort women" for Japanese troops and administrators. Bitterness over this issue still remains.

China, too, is turning into a true superpower, and confrontations between Japan and China over disputed islands has risen in the past few years. Their disagreement is over some uninhabited small "rocks" in the East China Sea (known in Japan as the Senkaku islands). These "rocks" are under Japan's control, but the Chinese want them. Their location is strategic, affecting China's ability to control the sea lines of communication, and is positioned near important oil and gas reserves.

But much more is involved as China grows stronger. China thinks of its perimeter as two imaginary boundaries, the inner boundary already clearly under China's control; the outer one coming under its control as China expands its navy and develops new weapons that can challenge America's aircraft carriers and nuclear submarines.

The United States has been trying to beef up its Pacific presence. The bases in Japan offset, to a degree, China's growing military power, but will that be enough?

The last test of military power in the region took place in the Taiwan Straits from July 21, 1995 to March 23, 1996. In that period China carried out an "exercise" that included closing sea and air traffic in and around the Taiwan straits as China launched missiles, mobilized its land forces, and prepared its naval forces to support what looked like an invasion of Taiwan itself. Would the US respond to China's provocation? Would China challenge the United States or back off?

The evidence shows that America delayed responding and finally put two aircraft carrier task forces on patrol near the Straits. China, if it really planned to strike Taiwan, backed away and the crisis ended. China blinked.

It is far from clear whether a repeat performance would be met resolutely by Washington. Even if America did move its naval and air forces to face China, China might not cut and run. There are many scenarios that could trigger a confrontation: disputed territories, Taiwan, conflict on the Korean peninsula.

Americans tend to forget that we faced Chinese "volunteers" in the Korean War, and proxy wars involving China and Russia in Vietnam, Laos and Cambodia.

This brings us back to Japan and the dilemma Japanese policy makers' face.

Can Japan depend on the United States for its protection? Should a confrontation unfold that directly impacts Japan, there is reason to believe, based on the worsening geopolitical posture of the United States and the drawdown of defense assets, which the United States might dawdle, seek diplomatic remedies, and try not to engage.

There have already been a number of incidents between China and Japan (for an excellent assessment see Sheila A. Smith, a senior fellow for Japan at the Council for Foreign Relations, "A Sino-Japanese Clash in the East China Sea"). So far they have been small scale and contained, but these were probes by China to judge not only Japan's behavior, but to understand what America might do. So far at least, the Japanese have worked to contain any incident and the United States has not needed to take any direct role. But this can change at any time. If China wants to do so she can ratchet up trouble at any time.

Japan is caught in a dilemma. Its military forces are weak compared to China and there is little chance much can be done to strengthen it in the next five years. Japan can compensate a little by buying new weapons. Japan has agreed to procure F-35 Joint Strike Fighters. But these airplanes are years away from delivery, and they are tactical aircraft and will not be regarded by China as any sort of deterrent. Japan really wanted the F-22, a true stealth penetration bomber capable of long range operations. The United States rejected Japan's attempt to buy them.

Japan, therefore, has few options. But there is one direction Japan can go, and it has the resources, know how, and delivery systems to get there. That is to build nuclear weapons. Doing this will surely antagonize the United States, China and North Korea, but Japan could nevertheless decide it is worth it. Some suspect Japan may be laying the foundation for such a step. For example Japan has been energetically building long range rockets. It is hard to believe Japan would invest so much effort in rockets and space unless the investment was regarded as an important part of a future strategic system.

Japan had an atomic bomb program in World War II divided into two main programs, one run by the Army and the other by the Navy. It had major facilities throughout Japan, and the Navy ran a secret operation in northern Korea that was taken over by the Russians at the end of World War II. That facility, which produced thorium for the Russians, was bombed by B-29's in 1950 in the early days of the Korean War. In addition, Japan had a highly capable scientific community with excellent nuclear physicists and chemists. Major Japanese companies built equipment including cyclotrons and gas centrifuges for Japan's atomic program and some participated in uranium extraction and enrichment.

Would Japan return to nuclear weapons after the devastation of Hiroshima and Nagasaki and the strong anti-nuclear feeling that permeates Japan's politics? That would depend on whether Japan felt sufficiently threatened by North Korea and China to do so. A few islands are probably not enough to cause a major change in policy. But minor clashes can turn into bigger ones, and the United States, its prestige in tatters and in retreat around the world, may not be able to play a role as Japan's defender. Then we will see.

FEB 09 2015

LENIN IS IN POLAND

There is an old and rather awful joke that goes like this. The Russian Revolution has succeeded and the Communists are now in Power. Lenin is feeling very good about his great success and thinks there is a chance to convince some other countries to go Communist. He decides to go to Poland.

Meanwhile the Kremlin wants to honor the momentous occasion and commission a painting celebrating Lenin's trip. The day arrives to unveil the painting and all of official Moscow has assembled. But alas, when the shroud over the painting is dropped there is a picture of a man in bed with a woman.

"What's this exclaim the top Russian leaders? This," the painter says, "is a painting of Trotsky, in bed with Krupskaya, Lenin's wife." And the painter explains, the title of the picture is "Lenin is in Poland."

Today Lenin, in the form of Putin, is in the Ukraine, somewhere he surely does not belong. No one would dare to make a painting honoring the occasion.

Meanwhile the Western allies are in some turmoil. The Europeans are threatening more sanctions unless Putin pulls his forces out and wholeheartedly supports a peace effort (whatever that means). The United

States is threatening to arm Ukraine with lethal weapons, as if there is some other kind of weapon useful to the Ukrainian military.

The country is in a mess. Ukraine is no match for Russia's army, who are better trained and well equipped; there is not much chance that the Ukrainians can prevail without outside help.

Technically Ukraine is not a NATO problem because the Ukraine was never admitted to NATO membership. In fact the Ukraine's bid for such membership was one of the contributing causes (but not the only one) to the Russian-sponsored war that is enveloping the country.

What is worse, NATO is far from having a single mind about the subject of Ukraine. Right now Angela Merkel and Francois Hollande are taking the lead as European leaders, not necessarily as NATO leaders, arguing for a cease fire and a peace process. Their chance for success is very small.

NATO itself is not what it used to be. NATO is a collective security system which was organized as the Soviet Union turned Eastern Europe into Communist puppet states under Communist Russia's full control. The NATO idea and part of the Treaty agreement is that any attack on a NATO member can be met by collective force. But for NATO to act, all members must agree. When the United States asked NATO to join it after 9/11 to take down the Taliban, NATO could not agree. Keeping in mind that it was the same European states that pressured America into entering the war in Bosnia, NATO's refusal to use collective defense on behalf of one of its members, in fact its most important member, was an especially rude slap in the face.

NATO also is paltry as a military operation. Many of the NATO countries reduced their armed forces after the collapse of the Soviet Union and major armor units were disbanded with land war equipment either sold or scrapped. Today NATO countries have an ability to launch a fight against the Taliban, but no ability to win the fight. That is the real reason Obama is pulling the US out of Afghanistan. The British are doing the same and most of the others are only providing humanitarian aid.

Years ago in a meeting in the Senate Foreign Relations Committee over problems in Lebanon one of the Senators asked Dr. Henry Kissinger about French insistence to have a role in the affair. Where is their Navy, opined Kissinger, or their Army? Without a military capability and willingness to commit it, Kissinger had no interest or regard for the participation of the French, even though years ago they ran Lebanon for the League of Nations under a Mandate (1923-1946).

Today we have a rather parallel situation. Neither Germany nor France will commit one single soldier to any fight in the Ukraine. So their intervention with Putin lacks credibility. Putin's only conceivable interest compelling his attention is European sanctions, but he has cards of his own he can play if he wants (like cutting off natural gas supplies to Germany or threatening other countries such as Poland or Estonia). For this reason Europe cannot risk war, and neither can the United States, because our country, like the rest of NATO, is woefully unprepared. Had America delivered on its promises to the Ukraine years earlier, after Ukraine got rid of Backfire bombers and other strategic assets, the situation today might have been different. But it isn't and no one knows how to change history or make hindsight into a constructive tool.

There is also the problem that the NATO partners, aside from the bombastic statements by President Obama and Vice President Biden on Ukraine, do not see eye to eye. Greece has a new leftist leader friendly to the Kremlin. Will Greece be willing to vote for more sanctions on the Russians? From the Greek point of view they already have enough sanctions laid on themselves by European bankers. Or will Italy want to get into this quagmire, with Russia an important trading nation? Or for that matter will the Germans back up Mrs. Merkel? Russia is a very important trading partner for Germany, the source of a significant flow of energy, and trades important raw materials in exchange for German manufactured goods. Merkel's flexibility has to be extremely limited and her political future is far from assured. Loss of jobs may well trump applying sanctions.

AS a result, these are not happy times either for Europe, for the United States, and certainly for the Ukrainian people who have been treated to a tap dance by the West's leaders in place of a functional alliance. There is only so much of this sort of thing before things turn even more tragic.

Interestingly, despite the fissures and extreme problems with NATO, all the Western players are marching around and around without getting to some core issues that must be addressed for the future. At risk today is not only NATO survival, but peace in Europe. Putin is not Hitler, notwithstanding the rhetoric that has been coming from the United Kingdom. But Putin is an aggressive minded Russian leader who is filling a vacuum. He already learned he could get away with aggression in Georgia. And now he is taking advantage because he knows NATO has mutated into a paper tiger.

We need to wake up. We don't want Putin in Poland.

JAN 27 2015

Greece Will Need a New Currency

The new Greek government, mainly composed of former Communists and other leftists, with a dash of a far right political party giving Syriza enough support to form a government, faces a huge task in trying to reform Greece's economy. The idea that it can be done in negotiations with the European Central Bank and the key economic power, Germany, is wishful thinking at best.

The German government has already made clear it is not prepared to write off Greek debts. Furthermore the Germans and the bankers expect Greece to pay back its loans and to retain an austerity program in order to squeeze enough resources out to make the required payments.

It is unlikely Greece can, or will comply. What is more certain is that the new government will raise salaries, cut some taxes (but not to the rich), and hire back many unemployed State workers. Of course this is impossible if the euro remains Greece's currency.

Once the government gets organized and starts imposing its "cure" Greek repayments will have to cease, bond prices will escalate and will be chasing investors who will be running for cover, and the situation will rapidly become quite explosive.

At this point both the Greeks and the Europeans will have to make choices. In such an environment, the most likely result is that Greece will have to replace the euro with a local currency. For our purposes let's call it the "New Drachma."

Greece can get along with the New Drachma. But a better solution for Greece is a hybrid approach: if possible retaining the euro and support a New Drachma –in other words, two currencies.

There are two ways this can be done. One is a formal agreement with the European banks that will give Greece room for maneuver by stretching out loan repayments and making other credit provisions that are reasonable. With a second, "local" currency Greece can pay its civil servants and encourage private business to also use the local currency for all internal transactions. André Cabannes, a professor at Stanford University, outlined this approach for Greece a few years ago, and his proposal remains the best one for Greece and for other weak players in the euro community such as Spain and Italy.

A New Drachma will start off in parity with the euro, but won't stay there for long. Unless the government exercises some discipline and restraint and builds confidence in the banking and business community, the New Drachma will rapidly lose value. The real challenge for a radical Greek government is whether it can come up with a program that can be managed properly, kept sensible, and will be able to have the support of the financial community.

Europe cannot really afford to write off Greece. Nor can the new Greek government survive if it is reckless or obnoxiously ideological. It would help both sides in the argument to find independent experts who can structure a workable program for a second currency while keeping the euro alive.

JAN 12 2015

NOW IT IS CENTCOM: BUT IT IS JUST THE TIP OF THE ICEBERG

You don't have to be real smart to know that social media accounts are not private, even if you are told by their owners and operators that they are. Social sites, all of them, are easily hacked by outsiders, and even the companies that offer own them exploit them to make money. The monetization of privacy in the United States is highly advanced and represents a multibillion dollar, unstoppable, business.

But folks are starting to figure out that a major danger is lurking.

For this reason the French gendarmes and counter terrorism forces have been order to close any personal social media accounts they have and to do so immediately.

You would have thought that America's Central Command, which focuses on the Middle East and plays a vital role in dealing with radical Islamic terrorism, would recognize social media risks and would have, long ago, taken security measures to protect sensitive information. But that did not happen. In fact, CENTCOM (as it is known) has been merrily running Twitter and YouTube sites without any care.

So now we know that ISIS hacked CENTCOM and published the names and addresses of top officials including four star generals, making the information generally available to any operational terror cells including some who may be lie embedded in the United States. US Cyber Command is only the tip of the iceberg. ISIS could have got all the information and passed it to terror organization without defacing the CENTCOM twitter account and other CENTCOM-sponsored sites. In this way Central Command would not know that critical information about their top personnel was in the hands of a vicious Islamic terror organization. But ISIS wanted to get the propaganda value out of its hack, so they made a lot of noise. No one knows how long they have been mucking about in CENTCOM's operations.

The Pentagon says it was all a prank and is of no concern. With this mindset anyone hoping there was a chance that the Pentagon might try and fix a looming problem now knows better: they are the problem.

But, under pressure, the Pentagon changed its mind.

Huh?

Is CENTCOM an exception? Hardly. Americans, despite countless articles pointing out obvious vulnerabilities in social networking and media sites, continue with their obsession to leak information that compromises personal and organizational security. It is a good bet that virtually every American military base, office, organization and unit is leaking away using Facebook, Twitter, LinkedIn, Pinterest and all the others. So too are folks at Homeland Security, the State Department, FBI and on and on.

The truth is we do not know just how much sensitive information is in the hands of terrorists, but if we have learned anything watching al-Qaeda, ISIS, the Iranians, the Syrian Electronic Army and all their brethren is that they certainly know how to exploit social media and build powerful attack databases.

They have already used their laptop computers and the lists they have generated and passed around on memory sticks to identify and kill their enemies in Iraq and Syria. It would be foolish to think they have confined themselves to the Middle East –indeed we know they have not.

In France the attacks on the Jewish community, for example, are not random. Names, addresses and other information were gathered by the terrorists from social media sources, especially Facebook. This exposed not only the targeted individuals, but also their families. Even the Charlie Hebdo attack was precisely targeted. The killers had the ID and photos of their victims well in advance.

For a long time the French government, trying to be politically correct in the French context, did almost nothing to protect its citizens from terrorists, especially its Jews.

Now, in the wake of Charlie Hebdo and Hyper Cacher, a Kosher supermarket in Paris, the French government has taken an about face and decided to try and protect synagogues and religious schools. To this end the French government has assigned 10,000 soldiers. But soldiers can't protect someone in their home or walking down the street. In the last decade Jews in France have been murdered, shot add, beaten up, raped and terrorized. How to protect exposed individuals, their families and friends?

The American situation is not much better. For years we have allowed terrorist organization free rein on the Internet, and have done little or nothing to stop them. The fact that ISIS can get away with launching cyber attacks tells you all you really need to know. Despite investing billions in so-called cyber security, and even creating a Pentagon unit ("Plan X") that is supposed to deal with the bad guys, everyone is still looking at their thumbs. US security policy is frozen, blindsided, hamstrung and inept. The Pentagon can't figure out which end us up, has not given direction to its millions of military and civilian employees, and has not engaged the enemy or tried to shut them down. Remember what happened in Boston.

Security comes down to protecting people, and if you can't do that your security system is faulty. A quick way to provide some modicum of protection is to purge social media of sensitive information that puts people directly at risk. The bigger job is to provide real aggressive leadership to take down the connections being exploited over the Internet by the Islamic terrorists. The Pentagon can do the job; they just need to be told to launch the effort.

SPRING 2014

THE REAL REALPOLITIK

Courtesy inFocus Quarterly

Iraq is in turmoil; Egypt is an outcast to the United States and starting to buy weapons from Russia; Iran is ascendant and increasingly aggressive; and the allied effort in Afghanistan is close to collapse. America has little or no credibility or influence. China is growing stronger, the Russians are assertive and brazen in Crimea, and our allies are increasingly uncertain and uneasy. Why?

The legendary Hans Morgenthau, master of Realpolitik, would say the United States has not pursued its national interest or applied a wise policy in support of those interests. This, in the end, is a policy and a moral failure, wasting economic and human resources and risking of lives of millions of people around the globe. Political realism, at its best, and Morgenthau was its best, was different from Realpolitik in one crucial way: under its adherence to the wise and constructive use of power was a profound moral message. You are not a great power because you can launch drones from afar, or mow down your enemies with flying gunships. You are a great power when you articulate strategic objectives aimed at preventing aggression and upheaval, and using force, if needed, to drive home the point.

America is a superpower, and as a result has a responsibility it probably does not want but cannot escape. Our government's inability to find a coherent foreign policy and execute it in a clear and sensible manner stokes the isolationism coursing through the country. We need to rethink what we are doing and get it right; Morgenthau can help.

Morgenthau postulated a theory of how nations behave, or should behave, based a modernized form of older, German thinking on international politics known as Realpolitik. In its essence, Realpolitik means that international politics is primarily based on military and industrial power and not on moralistic ideas. A key modern example is Richard Nixon's decision to recognize the People's Republic of China. Prompted strongly by Henry Kissinger (often wrongly cited as the originator of Realpolitik), the Nixon-China embrace came at the expense of Taiwan, which was not asked, but was simply de-recognized.

The embrace of China was to try to balance the hostile Soviet Union. For Nixon and Kissinger, the fact that China was at the time more extreme in its Communist views than the Soviet Union was of little importance. The Nixon-Kissinger goal was to tighten the noose around the USSR. Nixon and Kissinger had earlier pushed the idea of "detente" with the Soviet Union, thinking that the U.S. could use its economic power to dissuade the Russians from confrontation. But the Russians had other ideas, and continued their military build-up featuring the famous SS-21 mobile short-range nuclear missile aimed at Western Europe. With "detente" largely shredded and our European allies flirting more and more with the Soviets to avoid Russian political and military pressure, the China card was a way for the U.S. to draw off some of Russia's military forces from Europe, especially nuclear missiles, which the administration hoped would shift to face China.

China was well aware that it was being used, but the benefits were considerable. The key to China's future as a growing power was Western technology, especially American microelectronics and computer technology. China also was promised arms cooperation. In the early 1980's, the Reagan administration jumped on the opportunity to help China modernize its arms industry, supplying important aerospace and underwater systems, including advanced torpedoes.

The Tiananmen Square massacre put an end to burgeoning U.S. and European military cooperation with China, although some of the Tiananmen sanctions (on nuclear power plants and equipment and on space launch) were later substantially eased.

But the transfer of advanced dual-use technology persists even today, long after the strategic idea behind it ceased to exist. The need to offset Soviet power evaporated with the collapse of the Soviet Union and the disintegration of the Russian empire (something Putin is working tirelessly to restore). The Tiananmen sanctions never addressed the transfers of critical technology to China. By the time sanctions were imposed, trade with China was too lucrative for the U.S. and its European partners to sacrifice trade for any principle of democracy or human rights.

Political realist Morgenthau and his predecessors would cringe looking at Western policy toward China, because of its clearly self-defeating and risky nature.

The Chinese understand that they need continuing access to Western technology for both civilian and military development. For that reason, China uses the benefits of trade as a lever to extract advanced technology from the West, especially from the United States. China has a huge cyber espionage operation to learn as much as possible about American weapons systems (including the F-35 Joint Strike Fighter) and to apply the technology to similar local programs. The U.S., afraid that China might stop "investing" in U.S. Treasury bonds and other financial instruments, does little to stop it.

A current analogous case is Iran. The U.S. unilaterally lifted some sanctions on Iran claiming that the lifting of sanctions would lead to a comprehensive deal to stop Iran's nuclear bomb building program.

The notion was flawed from the start because of the difficulty of verification and the fact that some "military" installations were off limits. The deal did not include delivery systems, especially long-range missiles, which Iran continues to develop. And the sanctions, once lifted, created a frenzy of trade and business activity with European and American companies flocking to Iran to set up deals. And the State Department, which steadfastly had urged its European allies to restrain themselves from running to do deals in Iran, officially "encouraged" U.S. aerospace companies to apply for licenses to ship jet engines for Iran's air fleet, the same air fleet that ferries supplies and troops in Syria.

Morgenthau would be appalled. Iran is an expansionist country causing havoc in Syria, Lebanon, and Iraq, and expanding its influences far and wide, including in the Americas. Iran continues to threaten Israel. The commander of Iran's Revolutionary Guard Corps was quoted by Iran's Fars news agency saying Iran's military has its finger on the trigger to destroy Israel as soon as it receives the order; the capacity to execute is irrelevant. In fact, Iran's policies are not moderate and do not lead to any regional accommodation. The U.S. nuclear proposal fails to take any of this into account, and so is strategically flawed and destabilizing.

Morgenthau explained political realism as "national interest defined in terms of power," while guarding against two fallacies: concern with motives and concern with ideological preferences. The core idea is that a rational international actor will follow the real interests of the state and, to a somewhat lesser degree, the real interests of the international community. An outside observer should be able to discern a country's national interests and goals in its foreign policy, and how that aligns with national power defined in both military and economic terms. In short, it is possible to observe whether a country has a rational policy, or one that deviates from rational.

At present, there are questions about the goals and objectives of U.S. foreign policy. But if we follow political realism and Morgenthau's prescription, we should be able to determine what our policy actually is, and whether it is coherent and aligned with our fundamental interests.

It is, of course, entirely possible to have a disastrous foreign policy even if it is coherent and aligned with our interests. The U.S. has been grappling with this problem since the middle 1970's, if not before, but it came into greater focus with the Iraq and Afghanistan wars.

Before Iraq, the most important and costly conflicts in which the U.S. was directly involved were Korea and Vietnam. In the former, the U.S. and its allies were unable to achieve anything more than a truce, which has remained in effect since 1953. General MacArthur and President Truman had a serious argument over Truman's approach to the war. Although at one point the U.S. considered using nuclear weapons against China and even went so far as to transfer authority to the Army for their use, the real flash point was over MacArthur's vision of challenging the Chinese and pushing them out of Korea altogether, and Truman's vision of negotiated deal. Ultimately, Truman relieved MacArthur from command.

While Korea ended in a stalemate, Vietnam ended in a defeat for the United States. Despite constant support for North Vietnam by the USSR and China, the U.S. did not attack China or even propose the idea. Instead the U.S. tried to defeat North Vietnam through conventional battles on South Vietnamese territory, and an extensive bombing campaign aimed at supply routes (the Ho Chi Minh Trail) into South Vietnam from North Vietnam, Laos and a corner of Cambodia. Operating in heavily foliated areas and using networks of underground bunkers as storage depots, the North Vietnamese were able to continue supplying their forces operating in the South. After Kissinger negotiated an accord with the North in Paris, the ARVN (South Vietnam's army) had to carry on the fight alone. In April 1975, Saigon fell.

Both the Korean and the Vietnam wars were limited because bigger players were either involved or lurking in the background. Was either conflict in the U.S. interest? Surely stopping China's operation in Korea, which would have resulted in all of Korea in Chinese hands, was the correct policy. Keeping South Korea free was an important message that has, since that war, helped restrain China.

Vietnam is different. While the U.S. was worried about a domino effect (Vietnam, Laos, Cambodia and more), the U.S. defeat and its aftermath did not work out the way we feared. Cambodia fell to the indigenous Khmer Rouge even before South Vietnam collapsed. Today, the U.S. has reconciled with communist Vietnam, and while Cambodia is still poor, it has a multi-party government. Laos is a socialist, single party country, poor, and with a poor human rights record. In sum, the U.S. investment in Vietnam, and in supporting Laos and Cambodia, was not really in the U.S. national interest. American willingness to fight there, and involve its allies (South Korea, Thailand, Australia, New Zealand, and the Philippines), had no positive result for the United States and even less for the victims.

Both Korea and Vietnam were so-called "limited" wars because of the threat of outside power intervention. However, neither the war in Afghanistan nor the war in Iraq is limited by any threat of outside intervention. Both are one-sided wars in the sense that it is a big power (and its allies) against far less powerful countries.

The first Iraq war was caused by Saddam Hussein's invasion of Kuwait, which threatened Saudi Arabia, threatened oil supplies and supply systems to the U.S. and to America's allies, and thus ensured that the United States would intervene. Had the U.S. taken a pass, a chaotic situation might have destroyed the global economy. Intervention thus made sense from the point of view of vital American interests and in terms of global stability. What made less sense was to let the first Iraq war end without putting an end to other potential threats coming from Iraq in the form of chemical, biological and nuclear weapons and delivery systems that could threaten the entire region. While the U.S. and the allies took steps to "manage" Saddam, the better solution would have been to topple the regime when they had the opportunity, replace Saddam with a government chosen from Iraqis in exile, and then leave.

American leaders instead confused themselves, their supporters, and the public. The result was a geopolitical blunder and a much longer conflict that did not serve either American or regional interests. It paved the way for al-Qaeda and for Syrian and Iranian trouble making. Per Morgenthau, the blunder seems to have been caused by a faulty moral idea—that allied destruction of Iraqi forces, particularly the bombing of retreating Iraqi forces along the Kuwait-Iraq highway (dubbed the Highway of Death) was an improper use of force. Thus President George H. W. Bush, on advice from his National Security Adviser, Gen. Colin Powell, declared a ceasefire on February 28, 1991.

Letting Saddam Hussein off the hook set the stage for related tragedies, including the decimation of the southern Shiite Marsh Arabs, whose revolt was encouraged by the United States, which then abandoned them to Saddam's helicopters and poison gas. The U.S. would return to Iraq, defeat the army, remove Saddam, and replace his regime with the costly and bloody American occupation. Disbanding but not disarming the Iraqi Army in 2003 was another faulty moral idea that encouraged the rise of militias full of armed, unemployed, and humiliated young men.

In at the end, the U.S. would pull out, abandoning the rest of the country as it did the Marsh Arabs twenty years earlier, this time creating a power vacuum that Iran quickly filled.

The U.S. could have done better, avoiding the occupation, strengthening bases in the area and stabilizing the region with a rapid action force. The U.S. could have created an independent Kurdish state—an area with significant oil resources and with a pro-American outlook. But lacking a strategy, and violating the fundamental principle of political realism, the U.S. wasted human and economic resources and failed to confront its emerging enemy, Iran.

Similarly in Afghanistan, in a war that has virtually no strategic importance, the U.S. has invested its prestige, and that of its coalition allies, in trying to stabilize a corrupt government. It has failed to stop either al-Qaeda or the Taliban, the latter being well-positioned to grab power after the U.S. and its allies leave. In the meantime, with very limited rules of engagement and unclear objectives, our forces continue to take casualties—including from "friendly" Afghan forces—and burn scarce resources.

The big picture is that the U.S. is not acting as a great power or following the basic rules of political realism as laid out by Morgenthau. From the mistakes the U.S. continues to make in the Middle East, in North Africa, and elsewhere, it is not surprising that foreign leaders no longer look to Washington for guidance and help—or even with respect.

Morgenthau did not live to see all this; perhaps it is best.

OCT 30 2014

The Obama Administration is Failing the Reliability Test

It would not surprise me if Israel's Prime Minister Benjamin Netanyahu does not soon wind up in Moscow working out a strategic deal with Russia's President, Vladimir Putin. The reason would not be hard to find. Israel is facing an existential threat from Iran, has lost all trust in the Obama administration, and has been vilified by unnamed Obama administration people.

There is an old political story that starts out when the late Senator John Sherman Cooper was asked to campaign for a friend. Arriving at a country store and standing on a soapbox, the good Senator delivered his campaign talk. Just halfway through a voice in the back hollered, "You're full of beans!" (The actual word is not beans, but as a matter of propriety I will tell the story my way.) The Senator, taken aback, regained his composure and continued, only to be once again greeted by the same exclamation from the old man in the back of the room. At this point, he rapidly concluded his remarks and got down from the soapbox. A number of local folks gathered around and apologetically told him, "please don't believe what that old man hollered to you. He is addle-minded. He just says what he hears."

In fact, the anonymous words directed contemptuously toward Netanyahu had to come from the top. This is why the White House, trying to mitigate the harm done, could not apologize. The boss would not tolerate an apology and anyway no one would have the guts to ask him. So, as they say the White House just put out that openly saying such things was counterproductive.

Any second-rate analyst in Israel would already understand that the statement came from the top. From this what would they conclude?

Aside from confirming what they already understood regarding personal relationships between Obama and Netanyahu, there was no surprise. But a deeper look reveals much more. The United States was not any longer a reliable partner.

The question about American reliability has been growing for some time. It has two dimensions: the strategic posture of the United States in the Middle East; the US-Israel "alliance" as the second.

The US has moved far ahead in jettisoning its friends in the Middle East, denouncing Egypt, faking it with Saudi Arabia, tolerating Turkey's suppression of their military leaders who for decades supported the United States, and playing fast and loose with Israel's security.

The US relationship with Iran has shifted significantly and the US has unleashed strategic trade deals with Iran, using its more than willing European allies as a front --all of this to grease the wheels of a nuclear deal that will be announced after the mid-term elections. There is a good probability that the Iran nuclear deal will have side arrangements that won't be made public. One suspects the Israelis may already be tracking them.

In the recent Gaza war the United States froze the delivery of Hellfire missiles. Hellfire missiles, as the Pentagon will tell you, are precision tools to be used to remove targets with as little collateral damage as possible. Freezing their delivery effectively pushed Israel into using other weapons to counter Hamas' rockets. So why did the administration do it? To show its ire at Israel, possibly, but also in a truly Machiavellian twist, to force the Israelis to cause more Palestinian casualties. This hardly qualifies how an ally should treat its partner. It is paradoxical that in the White House briefing over the "chicken s..t" comments, the Press Secretary was anxious to put across how the US helps Israel and that it was Obama who led the charge to get Israel's Iron Dome program funded.

From the inception of the Jewish state there was always a Russian hope, based on the fact that many of the Palestinian Jews were either socialists or communists, that Russia could strategically align with Israel. The USSR was the first state to recognize Israel diplomatically. A few years later the Russians decided that the Jewish state was going to be anti-communist, so the Russians embraced Arab socialism and dropped Israel. Today Russia is not communist and Putin and Netanyahu have a positive relationship. Israel has an interest in persuading the Russians to help stop the Iranian march to nuclear weapons. Putin has an interest in putting as much pressure as possible on the United States. This creates options for both countries.

The Obama administration's side switching and unreliability is very costly and dangerous. American power and influence in the Middle East is at an all time low.

SEP 24 2014

WHAT DURA EUROPOS MEANS TO JEWS AND CHRISTIANS

The ancient city sits ninety meters above the Euphrates river. Known in ancient times as Dura Europos, its history spans the most important time for change and strife for Jews and the formative period of Christianity. Dura Europos (the nearest Syrian village is Salhiyé) is now under ISIS control. ISIS has put diggers there who are pick-pocketing the artifacts of the city and selling them to brokers on the spot.

Dura Europos has three sanctuaries, a synagogue, an early Christian church and a Roman temple. The city was founded by the Seleucids in 303 BC. It would be captured by the Romans in 165 AD who held it until 256 or 257 AD. Established as a trade hub for caravans and river traffic, Dura Europos also was a melting pot of culture and a place of religious ferment.

The period between from 303 BC to 250 AD marks a time of great change in Judaism and Christianity. It is the period of struggle between the Roman occupiers and Jewish zealots who believed the Romans were polluting the Temple and undermining religion. It is a period where notions of a savior took hold in both the Jewish and Christian communities and where it was not always possible to distinguish between Christians and Jews. In the finds at Qumran (popularly known as the site where the Dead Sea scrolls were discovered) we can get an extraordinary insight into the religious fervor, the striving for purity, the anticipation of a messiah that became the core idea of Christianity.

Of particular importance is the work of the prophet Ezekiel. He was Ezekiel ben-Buzi who lived in exile in Babylonia between 593 and 571 BC. Ezekiel's writings were modified and added to many times, so it is uncertain what truly belongs to him and what his successors added over the years.

Chapter 37 by Ezekiel is most famously known as "dry bones."

"The hand of the Lord was on me, and he brought me out by the Spirit of the Lord and set me in the middle of a valley; it was full of bones. He led me back and forth among them, and I saw a great many bones on the floor of the valley, bones that were very dry. He asked me, "Son of man, can these bones live?"

"I said, "Sovereign Lord, you alone know."

" Then he said to me, "Prophesy to these bones and say to them, 'Dry bones, hear the word of the Lord! This is what the Sovereign Lord says to these bones: I will make breath enter you, and you will come to life. I will attach tendons to you and make flesh come upon you and cover you with skin; I will put breath in you, and you will come to life. Then you will know that I am the Lord.'"

" So I prophesied as I was commanded. And as I was prophesying, there was a noise, a rattling sound, and the bones came together, bone to bone. I looked, and tendons and flesh appeared on them and skin covered them, but there was no breath in them.

"Then he said to me, "Prophesy to the breath; prophesy, son of man, and say to it, 'This is what the Sovereign Lord says: Come, breath, from the four winds and breathe into these slain, that they may live.'" So I prophesied as he commanded me, and breath entered them; they came to life and stood up on their feet—a vast army."

"Then he said to me: "Son of man, these bones are the people of Israel. They say, 'Our bones are dried up and our hope is gone; we are cut off.' Therefore prophesy and say to them: 'this is what the Sovereign Lord says: My people, I am going to open your graves and bring you up from them; I will bring you back to the land of Israel. Then you, my people, will know that I am the Lord, when I open your graves and bring you up from them. I will put my Spirit in you and you will live, and I will settle you in your own land. Then you will know that I the Lord have spoken, and I have done it, declares the Lord.'"

These verses speak for themselves and it is this vision that takes hold and dominates Qumran and early Christianity.

"Duraeuropa-1-" by Unknown - http://www.library.yale.edu/exhibition/judaica/jcsml.2.html. Licensed under Public Domain via Wikimedia Commons - ttp://commons.wikimedia.org/wiki/File:Duraeuropa-1-.gif#/media/File:Duraeuropa-1-.gif

The incredible Dry Bones mural from Dura Europos - By Anonymous [Public domain], via Wikimedia Commons

Civilization is possible thanks to historical memory, and the artifacts of the past intensify and validate the integrity of our culture and give proof that our beliefs grow out of the struggles of our forbearers. We cannot describe in words what we owe to them, but when they leave behind remnants of their vision it moves us spiritually and emotionally.

The Dura Europos synagogue is now threatened as never before by ISIS. What a tragedy for all of us if we lose this precious symbol of our religious heritage.

JUN 13 2014

Iraq– A National Security Disaster

Iraq is in crisis, and the crisis is fatal. The administration, without any support at all from the American people, is privately asking the Iranians to help the Iraqi regime. The Iranians will extract a huge price, but in fact Iran cannot do anything much to help the rapidly collapsing situation. Iraq is no longer a single country –what it will actually become is still in doubt.

All of this has been brought about largely through the deliberate ignorance of the current administration. Thinking they somehow could defeat Saddam and, following that, al-Qaeda in Iraq, Obama pulled US troops out of the country and declared victory.

From the start the post Saddam reconstituted Iraq state did not have a chance. To begin with there are massive sectarian hatreds that are still sorting out. US training and equipment supply to Iraq's army and police made it look like we were accomplishing something. But no one asked the obvious questions: are the Iraqi military and police coherent organizations and will they fight for the new government? The answer is now crystal clear. The military and police did not fight. The only fighting force willing to fight, outside of the Sunni al-Qaeda like insurgents are the Kurdish forces. The Kurds, who have always been despised by Washington because their cause was not "convenient," have a real territorial claim, a genuine sense of identity, and deep historical ties to the land. They are not, unlike all the other players, the pawn of some foreign regime (whether American, Saudi, Turkish, Syrian or Iranian).

The goal of the al-Qaeda-like insurgency is to create a Caliphate that will stretch across Syria, Iraq and Jordan for starters. If they are successful they will form a powerful and dangerous force. They are determined, very well equipped (and now helping themselves to stores of equipment and ammunition generously provided by the American taxpayer), rich, absolutely ruthless and inflexible in the extreme.

These are Islamic Jihadis. They are the same people the Obama administration has been playing footsie with for far too long, destabilizing the Middle East, alienating virtually all the allies we have in the region. Single handedly the Obama administration has destroyed America's relationship with Egypt, made a total mess of their constant pounding on Israel, and showed themselves as both toothless and worthless at every turn. The constant hectoring by both former Secretary of State Clinton and her successor, the none-too-adept, John Kerry has just poured napalm onto the fire. The President, who has a strange romantic notion about Islam and Muslims, has made it far worse. By now he has lost the respect of the foreign leaders he needs to work with, such as Merkel in Germany and Putin in Russia. So too has his "team" been discredited. Senator John McCain has gone so far as to call for the resignation of the entire National Security Council. He should extend his argument to large parts of the State Department and CIA, who have proven themselves unsuitable to run US national security policy.

Should the Jihadists get control of Baghdad, their next task will be to try and consolidate territorial gains. This may take some time and it will mean that the lower third of Iraq, which is Sh'ia, probably will form an independent breakaway state. The Kurds too will have virtual independence.

So what should the US do? By all means there is no chance at this late moment to defend a failed government in Baghdad which is currently under practical Sh'ia control. The remnants of the Baghdad government will probably retreat to the south and try and reestablish itself in Basra (itself a key oil port). Whether it can do so, and get the backing of the various Sh'ia factions, some pro-Iranians, others not, is far from certain.

The Pentagon must vigorously resist any proposed suicide-type military missions to save and un-savable Baghdad government.

The Kurds will probably, under these circumstances, declare their independence. If the US was smart, which is in serious doubt, it would recognize a Kurdish state provided agreement can be reached on boundaries, especially the sensitive boundary with Turkey, which has a large, restless, Kurdish population.

Jordan and Israel also need to be more strongly supported. If Jordan comes under Jihadi attack, as seems highly probable, Jordan may need help. Israel has bailed out Jordan before, most notably in 1970 when the Syrians threatened King Hussein. They may need to help again by providing tactical support and real time intelligence.

It bears mentioning that Israel also has to be prepared for a Palestinian threat, from Hamas and from the now clearly compromised West Bank government.

The US also has to significantly improve its tattered relationship with Egypt. Like it or not, Egypt is a big power. If it is cast adrift, as now seems the case, it will inevitably be another tinder box for the Jihadis.

America's relationship to Saudi Arabia also is in a mess. The Saudis feel they were not really supported in the fight in Syria, which is true. But even worse has been the US policy to Iran, which has left the Saudis totally exposed to nuclear extortion. Anyone who believes the nuclear deal in Iran is real probably also likes smoking dope. We need to realize that thanks to our machinations with the Iranians, Saudi Arabia's stability and its future is now deeply in doubt.

Finally we have to realize that this is a massive defeat for the United States which put all its support into the Baghdad government. The US defeat is well understood in the region, and will trigger trouble far and wide.

June 02 2014

Bergdahl and Alan Gross, The One Who Did Not Walk Away

[Editor's Note: Alan Gross was released from a Cuban prison on December 17, 2014. The United States released three Cuban spies who had been in an American prison since 2001; in exchange, Cuba released an agent for United States intelligence who had been imprisoned for nearly 20 years and released Gross, although it was claimed that Gross was released on humanitarian grounds.

On March 25, 2015, the Army announced that Bergdahl had been charged with two counts under the Uniform Code of Military Justice: one count of "desertion with intent to shirk important or hazardous duty" and one count of "misbehavior before the enemy by endangering the safety of a command, unit or place]

I have been trying to stay away from the story of Army Sgt. Bowe Bergdahl, the chap who we traded Taliban murderers for, and who knows what else.

The spin doctors tried to put out a story that the Sergeant's health was rapidly declining and that freeing him was an urgent matter for the administration. They also characterized, and continue to say, that Bergdahl fell into the hands of the enemy while he was on patrol, leaving open the suggestion that either he was in the front or at the rear of a line of soldiers on patrol in the wilderness of Afghanistan.

But it seems that story was false. The truth is that Bergdahl was not on patrol. He had been on guard duty around a FOB, or Forward Operating Base and seems to have disappeared shortly after completing his guard assignment. According to what his comrades at the outpost say, Bergdahl left behind his weapon and his body armor, all arranged in a neat stack, and walked off, taking with him only his compass. Where would he have been going in the middle of the night?

It would seem likely that either Bergdahl knew more or less where the "enemy" was, or he had some prior contact perhaps through a third party to give him instructions on what to do and where to go and who to meet. We don't know that any of this is the case, but it seems bizarre to just wander off and take your chances, since the perimeter of this FOB was far from secure and all the soldiers on the base knew that they were in harm's way.

So too does the story seem false that the trade was made for Bergdahl because he was ill. The administration has suggested that he lost a lot of weight, or that he was suffering some incurable illness.

The Associated Press reports as follows on the health issue: "'Had we waited and lost him,' said national security adviser Susan Rice, 'I don't think anybody would have forgiven the United States government.' She said he had lost considerable weight and faced an "acute" situation. Yet she also said he appeared to be 'in good physical condition.'"

If he was in good physical condition, then we are to suppose he had a mental problem? How that could be diagnosed in conversations with a kid who in talking to his father only spoke in Pashto, claiming he had "forgotten" English, his native language?

The AP also reports that two administration officials said that the Taliban may have been concerned about his health, as well, since the US had sent the message that it would respond harshly if any harm befell him in captivity.

There is a serious problem with what the unidentified administration officials are saying. Bergdahl was not a prisoner of the Taliban. He was a "prisoner" of the Haqqani Network. While the Taliban and the Haqqani Network sometimes work together, the Haqqani is also closely linked to al-Qaeda and is probably the organization that facilitated Osama bin Laden's transfer from Afghanistan to Pakistan. So it is fair to ask, what did the Haqqani network get out of the deal with Washington? Certainly not the release of five Taliban terrorists. Was it money? Or something else?

Finally, the AP reports that in 2010 the Defense Department concluded that Bergdahl walked away from his post, and this led to a decision to call off the active hunt for him. Instead of rescuing him, says the AP, the Defense Department would use only diplomatic means to get him released if at all possible.

The release of terrorists in exchange for a US soldier paints a target on the back of every American soldier. The Taliban, well aware of their great victory over the United States and the American military, are making their success loud and clear. Every tin horn terrorist now knows that he (or she) can benefit by snagging an American soldier.

Alan Gross with his wife Judy, attorney Scott Gilbert, Rep. Chris Van Hollen, D-Md., Sen. Patrick Leahy, D-Vt., and Sen. Jeff Flake, R-Ariz. watch television onboard a government plane headed back to the US as the news breaks of his release, Dec. 17, 2014. (Official White House Photo by Lawrence Jackson) [Public domain], via Wikimedia Commons

Today there are Americans who are incarcerated where, it seems, the administration has done nothing. The case of Alan Gross, who worked for the State Department, is a case in point. He was "convicted" and thrown into a Cuban prison in 2009. It would be easy to get him back if we traded some jailed Cuban spies in the US for him. But the administration, despite the pleas of the Gross family and many in the Jewish community who worked with Alan trying to aid Jews in Cuba, has not brought Alan home. He was working for them and he did not walk away.

Addendum: I want to call reader's attention to a devastating story carried in the London Daily Mail newspaper. The story tells of an Army officer who died trying to "rescue" Bergdahl from his captors in 2009.

There is one further point that needs to be made. The "freeing" of Bergdahl is obviously a cover for something else. Bergdahl is a little fish in a much bigger pond. What the administration is actually doing is negotiating a deal with the Taliban to take over Afghanistan. I feel really certain this is the case. The Bergdahl father had a channel to the Taliban, and I think the administration wanted to use this "innocent" seeming channel to negotiate something far bigger. All the rest is simply noise, but the noise is unfortunately terribly harmful to the families who have suffered over the Bergdahl matter, and the prisoners who remain prisoners, because the administration has no interest in them, the most obvious case, Alan Gross.

After a long wait, Alan Gross was finally released from a Cuban prison on December 17, 2014, after more than five years in captivity.

FALL 2014

Will NATO Fight, Talk or Trade?

Courtesy inFocus Quarterly

With the end of the Cold War and the collapse of the Soviet Union and Warsaw Pact, the NATO alliance could have folded, and maybe should have folded with its raison d'être gone. But not only did the alliance continue, it aggressively pursued an expanded membership base and broader non-member relationships under the Partnership Action Plan. Attempts to bring Ukraine and Georgia into NATO, and partnerships with Azerbaijan, Armenia, Kazakhstan, and Moldova caused considerable angst in Russia where they were seen treading on the Russian sphere of influence.

But as NATO has become wider, it has become shallower and less able to meet its own standards for the defense of its members. And a weak NATO may in fact be worse than no NATO at all, inviting aggression against it. Russia, for all its bluster, still fears NATO encirclement and does not trust the United States. Leaving NATO in a posture where it lacks any real ability to fight is the worst of all possible worlds.

NATO Has Been Busy
The NATO alliance has taken on a number of non-core missions since 1991.

In 1992, NATO entered the Bosnian-Serbian war and on February 28, 1994 US F-16s, operating under NATO command, shot down four

Serbian J-21 jets near Banja Luka, marking the first time in NATO's history that the alliance engaged in actual combat. The allied bombing campaign and on-the-ground enforcement activities led to the Dayton Accords and a negotiated settlement, contingent on the presence of 60,000 NATO peacekeepers that remained in one form or another until 2004.

The Bosnia operation was extended to Kosovo with the stabilization force known as KFOR deriving its mandate from the UN Security Council and the Military-Technical Agreement between NATO and the Federal Republic of Yugoslavia and Serbia. In 2008, Kosovo declared independence from Serbia, an announcement strongly rejected by the Russians—although Russia used the Kosovo "precedent" as a justification for Crimea's independence in 2014.

In 2003, NATO set up the International Security Assistance Force for Afghanistan to conduct security operations in that country. ISAF, too, was backed by the United Nations and consisted of both NATO and non-NATO countries. The largest contingent was American (30,700). Most countries provided only small numbers, with Britain (3,936) the only other country to exceed 1,000 personnel.

In 2011, NATO launched Operation Unified Protector in Libya, based on UN resolutions that imposed sanctions on key members of the Gaddafi government and authorized NATO to implement an arms embargo and no-fly zone, and to use all means necessary, short of foreign occupation, to protect Libyan civilians and civilian populated areas.

The recent NATO decision to create a "rapid reaction force" to protect Eastern Europe from Russia was created in response to the situation in the Ukraine.

Overall, NATO—in its new clothes—has conducted a number of military operations with mixed success. Its record overall is blemished by a number of unfortunate incidents including the massacre at Srebrenica that should have been prevented by Dutch peacekeeping forces; the bombing of a civilian train at Grdelica (300km south of

Belgrade); and the "accidental" bombing of the Chinese embassy in Belgrade. Similar mistakes were made in Kosovo. In Afghanistan, airstrikes have killed many civilians, and the entire effort seems close to collapse as the US prepares to withdraw. Gaddafi was ousted but today Islamists occupy Tripoli and the US Embassy there.

What does it mean to be NATO?
NATO was formed in 1949 in response to the Russian-precipitated Czech crisis and denial of land access to Berlin in the Russian Occupation Zone. In response, the US and its allies organized an airlift of supplies—the celebrated Berlin Airlift—that not only replaced supplies previously going by rail, but exceeded the amounts delivered under normal conditions. The result was the creation of two German states and the formal division of Berlin itself. And the Cold War in Europe.

At its inception, NATO included the US, Britain, Canada, France, Iceland, Italy, Luxembourg, Netherlands, Norway, and Portugal. In 1952, Greece and Turkey were added as both emerged from Soviet/Communist challenges, followed by The Federal Republic of Germany in 1955 and Spain in 1982. Since the collapse of the USSR, a number of Eastern European countries have been added. While France continued to participate in NATO's political meetings, it removed itself from military participation between 1966 and 2009.

The key to NATO is collective defense, embodied in Article V of its Charter, which states that "an armed attack against one" state or more "shall be considered an attack against them all." Moreover, member states each agree to "assist the Party or Parties so attacked by taking forthwith, individually and in concert with the other Parties, such action as it deems necessary, including the use of armed force."

Because Article V can be exercised by any state individually and in concert with other Parties, no formal NATO approval is required—meaning that no single state could object to action under this Article. That is the best that can be said. Article V authorizes each state to respond "as it deems necessary" but there is no obligation for any state to respond and no assurance that all the states will respond.

No one can say what NATO would do under conditions of an actual attack. We do know that when the US was attacked on September 11, 2001, it asked NATO to consider it to be an attack under Article V. NATO agreed that the United States was attacked but did not determine that the attack was directed from abroad. Therefore NATO did not see the 9/11 attacks on the US as qualifying under Article V. Since 9/11 there have been a number of attacks on NATO member countries by terrorist organizations with clear foreign connections. NATO has remained inert.

Article V, furthermore, presumes that it is a state actor that leads the attack. As the Russians have amply demonstrated in Ukraine, non-state surrogates can always be used to accomplish state goals. While Russia's backing of these non-state actors is clear, would that be enough to trigger a NATO response were Ukraine a NATO member? If the precedent of 9/11 is any guide, the answer is that such a surrogate attack would not qualify.

This is only one of the weaknesses in NATO's collective defense agreement.

Another is that Article V allows for member states to decide what response is appropriate, whether military force or short of that. This is particularly important because presumed front line states, such as Poland or Estonia, could be exposed to political-military subversion, some of it involving armed violence, which under NATO rules would not trigger an Article V reaction.

The Bronze Soldier of Tallinn

The Bronze Soldier is a monument erected in September 1944 by then-Soviet controlled Estonian authorities commemorating the expulsion of the Nazis. Estonian nationalists regarded it as a symbol of Soviet occupation. In 2007, the now-independent Estonian government decided to relocate the monument, causing a bitter fight with Russians living in Estonia and with the Russian government.

On April 27, 2007, websites of Estonian organizations, including the parliament, banks, ministries, newspapers, and broadcasters, were hit by strong cyber attacks coming from Russia. Until then, the major example of an attack on parts of a country's critical infrastructure was a three-year Chinese attack on American assets culminating in 2003. Called "Titan Rain" by the US government, the attacks struck defense contractor computer networks.

The Estonia attacks were directly connected to political events. They damaged parts of the critical infrastructure and contained much that was new and unexpected. Certain hidden network locations for sensitive banking and finance systems and telecoms were identified and hit, which greatly surprised Estonian security authorities. Intending to demonstrate its ire toward the Estonian government, Russia also demonstrated that it could do considerable damage short of an actual military invasion.

At the time, the Russians had the option to cause much more trouble, even to the point of sponsoring local terrorist attacks. They did not do so then, but what about the future?

A cyber attack on critical infrastructure, even when the source is known (as it surely was in Estonia), is apparently not an attack under Article V because it is not what is conventionally thought of as an "armed attack." Suppose, instead, the Russians decided to use an EMP attack (electro-magnetic pulse)? Would that be actionable under Article V? The truth is that NATO has never tested the definition of "armed attack," while demonstrating a strange variability when it came to protecting the United States after 9/11.

Can NATO really fight?

In 1953, the United States had over 450,000 soldiers overseas in NATO countries, spread across 1,200 different sites. Army, Air Force, Marine, and Naval forces presented a formidable obstacle and trip wire to any possible

Soviet invasion of Western Europe, and certainly against an attack against a single country. By 1990, that number was reduced to 213,000 American military personnel, and over the next three years it was reduced to 122,000 troops. Today there are 64,000 American troops in Europe, mostly supporting US operations elsewhere, including Afghanistan.

In addition, in 2013 the US deactivated an A-10 ground attack jet fighter squadron from Germany. Also in 2013, the US deactivated an Air Control Squadron from Italy, vital to US operations in Africa and the Middle East. The 170th and the 172nd Brigade combat teams were deactivated in 2013 and 2014 respectively, removing all US Army heavy armor capability from Europe.

These cutbacks may have been acceptable had intelligence supported the idea that Russia would not launch a land attack against NATO countries, as all the assets removed (not counting the soldiers) focused on protecting against a massed land attack. But the convoys of tank transporters moving heavy tanks, artillery and anti-aircraft systems moving into Ukraine from Russia indicates that they either intend to use these assets themselves or provide them to pro-Russia forces inside Ukraine. Ukraine could certainly be a dress rehearsal for other, even more provocative, operations.

The bottom line is that the American ability to support ground operations in Europe, should it be needed, is very limited. About the only response the US could mount would use American aircraft already in Europe, of which there are not many.

Zapad 2013

Zapad ("West") 2013 was a major Russia/Belarus military exercise that took place in September 2013. By combining anti-terrorist operations and urban warfare into major conventional operations, the exercise suggested a renewed Russian focus on a large scale war doctrine. Most interestingly, Zapad 2013 featured the air transport of some 70,000 troops, a huge number considering that NATO's answer to Zapad 2013, "Steadfast Jazz," transported at most 6,000. Zapad 2013 deliberately did not show tactical nuclear weapons, but Russian doctrine is to back up its conventional forces with tactical nuclear weapons of various types including missile and artillery based systems.

Russian President Putin With Belarusian President Alexander Lukashenko at the Gozhsky test ground during the final stage of the Zapad-2013 Russian-Belarusian strategic military exercises

Kremlin.ru [CC BY 3.0 (http://creativecommons.org/licenses/by/3.0)], via Wikimedia Commons

Europe's Economic Dependency

In deciding how NATO might respond to a rapidly expanding challenge, it is important to understand that Europe's economic relationship with Russia has changed since the end of the Cold War. Europe's energy dependency on Russia continues to grow, and Europe enjoys considerable export advantages to Russia and the former Soviet states.

Russia is Germany's 11th biggest trading partner at more than $104 billion annually. Germany is also one of the biggest investors in Russia, putting in $22 billion last year. Most important, Germany is a big customer for Russian gas and oil, receiving over 35% of its supplies from Russia. According to surveys, Germans approve of the relationship with Russia and oppose sanctions on the Russian government. While NATO has put sanctions in place as a result of Ukraine, it is far from clear Germany will adhere to them.

Dependency on Russian energy exports, particularly natural gas, is very high for many European countries. Should an emergency result in the shutdown of these supplies, it would have a devastating impact on Europe's already slumping economies.

This creates an advantage for Russia in assuring that NATO won't respond strongly to challenges on the non-NATO periphery, such as Georgia or Ukraine. What would happen if the challenge was directed against a NATO member is harder to judge, but NATO members would struggle, given the potential economic and social consequences to their people. It would take a tremendous challenge to force the Europeans to respond militarily, and even then the capacity for a meaningful response is limited.

Such an assault would not be cost-free for Russia. Putin can continue to point out that Russia is a force to be reckoned with, but if he finds his tactics leading him to a real military confrontation, the long-term consequences are neither predictable nor optimistic insofar as Russia's stability and integrity are concerned. That may prove small comfort to both sides if a weak NATO is forced to respond militarily to Russian aggression.

MAR 10 2014

THE KLOS-C MISSILES -- TARGET ISRAEL OR EGYPT?

On early Wednesday morning (Israel time), March 5th, an Israeli commando force known as Shayetet 13 (Flotilla 13) stormed on board a freighter, the Klos-C, in the Red Sea sailing under a Panamanian flag. Shayetet 13 is roughly equivalent to the US Navy Seals –its motto is Never Again. Jamie Frater counts this naval commando force as one of the "Top Ten Badasses of the World's Special Forces." The raid on the Klos-C was the result of extensive intelligence gathering including close cooperation between the US and Israel.

By IDF Spokesperson Unit (Israel Defense Force) [CC BY-SA 3.0 (http://creativecommons.org/licenses/by-sa/3.0)], via Wikimedia Commons. Hidden on board the vessel, sandwiched under bags of cement with "Made in Iran" stamped on them, were some forty M-302 missiles, 181 120mm mortars and 400,000 rounds of 7.62 ammunition.

According to Israel and fully supported by the US, the missiles originated in Syria. They were air-shipped to Iran (probably on Russian-made IL-76 aircraft), put on the Klos-C freighter, which departed Iran's port of Bandar Abbas, sailed on to Iraq and planned to drop off the weapons on the Sinai coast where they would eventually be smuggled to Gaza or, alternatively, set up in the Sinai but aimed at Israeli cities. According to the Israel Defense Forces (IDF) from launching sites in Gaza or Sinai, the rockets are in range of most of Israel.

The M-302 is manufactured in Syria and previously was supplied to Hezbollah. In 2006 a number of these rockets were fired at northern Israel. The M-302 is available in different versions, has a range in excess of 125 miles, and a fairly large warhead coming in at over 144kilograms (318 pounds).

The M-302 is otherwise known as the Khaibar. Khaibar (or Khaybar) is an Oasis located near Medina in Saudi Arabia. Khaybar itself was the scene of an important series of battles starting in 629AD between the Jewish community living in that area and an invasion force launched under the guidance of Mohammed. Known as the Battle of Khaybar, it is an interesting and complex story that resulted in the defeat of the Jewish community and a negotiated surrender. Under the surrender terms, the Jews were to be allowed to continue living in the Khaybar area, said protection agreed under a signed treaty. However, in 642AD the Jewish community was expelled from the area, violating the treaty terms.

It is hard to miss the significance of the name of the missile.

FEB 03 2014

THE SODASTREAM FACTORY AND PEACE IN THE MIDDLE EAST

It is an industrial park located about ten minutes drive from Jerusalem. This industrial park is named Mishor Adumim. The name denotes a plain or flat area made up of red earth. This industrial park is in the West Bank and it is the home of Sodastream.

Sodastream is the largest private employer of Palestinians on the West Bank, and it also employs Jews drawn mainly from the nearby settlement of Ma'ale Adumim. Ma'ale Adumim's name is taken from the book of Joshua in the Bible, and literally means the Red Ascent, meaning the trek up from the Dead Sea where the rock faces are red in color. The population of the town is over 39,000 and the place was historically the border area between the Jewish tribes of Judah and Benjamin.

Sodastream has now become famous principally because its spokesperson, the attractive actress Scarlett Johansson, came under attack from Oxfam International on the grounds that supporting Sodastream violated Palestinian rights. The result of the argument was that Johansson resigned from Oxfam as their "ambassador" and continues her support of Sodastream. This was highlighted by a Sodastream advertisement during the Super Bowl.

Whatever one wants to say pro or con on the relationship between Israel, the Palestinians, and the West Bank territories, there is no way one can say that Palestinian rights are being violated by Sodastream. The company goes out of its way to treat all its employees equitably. Palestinians and Jews make the same money and enjoy the same benefits in the company. The Palestinian employees are, in some cases, taking home three times the pay of their counterparts in the West Bank that is if their counterparts have employment. Unfortunately unemployment is discouragingly high in the West Bank. The Palestinian authority puts the current overall unemployment level at 27.1%, but the unemployment level of young people between 20 and 24 is 43.1%. If one adds in underemployment which is more the norm, the average person is having a hard time in the West Bank and, without a good job, is at risk.

It follows that part of the solution is more employment for Palestinian workers either in Israel or in companies located at or near Israeli West Bank settlements. And, in fact, that is the trend. Again, as reported by the Palestinian Authority and noted in the Israeli newspaper, Ha'aretz, "the number of Palestinians employed in Israel and the West Bank settlements increased in the third quarter (2013) over the second, to 103,000 from 96,000... Of that total, 51,000 Palestinians had work permits [in Israel]; another 34,600 were working without permits, and 17,600 had an Israeli identity card or foreign passport. Some 20,000 of them were working in West Bank settlements, the rest in Israel, the bureau said."

What hinders the growth of employment for Palestinians is the pressure put on potential workers by Palestinian officials and by various pressure groups inside and outside the West Bank, by incessant anti-Israel propaganda in the West Bank, especially in the media and in all schools, by threats from shadowy terrorist organizations, and by security concerns on the Israeli side that a worker coming from the West Bank may intend harm against Israel. We can add to this the fact that European and American organizations, who should know better, are stirring up trouble. Oxfam is one of them.

Even so, the picture is a little brighter than what happened in the Erez Industrial Zone in the Gaza strip. The Erez Industrial Zone in the Gaza strip housed 187 businesses including carpentry shops, textile factories, metal works and garages and employed about 5,000 Gazans. The trouble started well before the Israeli unilateral pullout from the Gaza strip starting in 2004. It was largely due to the Palestinian Intifada (or uprising) and the murder of numerous Jewish businessmen and workers in the Erez Industrial Zone. In turn this sparked the shutdowns of businesses in the Zone. At the same time, thanks to the Intifada and attacks launched by terrorists coming from Gaza into Israel, the border between Gaza and Israel, where thousands of Palestinians crossed everyday to work, was closed. Tens of thousands of Gazans were out of work as a result.

The general academic theory is that economic cooperation is a necessary prerequisite for normal political relationships. Many intellectuals have long believed that when people have jobs they are more likely to work out any differences that, if not settled, would cause them to lose their jobs.

In short, employment is an incentive for peace while unemployment is the enemy of peace.

The problem with the theory is that a small minority can destroy economic advances and set back the chance for political dialogue, perhaps indefinitely. That is precisely what happened in Gaza, and it is what threatens in the West Bank.

What is most peculiar is that the trouble making is not only local and it is hardly limited to Palestinians or even Arab pressure groups who sympathize with their cause. The fact is that groups in Europe and the United States, especially among academics, are lobbying governments to boycott Israeli business in the West Bank. Effectively their lobbying, if successful, denies Palestinians good jobs and brings them irreparable harm.

Even the US Secretary of State has threatened Israel saying that if it did not cooperate with him on his terms, Israel would end up suffering boycotts. This, in fact, creates incentives for boycotts and harms

Palestinians much more than Jews. No matter how the Secretary tries to explain his "observation," the damage is huge.

Daniel Birnbaum, the CEO of Sodastream, took over the company after it was acquired by outside investors. He has told journalists that it would not have been his first choice to support a manufacturing plant in Mishor Adumim, because of the implied investment risks for his company, and the threats and dangers to his employees and their families, Jewish and Palestinian. But since the factory was already there, he has worked hard to make it the best manufacturing facility it can be with the best employment opportunity for all its workers. He was incredibly lucky or really smart to have chosen as his spokesperson the gutsy Scarlett Johansson.

Let's hope the example will spread. Only good can come from it.

[Editor's Note: In October 2014, Sodastream announced that its factory in Ma'ale Adumim would be closed by the end of 2015 ostensibly as a cost saving measure but in fact to put an end to Palestinian political activity. The plant's operations will then be transferred to Lehavim, where it will "employ a significant number of Bedouin Arabs," not Palestinians. Once again the Palestinians and their cohorts have been successful in destroying an opportunity vital to economic development."

JAN 27 2014

CHEMICAL WEAPONS: IRAQ AND A HISTORY OF ABUSE

He was 70 years old on February 23rd, 1991. Legendary violinist Isaac Stern was in Jerusalem as the virtuoso performer of Mozart's Third Violin concerto. But, as the philharmonic orchestra and Stern performed, air raid sirens blasted. The orchestra stopped and left the stage to get their gas masks. The audience, with their gas mask containers at the ready, put them on. There was neither chaos nor panic.

Stern, alone, returned to the stage carrying, but not wearing his gas mask. He had come to Israel as a gesture of solidarity with the Israeli people, then under attack from Scud missiles fired by Saddam Hussein's forces. Amazingly, under heavy political pressure from the United States, Israel did not retaliate. Back on the stage, Stern played for the audience in a surreal scene that captivated the world. He chose Bach's Adagio for Violin. The Adagio is a prophetic piece of music, powerful, moving and modern, as if its message is the human condition of today, not of Bach's time. The audience understood the meaning of the music and Stern's extraordinary performance. When he finished they stood and cheered. Then the all-clear siren rang out.

The Iraqi attacks on Israel during the first Gulf War are difficult to explain. Israel was not a combatant in the Gulf War, and Saddam's weapons were far from sufficient to do much more than random destruction.

Saddam Hussein was well aware, even in 1991, that Israel was more than capable of reaching targets in Iraq. Ten years before the Gulf war, Israeli F-15's and F-16's successfully destroyed the Osirak nuclear reactor a little less than 11 miles southeast of Baghdad. The raid, called "Operation Opera" by Israel's IDF and "Operation Babylon" outside of Israel, perfectly pinpointed the reactor and took it out. While since that time Saddam improved his air defense capabilities and acquired modern interceptor aircraft including the MIG 25, his electronic warfare capabilities were poor and his air force was never able to put up a serious fight against modern Western aircraft equipped with radar jammers and supported by AWACS (Airborne Warning and Control Systems).

Israel feared that Saddam would equip his Scud missiles with chemical weapons, or chemical and biological weapons. Iraqi fixed and rotary wing (helicopters) aircraft had attacked the village of Halabja on Bloody Friday, March 16, 1988. Halabja was a Kurdish village in north-eastern Iraq that had fallen to Iranian forces and Kurdish guerillas. The attack killed around 5,000 people, mainly women, children and the elderly, and sickened thousands of others, many of whom later died from exposure to the gas.

Iraq used mustard gas, Sarin and Tabun (both nerve gases) and possibly VX, another nerve gas. There is strong evidence that some of the gas canisters also contained hydrogen cyanide, and possibly biological agents including anthrax. While most of the survivors had blistering and lung damage consistent with mustard gas, evidence points to nerve gases as causing the most deaths.

Iraq also used chemical weapons against Iran. The most famous battle of al Faw saw the extensive use of Sarin nerve gas by Iraq against Iranian forces. At the time, Iran had mustard gas but no nerve gas. The battle on April 17, 1988, in a major operation named "Ramadan Mubarak" aimed to clear the Iranian forces from the al-Faw area. The Iraqis were successful, in large part because of US clandestine help that included satellite imagery supplied to Saddam Hussein, American military advisors and the supply of atropine injectors for Iraq's army. The problem with Sarin or any other nerve agent, is that when you fire artillery shells filled with nerve gas a relatively close range, a shift in the wind can affect your own forces. The supply of atropine injectors was a key strategic item for Saddam's army, permitting them to confidently use Sarin.

Israel had long worried about the appearance of Weapons of Mass Destruction in its neighborhood. Egypt had a large chemical arsenal, and used mustard gas in Yemen. A well documented case was the attack on the villages of Bnei Sham and Shaukan in Yemen on 2 June, 1967. While the number of dead (again unsuspecting villagers and animals) was less than 100, the Red Cross determined that the villagers experienced symptoms consistent with mustard gas. Syria also had a chemical weapons program and a large stockpile of mustard and nerve gas. But Iraq was the leader in the WMD contest, and had invested heavily in developing chemical and biological weapons and delivery systems for them, including work on so-called binary chemical weapons.

A binary chemical weapon makes it possible to mount chemical weapons on missiles without the need to go through a lengthy and dangerous fueling process in the field. Essentially a binary weapon separates the active agents that make the weapon lethal, generally with a membrane that can be burst after a missile launch. Iraq was also at work on efficient chemical weapons dispersion systems —essentially means of atomizing the chemical weapon contents in a way to cause the maximum damage in the targeted area.

Iraq had three delivery systems for its chemical weapons. The most common was long range artillery where artillery shells are filled with mustard gas, nerve agent, or some mixture of agents, and fired against land targets. The second were aircraft and helicopters. Some of these just dropped canistered weapons. Others, especially the helicopters were equipped with sprayer units, the same as are used in agriculture to spread pesticides. The third was missiles including the Frog and Scud. The Frog is a short range missile with a range of around 70 km. The Scud missile is a Russian-developed short range missile that can carry conventional, nuclear and chemical/biological warheads. It has a range typically of less than 200 miles; the Iranians modified the Scud by enlarging its fuel tanks and reducing the size of its warhead, achieving a range of up to 500 miles. Known as the al-Hussein, it was this modified Scud that was used to attack Israeli targets –and it was exactly these missile launching sites in Iraq that the Israeli Air Force was itching to destroy.

Iraq fired 42 Scud missiles at Israel and 46 Scud missiles at Saudi Arabia. One of the missiles scored a direct hit on a barrack in Dhahran, Saudi Arabia, killing 28 members of the Pennsylvania National Guard. Otherwise, one person in Israel died (from a heart attack) and one security guard in Saudi from missile fragments.

None of the missiles fired contained WMD materials. One of them reportedly contained a cement warhead and landed near the Israeli nuclear site of Dimona. If true (the story is not confirmed), this would have been extraordinarily reckless by Saddam, because the Israelis could have interpreted the incoming missile as a nuclear threat and reacted accordingly.

Saddam clearly took extraordinary risks in using his Scuds. To begin with, equipped with conventional weapons the Scuds were not effective. While they clearly impacted civilian life in Israel and, to a lesser degree, in Saudi Arabia, they achieved very little otherwise. Moreover, they ran the risk for Saddam that his enemies could misinterpret Iraq's intent, confusing conventional with WMD attacks, as the Dimona story appears to illustrate.

The missiles also performed poorly. They were inaccurate and could only strike approximate geographical areas, not pinpoint targets as the Israelis demonstrated when they knocked out the Osirak reactor. The missile warheads tumbled as they approached target areas, sometimes exploding too soon before they struck the target. The Scuds lacked terminal guidance (later Russian-built Scuds have terminal guidance and stabilization for their warheads), and trajectories were generally predictable notwithstanding the tumbling of the missile warheads. Even so, the

US Patriot Air Defense system found it hard to destroy the Scuds, mostly because the Patriot warhead was undersized for the job and did not account for the wobbling incoming warheads. These weaknesses apparently have been corrected as a result of the Gulf War.

An Israeli researcher named Adam Golov at Israel's Institute for National Security Studies has analyzed tape recordings made by Saddam Hussein when he met with Iraqi officials and foreign visitors. Hussein had the same penchant for recording as have a number of American Presidents, a disease also shared by many other world leaders. One of the tapes, from April 1990, involved Hussein meeting with Yasser Arafat, then the PLO head. The tape, broadcast for the first time by Israel's Channel 2 on January 24th 2014, has Saddam Hussein telling Arafat (four months before the Gulf War) that "Iraq has chemical weapons it has successfully used against the Iranians" and that Iraq "won't hesitate to use them against Tel Aviv." In another tape recorded in 1991 Hussein orders his vice president Izzat Ibrahim al-Douri to launch missile strikes at Israel at night. Asked about targets, Hussein tells al-Douri that any Israeli city is a target. The tapes also show that Saddam regarded his chemical weapons as a trump card. If his regime was threatened, or if somehow Saddam was cut off from his general staff, missiles armed with chemical weapons should be launched at Israel at a variety of targets that included Israeli's major scientific research institute, the Technion.

Saddam's threats and the orders he gave were certainly understood by Israel and by the United States. His likely goal was to keep Israel out of the war, which was the same objective the US had. One of his conduits, Yasser Arafat, was regarded as a good channel to alert the Israelis. His warnings, which are only part of the intelligence matrix, permitted Israel to prepare its population with kits that included gas masks and atropine injectors to protect against nerve gas. Israeli also created a program where safe rooms were put in place in every shelter in the country (called "sealed rooms") and air raid alert sirens to warn of attacks. No other population in the world is so protected.

Saddam Hussein is no more. He was executed in Iraq on December 30th, 2006. Israel retains its civilian defense system, although with the apparent liquidation of the Syrian chemical arsenal, Israel has suspended the distribution of gas masks. The decision is not without controversy. Some doubt that Syria will get rid of all its chemical weapons. The Syrian government has already halted transit of chemical weapons out of the country on the claim that the roads are not safe from terrorists. There also is an unknown amount of chemical agents in the hands of Iraq's insurgents, many of them radicals.

Iran continues to manufacture chemical weapons even though it signed the Chemical Weapons Convention in 1993 and ratified it in 1997. Libya got rid of most of its chemical weapons and all but one of its manufacturing plants, but stockpiles of weapons and shells were not liquidated. Some of them fell into the hands of Libyan insurgents, and others were transferred to al-Qaeda, as reported by the London Daily Telegraph and based on intelligence supplied by a Spanish intelligence official. Many other countries in the Middle East and elsewhere have a chemical weapons capability. Even in the US which has destroyed its chemical and biological weapons stockpiles, research continues. The same is true of Russia and China.

We are a long way from ending the scourge of chemical weapons.

JAN 14 2014

THE ISRAELI DEFENSE MINISTER SPEAKS OUT

Years ago when I worked for Senator Clifford Case (R-NJ) on the US Senate Foreign Relations Committee, the Senator was especially fond of telling a story about his colleague and friend, John Sherman Cooper.

Senator Cooper (R-KY, born 1901 died 1991) was down south campaigning for a friend. Stopping off in a little hamlet, so the story Case told goes, Cooper gave a little speech promoting the candidacy of his friend. In the midst of the speech, which was in a small country store crowded with older gents, a voice in the back hollered "That, sir, is a crock of beans." "Beans" is not the word, but you get the drift. Cooper, a southern gentleman himself to the core, was taken aback by the chilling voice from the back of the crowd, but he mustered his strength and continued a little longer until the same old man again hollered, "That, sir, is a crock of beans." At this point Cooper stepped down from the box he was standing on to give his campaign talk. A number of the older fellows gathered around, and to soothe the Senator they told him, "Senator, don't pay any attention to that old man in the back there. He is truly addled. His outburst was, you know, really nothing. He just says what he hears."

This charming story Case used to make a point about what you say and hear in politics.

Maybe we can make the point again –this time in connection with the Israeli Defense Minister's comments about his opinion of Secretary of State John Kerry and his "peace mission" in Israel.

Israel has a lot of angst about the United States these days, and it is understandable. While officially regarded as a close ally, the US has rather gone out of its way to destabilize the region through its support for the Muslim Brotherhood in Egypt, which helped bring down the corrupt but reasonably reliable Mubarak regime, by Obama's coddling of Turkey as it trended more and more toward a more Islamist less democratic country, turning a blind eye to Turkey's under the table oil and gold deals with Iran, by the administration's failure to enforce its declared "red line" on chemical weapons use by the Syrian regime, by the US abrupt pullout from Iraq resulting in a growing collapse of stability and a tumble toward largely sectarian civil war, and most of all Obama and Kerry's decision to lift sanctions on Iran resulting in a rush by our friends in Europe to make deals with the Iranian regime, and more darkly making Iran's march to nuclear weapons power a certainty by removing any retaliatory threat to the regime.

All these things in Israeli eyes, and in the eyes of others in the region, most notably Saudi Arabia, create an existential danger and vastly diminish American power and prestige which is a vital ingredient of the balance of power.

A defense minister in Israel would have to be near the tipping point, or even completely exasperated when the American interlocutors hand him an absurd plan for creating a Palestinian state and assuring it's "peacefulness" with satellites and sensors and other technological trivia.

American Marines and the US Army know very well that Islamic terrorism is low tech but also incredibly ruthless. That is why, despite our best efforts, trying to hold a perimeter was not the best way to stop fanatics. The only way is to go on the offensive and root them out. Otherwise you are constantly dodging IED's and suicide bombers.

Over the past ten years, in a small way, my wife and I have been working with our wounded soldiers returned from Iraq and Afghanistan. I have never been more impressed with their resolve and commitment; with their fighting spirit, and their incredible dedication and optimism.

But at the same time, to sacrifice them by trying to hold territory and guard perimeters only creates more casualties and does not bring a lasting victory. My late colleague Fred Iklé (Dr. Fred Charles Iklé 1924–2011) used to say that you better define victory before you get into a fight.

The same is true in Israel. They have had their share of bombings and killings, of rockets and suicide killers. Because they are protecting a country, meaning a territory and borders, either they need a forward strategy to protect their population, or they will be victims of more and more attacks by radical Islamic forces. If Israel's Army is not able to hold the lid on the West Bank, in a minute the West Bank will be taken over by radicals and the war will be spread to every Israeli population center. A bunch of sensors and satellites is not ever going to stop it: only an army that can patrol the space and stop them before they bring harm and devastation. You don't get national security from remotely operated technology.

A good example of how technology is not a solution is the US use of drones equipped with Hellfire missiles. The US pursues al-Qaeda with drones. It has killed many al-Qaeda leaders and even more unfortunate civilians (which the administration does not talk about). It has not stopped al-Qaeda, which every report shows gathering more and more strength. In fact, the drone strikes make heroes out of al-Qaeda and their Taliban buddies.

This is what the Defense Minister of Israel, Moshe Ya'alon, was saying. He sees the Kerry mission as another deadly notch in the existential gun. And he has had enough. That, certainly, is why he spoke out.

But to think he is alone would be a mistake. Remember the old man in the back of the room.

While the US government is offended by rough

DEC 13 2013

WHAT REALLY HAPPENED IN NORTH KOREA?

The purge and execution of Jang Song Thaek in North Korea has touched off concern about the future of North Korea, and it has stimulated a variety of comments about what was behind Jang's fall.

A still image taken from North Korea's state-run KRT Television of December 9, 2013 showing Jang Song Thaek being removed from a meeting of the Political Bureau of the Central Committee in Pyongyang.

There are certain points to keep in mind in evaluating the North Korean situation.

1. The purge and execution of Jang Song Thaek was relatively quick. A few days before Jang Song Thaek was snatched by soldiers at a Politburo meeting in Pyongyang, reports leaked through sources in South Korea's intelligence organization that two of Jang Song Thaek's top aides had been executed. Even so, Jang went to the Politburo meeting where he was arrested, taken before a sort of military tribunal, and sentenced to death. It was only after the announcement of the execution that the official charges were announced by the North Korean mass media.
2. Jang's arrest and immediate execution are unprecedented by the standards of modern totalitarian regimes. In modern times the two most notorious, Stalin's Russia and China after Mao, behaved in a decidedly different manner. Typically, the subjects were arrested and held incognito for some time, in some cases as long as five years. Once matters were satisfactorily organized, state trials commenced. Many of these trials were public or semi-public in character, although others were secret trials. The accused were expected and, in many cases cooperated, in providing "confessions" of their "crimes." Some, but not all were executed, some were sentenced to execution but received reprieves, and others were sent to labor camps and Gulags.
3. In China and Stalin's Russia the purpose of the purges and trials was primarily the consolidation of power. The trials served the purpose of discrediting political factions and movements, creating a justification for the action of the state in making the arrests, and produced an aura of fear among those would-be opponents of the regimes. In Russia the purges of the old Bolsheviks morphed into the massive Great Purge that led to millions of deaths and a chain of prisons known as the Gulag Archipelago (the title of Aleksandr Solzhenitsyn's famous book).
4. Confessions are the essential element of a successful show trial. In some cases, the confessions that were given were filled with coded messages, put there by the victims, to try and communicate to

the global audience the real nature of their persecution. In other cases, such as Mao's wife Jiang Qing, the effort to obtain a confession failed; more recently in the case of Bo Xilai the "trial" was actually closed and only summaries were provided to the press (the actual court transcripts still are suppressed), because Bo, a powerful political figure, was uncooperative. He got a life sentence (his wife was previously convicted of murder and got a life sentence), but this saga is far from over.

5. In the case of Jang Song Thaek there was no confession, no open trial, no proceeding's summary, and no appeals. The sentence apparently was carried out immediately. In this circumstance, it more approximates what happened in the so-called trial of Nicolae and Elena Ceaușescu in Romania by a sort of revolutionary court. The couple was executed immediately on the conclusion of the proceeding, itself a shouting match. To add more insult to the affair, the condemned couple broke loose and ran around a courtyard until they were cut down by the executioners.

6. If we use the above as a guide, the execution of Jang is more like what happens in a revolution than in a power consolidation. But how can that be? How could Kim Jong Un be operating as a revolutionary? Only if his grip on power was so tenuous, and the situation so dire, that this was the only way he could survive.

7. Professor Kang Myong-do is the son in law of a former North Korean Prime Minister who is now a professor at Kyungmin University in South Korea. His explanation is one of the few that partly explains what is going on in North Korea. He says that Jang, in October, had traveled to China, probably Macao, which is a special administrative region of China and a former Portuguese colony and gambling center. He went there to take a monthly stipend to the older brother of Kim Jong Un, Kim Jong Nam. According to the Professor, this trip made Kim Jong Un very apprehensive and suspicious. It also conferred in Kim Jong Nam a much higher status than an exile who was passed over when power was transferred to Kim Jong Un. One recalls that Kim Jong Nam was poorly regarded, before this visit by Jang, and that he was passed over for succession by his father after it

was exposed that he traveled to Japan under a false passport, ostensibly to go to Disneyland. In the eyes of the North Koreans, he would either have been regarded as a defector or a traitor for the unauthorized trip.
8. It is extraordinary and unusual for a very high ranking official, technically the number two guy in North Korea, to personally deliver money to Kim Jong Nam. Kim Jong Nam was a special "guest" of the Chinese government, and it does not take much to see that the visit was regarded, and probably was, a plot to get rid of Kim Jong Un. This plot can be surmised to consist of Jang, regarded as a major pro-China partisan, and Kim Jong Nam, a sort of hapless fellow but useful if the idea was to replace Kim Jong Un.
9. We recall that Jang is officially accused of treason, of "day dreaming" about "being recognized as a new regime" and of plotting a "premeditated coup against" Kim Jong Un. It is also worth noting that the official charges talk about the "discovery and purging of the Jang group...." In short, Kim Jong Un was in serious trouble and feared for his life.
10. Professor Kang says that Kim Jong Un had been trying for some time to assassinate his older bother and that some of the agents sent to kill him had been arrested by the Chinese.
11. Jang was married to the biological aunt of Kim Jong Un. There was speculation she may also have been involved in the plot, but according to the latest leaks from North Korea, she was consulted about the imminent purge of Jang and supported it. This story is almost certainly fabricated, but Jang's execution and the threat to the aunt may have caused a great deal of panic in the larger family of the dictator. The leak was certainly designed to calm them down.
12. China's game in all this is not clear, but it appears that China probably supported a coup d'état and a more compliant North Korean leader in the form of Kim Jong Nam. Temporarily at least, China is the loser in the struggle. Kim Jong Un's intelligence apparatus sniffed out the threat and Kim Jong Un liquidated it by cutting off its head. It is said in China that a fish rots

from the head down. At least one of the heads, Jang's, is off. Kim Jong Nam has a lot to worry about these days.
13. Where does all of this lead? Most of the experts are saying that all of Jang's people will be purged. If this is true, there are some 20,000 who were directly dependent on Jang. If they are purged in a ruthless fashion, it could trigger heavy internal conflict. If the purge is gradual and measured, Kim Jong Un may survive for a while longer.
14. Meanwhile North Korea continues to fester and its economy continues to falter. The country is dysfunctional, and danger is always lurking when dealing with frightened and hungry people. That North Korea has nuclear weapons and rockets, and that the US failed completely to make a deal with North Korea, creates a danger that goes far beyond the Korean peninsula.

A Brief Update
Since the above was written two events have been reported. The first is that a series of Chinese military "exercises" have been shifted to locations along the northern border area of North Korea. Observers say that normally the Chinese Army (PLA) spends time scouting the exercise area and makes sure that the troops are properly equipped to work in the training environment. In this case, the PLA forces were moved quickly with no prior preparation, deployment of supplies, etc. China would not have taken these steps unless it had concern about any surprise moves by Kim Jong Un. Some reports say the Chinese are also concerned about refugees pouring into China in the midst of big purges that could occur there. This has long been a legitimate worry of the Chinese government, and in the past it has repatriated refugees to North Korea (who generally would meet an unpleasant end). On the Chinese side of the border the population is around forty percent Korean.

A second report is that North Korea is recalling businessmen that are in China, especially those in the north-eastern Chinese cities of Shenyang and Dandong. These businessmen are probably regarded as Jang's men, and if they go home they will be purged (meaning, most likely, either killed or put in North Korean gulags).

In sum, there is considerable tension between North Korea's Kim Jong Un's regime and China, reinforcing the point made in the article above that China was likely in on the plot to replace him with his older brother and a more pro-China leadership that would be more reliable. China has considerable economic and political interests in the Korean peninsula, and has friendly and positive relationships with the Government of South Korea. South Korean industry is strongly partnered with China these days, especially in electronic device manufacturing. China would want to control North Korea and prevent a rash of adventurism and nuclear saber rattling that hurts China's political, economic and strategic interests.

DEC 01 2013

Pre-Payment on the Iran Deal

"Enrichment, which is one part of our nuclear right, will continue, it is continuing today, and it will continue tomorrow and our enrichment will never stop and this is our red line," Hassan Rouhani was quoted as saying on Iran's state-run television.

By Stephen Bryen and Shoshana Bryen

The nuclear-related agreement signed between the P5+1 and the Iranian government is, on its face, one-sided. In essence, according to Senator Mark Kirk (R-IL), they get: billions in sanctions relief, 3,000 new centrifuges, a plutonium reactor and enough enriched uranium for one nuclear bomb. We get, essentially, nothing: no centrifuges dismantled; no uranium shipped out of the country or facilities closed; no delay at the Arak plutonium plant; and no stop to missile testing, terrorism or human rights abuses. But it is, actually, worse than that.

The administration's position is that the nuclear deal is separate from any other conversation with Iran, including the fate of Americans imprisoned there. Asked whether retired FBI agent Robert Levinson, former US Marine Amir Hekmati, and Iranian-American Pastor Saeed Abedini were discussed in Geneva, State Department spokesperson Jen Psaki said, "The P5+1 talks focused exclusively on nuclear issues, but we have raised – repeatedly raised [these cases] in our bilateral discussions with Iran."

In fact, the Obama administration appears to have paved the way to the nuclear talks with two steps in the direction of Iranian interests:

- Releasing high-value prisoners to Iran; and
- Separating US demands for access to Iran's bomb development complex at Parchin (and perhaps other military sites) from the nuclear talks.

Prisoners
American hikers Sarah Shourd, Josh Fattal and Shane Bauer were targets of opportunity, captured and imprisoned as spies by Iran in July 2009. Shourd was released in 2010, Bauer and Fattal in September 2011. As part of an arrangement or not, in 2012, the United States released Iranian prisoners Shahrzad Mir Gholikhan, Nosratollah Tajik, and Amir Hossein Seirafi. Unlike the Americans, however, the released Iranians were clearly working for the Islamic Republic's military establishment. Gholikhan had been convicted on three counts of weapons trafficking. Tajik, a former Iranian ambassador to Jordan, was caught attempting to buy night-vision goggles from US agents. Seirafi was convicted of attempting to purchase specialized vacuum pumps that could be used in the Iranian nuclear program.

It appears the price for the three hikers was three purchasers of illegal weapons for the Iranian government. The lopsided deal was made considerably odder by the later release of Mojtaba Atarodi, a top Iranian scientist.

The then-secret US-Iranian nuclear talks began in March 2013, after the three-for-three. In April, according to Kerry Picket at Breibart News the US released Atarodi who was arrested in 2011 for attempting to acquire equipment that could be used for Iran's military-nuclear programs. The Atarodi case is very problematic, beginning with why an Iranian scientist was allowed in the US. In cases involving theft of technology, charges are generally public and there is a trial. Atarodi's arraignment was secret and the US attorney refused to provide any public information. It appears Atarodi was to have been released to house arrest with electronic monitoring, due to concerns about his health, but the deal fell through and he was kept in a Federal detention facility in California. There is no information what he was attempting to acquire, but previous cases involving Iran have included very high speed cameras, very high frequency oscilloscopes, and nuclear trigger Krytrons. Atarodi would have been considered a high-value prisoner. Without further information, Atarodi's handling and subsequent release amounts to a cover up by the administration intended to pre-pay on the Iran uranium enrichment deal.

Meanwhile, the three Americans Levinson, Hekmati, and Abedini remained in jail in Iran. A balanced deal would have seen these three released. Levinson has been an Iranian prisoner since 2007. Hekmati was sentenced to death as a CIA spy, but while the Iranians set aside the death sentence and decided to have a new trial, it has not taken place. Abedini was sentenced to 8 years in prison for "anti-Iranian activities," which appears to mean having practiced his Christian faith while in Iran. He is currently housed in a "violent offenders" prison.

The fact that the US negotiators failed to have them released in exchange for Atarodi can be seen as a harbinger of the unbalanced deal to come. And it came with the Western decision to leave the military facility at Parchin out of any deal with Iran.

Parchin
The IAEA has been demanding to inspect the Parchin facility near Tehran since 2005, believing the site was used to test explosive triggers for a nuclear device. Satellite photography of Parchin shows the construction of a special explosives containment building that would serve precisely that purpose. Satellite imagery indicates major alterations in the Parchin site, including paving that would diminish "the ability of IAEA inspectors to collect environmental samples and other evidence that it could use

to determine whether nuclear weapons-related activities once took place there," according to the Institute for Science and International Security.

That would seem to make it essential even to the *strictly* nuclear-related conversation the State Department claims it was having with Iran. But Parchin was not part of the discussion and not part of the deal. In its "Fact Sheet" the White House alludes to Parchin saying "a number of issues" involving Iran's compliance with Security Council Resolutions need to be resolved including "questions concerning the possible military dimension of Iran's nuclear program, including Iran's activities at Parchin."

The Joint Plan of Action, the official name of the deal with Iran, says nothing about Parchin or about Marivan near the Iraq border, where large-scale nuclear-explosive testing is also reported to have taken place. There are probably dozens of other facilities in Iran where work on nuclear weapons is going on. None of the military facilities are part of the deal.

Conclusion
Anything the P5+1 believe it has achieved pales in comparison to what the deal cost. The West gave permission for Iran to continue uranium enrichment; permitted continued secrecy for a major military-related facility that the international community had demanded to inspect; and acquiesced to continued imprisonment for three Americans caught in the Iranian prison system while Iranians who were part of the nuclear program went free. And those are only the debits on nuclear-related issues. If Iran's human rights nightmare, support for the mass slaughter taking place in Syria, and support for terrorism around the world are factored in, the American pre-payment was a very bad deal for the West.

NOV 08 2013

SAUDI AND ISRAELI OPTIONS AFTER THE US-IRAN DEAL

[Editor's Note: Since the article below was written two years back the US and the other participants have agreed to a deal with the Iranians although the terms are disputed by the US, Iran and France and it is far from uncertain a final deal will be concluded in June, 2015.]

The United States has decided to cut its own deal on Iran's nuclear program, leaving in the dust both Israel, Saudi Arabia and their neighbors including Egypt and Jordan. The US already has abandoned Egypt, has cut off military aid, and has proven to be an unreliable friend. It has also abandoned Saudi Arabia, because for the Saudi state to survive it must now balance Iran's soon-to-be demonstrated nuclear weapons threat. This process, if it can be called that, has been evolving for some time.

The Saudis, like Israel, understand the threat and have been working for many years to be able to respond. For that reason Saudi Arabia has put in place an intermediate range ballistic missile system and reportedly has contracted with Pakistan for the delivery of nuclear warheads for these missiles.

Exactly when and if, nuclear weapons will appear in Saudi Arabia is anyone's guess, but the US rapprochement with the Iranian regime is very far advanced and a "deal" is likely to be signed fairly quickly. At that point, sanctions on Iran will evaporate and there will be a mad rush by European governments and manufacturers to sell advanced technology to the Iranians. Europe has lots of nuclear-related and conventional weapons technology, and has been selling equipment to Iran under the table for some time, while trying not to arouse the ire of the US government. Now the gloves are off, and both technology and bank credits will flow from Europe in a race to capture the Iranian market. Expect the Germans to be first in line, with the British, French and Italians just behind them. It will look like the kind of wanton transfer of technology, primarily by the Europeans, to Saddam Hussein of Iraq. Then everything went –nuclear reactors, poison gas technology, missile technology, communications and command and control equipment, systems for manufacturing nuclear and biological weapons. We are on the threshold of even bigger technology transfers to Iran.

As a result of these machinations, the US has all but lost any influence it may have in the region. This was demonstrated, most clearly, by the decision of the US not to enforce a Presidential "red line" on Syria and not to provide real support to Saudi Arabia in the Syrian civil war. President Assad has survived because of substantial assistance from Russia and Iran and a well armed Syrian Army and Air Force fighting against poorly equipped and disorganized foes, which sometimes fight each other. Now any settlement, if there is to be one, is in the hands of the Russians and Iranians. The US will go along with whatever they cook up and will be grateful for anything that will "end" the conflict.

US policy is, to say the least, incoherent. It is unprecedented that in the space of a few years the United States has managed to jettison critical relationships and surrender strategic assets that remain important to American global influence and to the American economy.

All of this leaves open what the former US allies in the region plan to do in the wake of these actions.

Israel has already said it rejects the US-Iranian deal. Saudi Arabia has done the same.

Israel's options, at the moment, are few. It can attempt to destroy Iran's growing nuclear capability, but this will not be easy to accomplish and carries many risks.

Israel can continue to try and sabotage Iran's nuclear program and its missile delivery systems. Unfortunately, Israel will get no help from the US because the US has vested itself in the Iranian deal. Nor will any help be forthcoming from the Europeans, if there ever was any. Nor will Israel get any help from Turkey, which –with the help of Washington– burned a number of Israeli agents in Iran, costing their lives. In fact, the US has been leaking vital intelligence information to the chagrin of Israel's leaders, in an attempt to undermine Netanyahu and weaken his efforts to derail the US-Iranian rapprochement. Trying to deal with the threat through Israeli covert operations, therefore, is already becoming difficult and may become nearly impossible because of US objections.

Israel can also more proactively challenge Iran's growing regional power by hitting Iran's operations outside its borders. This type of challenge might provoke Iran to try and respond prematurely, which could lead to a conventional conflict. The US can be expected to oppose all of these actions by Israel and will reject any claim by Israel that it is trying to protect its security.

Israel can also seek either covert or overt alliances.

One "alliance" that is possible, but extremely tricky, is between Israel and Saudi Arabia. There is already, some experts contend, Saudi-Israeli cooperation under the table. But there are strong ideological differences and considerable mistrust on both sides. Saudi Arabia is still sponsoring many terrorist groups who threaten Israel. Israel still has not achieved a settlement with the Palestinians, angering the Saudis. In addition, there are vast cultural differences between Israel and Saudi Arabia. These differences are serious and heavy. Even so, the most likely scenario is that Israel will provide intelligence on Iranian military activities to the Saudis, and help them understand Iranian deployments and grasp fully the Iranian nuclear infrastructure. It will, however, be more difficult for the Saudis to reciprocate.

Saudi Arabia, like Israel, knows that it cannot rely on the US for protection and that security promises from Washington are no longer credible. This is the driver that sends the Saudis in a search for help. One possible source of help comes from Israel's military and the fact that Israel already has a nuclear deterrent. How this can be "translated" and demonstrated given the political circumstances will require serious courage by Saudi leaders, more than by Israelis. A possible trigger will be whether Pakistan will, in fact, deliver the weapons the Saudis have ordered and already paid. If they are not delivered, Israel could be Saudi Arabia's only real option. Could one anticipate a secret mutual defense pact between them?

An alternative option that Israel and the Saudis have been exploring is trying to get Russian protection. For the most part this is just a show to try and motivate American policy makers to change course. Any real deal will be very costly to both countries and will weaken them at a critical moment.

Israel most of all, but also Saudi Arabia will face substantial pressure from the US trying to take down their nuclear programs. Over the years the Israelis have never declared they have nuclear weapons. One of the likely consequences of the Iranian rapprochement will be strong Iranian demands to dismantle Israel's nuclear arsenal. The Iranians will want American and European sanctions on Israel until the Israelis comply. Israel, of course, will not do so —but with a hostile US and a hostile Europe, Israel will face new political and economic threats.

On the whole the US has truncated and abandoned a security policy that has been in place since the end of the Yom Kippur war in 1973. That policy served both Democratic and Republican administrations. It is now gone. The result is a period of maximum risk and destabilization.

OCT 21 2013

What's Behind the Spying?

It's Much More than about Terrorism – It is about American Competitiveness
Now more revelations are coming in about US spying on friends and allies. The latest is found in stories in Germany's Der Spiegel and France's Le Monde. In the former case, Der Spiegel reveals extensive US spying in Mexico targeting the Mexican President, his cabinet officials, and Pemex, Mexico's mega-petroleum company. In the case of Le Monde, that newspaper reveals that the US was able to tap into France's undersea telephone and Internet cable system and access millions of fixed and mobile phone calls and an equal number of email accounts and data transfers. France regards the matter as so serious that the French Foreign Minister summoned the US Ambassador to complain.

One can expect in the days and weeks ahead, more spying stories. The tentacles of the NSA system are wound tightly around allied and friendly countries, around American citizens, and around hostile places too. Effectively, NSA has been able to exploit a key American advantage –virtually unlimited funds to carry out vast phone and internet tapping, and a technology advantage because most communications technology is designed in the United States (although much of it is manufactured in Asia).

The NSA "cover story" is that extensive spying is necessary to stop terrorism. But NSA has been hard pressed to demonstrate that its phone and Internet spying has actually helped stop terrorism, and targeting the

President of Mexico or key government and industrial leaders in France, Germany and many other countries, is absolutely divorced from having any linkage to terrorism.

In fact, the United States has been carrying out political and economic spying. Terrorism probably accounts for only a small portion of what the mighty NSA collection apparatus sweeps up.

Why is this? There are three explanations.

First, NSA's "customers" are US government agencies and organizations. Each of them wants information in their area of responsibility – for example, the State Department wants to know what is really going on in target countries, or the Commerce Department wants to know how to promote US business abroad.

For many years it was supposed that, unlike certain foreign intelligence gathering activities that are tightly linked to local industry and local financial interests, the US was a more benign operator: only supporting legitimate US government agency requirements. But the massive spying and wide range of targets suggests otherwise, leading to the notion that the US government is feeding not only its own government agencies, but also tipping American industry to help it compete more effectively.

Second, NSA is well placed to help secure a US economy that is barely surviving as US debt rises and as a vast number of US jobs are exported to Asia. This means manipulating money supplies, knowing what central banks in other countries will do, and trying to find some advantage in an increasingly dismal economic portfolio.

Thirdly, NSA may be helping "get back" some of the technological advantage the US has lost. A key area of concern is the erosion of the US commercial aerospace industry which has been successfully challenged by France. Boeing, trying to leapfrog technologically from a deepening lack of innovation, has spawned the 787 aircraft series –a nearly all composite airplane fraught with a multitude of problems. Knowing what Airbus in France is up to has to be a high priority not only for Boeing, but for the United States which needs to try and hold on to aerospace jobs and try and re-secure future aerospace leadership.

For many years US officials and their American industry partners ran around complaining that the French were stealing American aerospace technology. Yet they could not explain why the French commercial aircraft were innovative while the American ones were not (sort of the Detroit syndrome), and they also did not want to say that whatever technology France got, they bought (not stole) from American companies. Maybe these complaints were just a smokescreen to try and defend a sinking, though vital, industry. (We can recall that Airbus won the American refueling tanker competition, worth billions of dollars, only to have it stolen back by American politicians.)

The problem NSA now is encountering is that the work it is doing to strengthen US competitiveness and preserve the US economy and America's political standing, is being exposed. Maybe the American Ambassador in Paris can tell his counterparts: "We won't say we did it, but if we did, it gave us an advantage."

SEP 30 2013

THE NUCLEAR TIDE COMES IN

By Stephen Bryen and Shoshana Bryen

Reprinted from American Thinker.

President Obama's speech to the U.N. General Assembly contained his annual diplomatic overtures to the government of Iran, pointing to letters he has written to Iran's supreme leader and to President Rouhani and disavowing "regime change." Declaring "our" preference for the diplomatic path, President Obama enjoined Secretary of State Kerry to meet directly with Iranian Foreign Minister Zarif to begin the process of improving relations. His own attempt at diplomacy, however, was rebuffed when Iranian President Rouhani declined the American president's offer of a meeting at the U.N., calling it "complicated."

At the same time, the president told the General Assembly, "We are determined to prevent [Iran] from developing a nuclear weapon." But his "determination" carries little weight following the on-again-off-again American response to Syria's use of chemical weapons and the broad sense that Russia is the rising power in an area that had been America's domain. With a weakened United States, the impact of its newest diplomatic overture is likely to be a scramble for nuclear weapons — with important consequences for global stability.

Iran has already announced that it will not give up its quest for nuclear capability. It has invested far too much; it has a huge supporting infrastructure and a large set of international technology feeders, as well as a strongly ingrained belief that it is entitled. President Obama doesn't entirely disagree, saying it is "weapons," not "capabilities" that he forbids, insofar as he can forbid anything. But as enrichment continues and Iran's missile program continues, the space between nuclear capability and nuclear weapons capability shrinks. Iran is closing in on what Israel called "the zone of immunity," the point at which Iran no longer needs outside assistance to pursue its nuclear goals.

The first country likely to react to Iran's nuclear progress and America's regional diminution is Saudi Arabia, presently locked in a proxy battle with Iran in Iraq, Syria, and Lebanon. Sunni and virulently opposed to Shiite Iran, the Saudis will do everything they can to acquire nuclear weapons. Expect them to hook up with countries that already have nuclear know-how. After all, if Pakistan could get nuclear support from corrupt European governments and predatory companies, and Iran gets similar support, why not Saudi Arabia? Thanks to "diplomacy," the chances of American military intervention against Iran have gone to zero, and of Israeli intervention nearly to zero, leaving the Saudis on their own. While Saudi Arabia is still more likely to trust Israel than to put any faith in the United States, if it is to survive, it has to have a counterpunch.

Other American dependencies are also reading the tea leaves. Bahrain, Kuwait, Qatar, and Oman all fear Iranian hegemony. If the US is not going to defend its vital Middle Eastern interests, and has recklessly abandoned a large and important client such as Egypt, how can smaller states and sheikdoms expect the United States to guarantee their security? Oddly enough, American pressure on Israel at the behest of the Palestinians also makes the Gulf States nervous. If the US won't protect its political, social, and religious ally, Israel, how can states with essentially only a shared interest in oil claim American attention?

Any country that wants to survive will have to figure out how to do it on its own, or expect that its days will be numbered.

Farther east, Afghanistan will fall to the Taliban, and fairly soon. The Afghan government is engaged "peace talks" while the Taliban continues to attack both government and allied installations. Without Western troops and money to prop up President Karzai in Kabul, he is on his way out, whether he likes it or not. Iraq, which is fissured, may explode in a new civil war unless a new dictator emerges and the Iraqi army is strong enough to beat back its "enemies." In Syria, Assad will likely hold a third or more of the country, and the rest will remain in chaos. He will keep his chemical arsenal.

In Asia there will be some surprises. The United States sees China — like Russia — as a superpower competitor in economic and military terms. But China, like Iran, operates not *only* at the level of superpower confrontation. China, like Russia, has a "near abroad." Its regional interests are the capture of resources in the Western Pacific and the ouster of the United States from its "backyard," as Iran hopes to oust American from the Persian Gulf. China has begun to build on a disputed shoal in Philippine-claimed waters. Manila hopes the US will deter China's sprawl in the region, but with the US Navy shrinking, additional resources and a firm posture from the US are unlikely. With that, democratic Taiwan may be forced by circumstances to make a final deal with the mainland and end its independent journey.

These are conventional responses to China's conventional rise, but Japan poses a different set of issues. It will need to reconfigure itself to deal with China and take into account America's failure to divest North Korea of its nuclear program; both China and Korea are historic adversaries of Japan. Although it is living through a disaster in its nuclear power industry, Japan has lots of plutonium and solid-fueled long-range rockets, and may not be far from being able to become a nuclear weapons power. This can happen only with a right-wing political revolution in Japan, but Japanese sources note that conversations have already taken place in the government.

A US "deal" that leaves Iran capable of producing nuclear weapons will serve as a warning to the Japanese.

The Koreas, too, may see the American retreat as opening the possibility of a deal between North and South, as far-fetched as that may seem. North Korea is rapidly becoming a nuclear power, and satellite imagery shows that the Yongbyon reactor, capable of producing weapons-grade plutonium, has been restarted. China appears concerned and has announced restrictions on nuclear-related exports to North Korea. Rather than remaining a Chinese protectorate, the North Korean military could overthrow the Kim regime and look for a deal for power-sharing with the wealthy South, leading to reunification. Undersecretary of Defense Fred Ikle during the Reagan administration predicted that ultimately, North and South Korea would merge into an economically powerful, nuclear-armed, united peninsula. The decline of the United States in Asia might make South Korea more amenable.

These changes are massive, and it is unlikely that they all will happen, but with the absolute retreat of the United States, the natural inclination of smaller countries is to seek self-preservation and to maintain regional and local balances of power. Each country will weigh its weapons programs — conventional and non-conventional — and its alliances against the understanding that the American protective umbrella is folding. President Obama insisted to the U.N. General Assembly that the United States will not withdraw and not retreat.

Whether he is believed is another matter.

SEP 16 2013

THE UN REPORT ON SYRIAN CHEMICALS IS OUT –NO EVIL DOERS

The UN Report on Syrian chemical weapons (United Nations Mission to Investigate Allegations of the Use of Chemical Weapons in the Syrian Arab Republic: Report on the Alleged Use of Chemical Weapons in the Ghouta Area of Damascus on 21 August 2013) is out.

The Report confirms the heavy use of Sarin against the Syrian population in the Ghouta Area of Damascus.

The Report also contains valuable information on the weapon use, which is contained in Annex 5 of the Report. The weapon found by the UN inspectors was a rocket that carried between 56 and 62 liters of Sarin, a huge amount.

The Report shows the rocket components that were found at the site the UN inspected. The Report clearly states that the warhead portion of the rocket was not found in the crater where the remains of the rocket were found. The supposition of the inspectors was that the warhead probably burst its chemical payload somewhere above the building and that the rocket itself hit part of the building and impacted outside. The report includes photos of the rocket and shows its markings (the number 97-179 clearly visible).

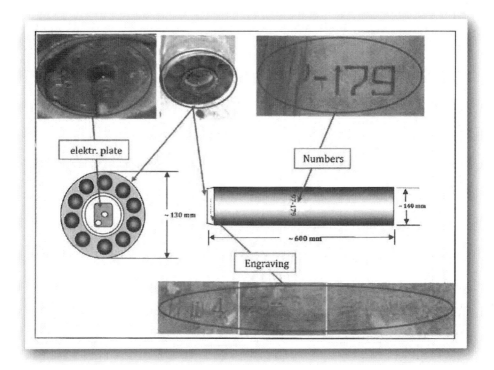

(Above)Diagram from UN Report.

This particular rocket is of Russian or Iranian manufacture. It is a very unusual design, to support the very heavy warhead. The entire munition is 2800 mm long and at least 333 mm in diameter. (This information is not in the Report.)

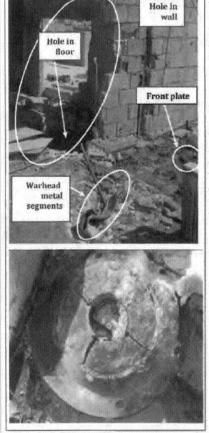

1. The rocket found by the sub-team on the roof penetrated a cinderblock wall and a rebar containing concrete floor before coming to rest in a room below. The suspected front plate of the warhead and other parts suspected of being the warhead casing were found in front of the first wall and not in the lower room. Additionally, they did not exhibit signs of significant deformation or damage due to kinetic impact. Based on the found evidence; there is an indication that the rocket warhead appeared to function prior to impacting on the roof, releasing its contents and depositing the discovered fragments before travelling through the structure to its terminal location. Apart from the rocket motor and the front central tube with the base plate, no other munition fragments were found in the lower room.

2. The front plate showed 6 symmetric threaded holes around the outline. It's unclear what part(s) are attached through these holes.

(Above) Photos and text from UN Report

The rocket with the warhead was likely launched on a platform called the Falaq-2.

Video of the launching of the munition is available and can be found on the same page noted above. Present at the launching are red beret Syrian soldiers. You will also notice a sophisticated, large vehicle of western manufacture that is used to place the rocket onto the launcher.

The UN Report does not name names —there is no Syrian Army, or Russians, or Iranians. It is as if none of them even exists.

This shows the futility of the UN and should give us ample warning that any supervision of the Syrian arsenal, as contemplated in the US-Russian agreement, is doomed to fail because the "inspectors" and "supervisors" will see no evil, hear no evil, and find no evil doers.

The UN reports a war crime without any war criminals! How inventive. How disgusting.

SEP 12 2013

PUTIN'S SPEECH (WELL, PUTIN'S OP ED)

[Editor's Note: The US, thanks to Russian cooperation, got a deal on Syria's chemical weapons, as imperfect as it is. But the US did not take the opportunity and the opening from Putin to work out an acceptable deal on Syria, or perhaps they tried but failed. No one can be sure. In any case, an opportunity was lost and the disaster in Syria, now spread to Iraq, Libya and Yemen, continues to fester out of control, taking countless lives, ruining others, and destroying artifacts of immense cultural and historical importance.]

I wanted to write about Putin's Speech, but since he wrote an Op Ed in the New York Times, I cannot be quite as dramatic as I might like. Even so, I will stick with my headline –Putin's Speech.

As this is being written, I am sure the politicos in the White House are wringing their hands, because they have been handed the second fait accompli by Putin in the space of a week.

First Putin took up Secretary Kerry's offer of a deal to remove chemical weapons from the hands of the Syrian regime. Next, Putin has made a powerful statement that will resonate with Americans, which contains the following three elements:

1. That Russia is willing to work out a political deal on Syria which could result in the end of the civil war;

2. That Russia is deeply concerned about radical Islamic terrorists, which Putin admits some are from Russia. He thinks American should be concerned about the same thing;
3. That America has gone too far in inserting itself in wars, "cobbling together" coalitions, which it will not win. Putin talks about the mess in Afghanistan, in Iraq and in Libya as examples. Putin points out that America cannot expect other countries to be instantly democratic; that becoming democratic is a struggle, and that people around the world need time to get there. Meanwhile Putin proposes that the United Nations process, with its veto system that was originally proposed and put in place by the United States, is the way to work out disagreements.

In short, Putin is saying that the United States has overreached and instead of demonstrating to the world that it is the bastion of democracy (and, by implication, human rights), we are looking like an interventionist country acting outside of international law. In the end this encourages countries to develop WMD weapons in order to protect themselves.

Putin says, "We must stop using the language of force and return to the path of civilized diplomatic and political settlement."

In his statement, which is extraordinary, unique and powerful Putin still says that it is the rebels and not the Syrian government that used chemical weapons. While all the evidence points the other way, this is the position the Russians have taken even though they have agreed to remove the Syrian regime's chemical weapons. It is on this point that Kerry has traveled to Geneva and where, it seems, the effort will be made to negotiate a deal.

Once the White House recovers from shock, it would be a good idea for the United States to negotiate with the Russians on the future of Syria. To get from here to there, the US government has to stop backing al Qaeda and other radical terrorists which it pretends it is not doing, but in fact is intervening in the Syrian civil war which is dominated by radical Islamic factions opposing the Assad regime. What lies behind the disaster in Libya and Egypt is the American pretension it could somehow embrace radicals and convert them to our side. This fundamental and inexcusable policy error has almost got us into World War III.

Putin's speech offers a way out.

SEP 09 2013

Cutting Off Supplies of Nerve Gas and WMD Equipment

[Author's Note: The article below was written before Secretary of State John Kerry suggested that Syria turn over its chemical weapons and before Vladimir Putin took up Kerry's offer and got the visiting foreign minister of Syria to all but accept the deal in principle. At this juncture, supposing that the details of an international supervisorship of Syria's chemical weapons can be worked out, the threat of war in the Middle East has been reduced significantly and the possibility of US retaliatory strikes vitiated. So we can say that a crisis has been avoided for the time being, but as they say the devil is in the details and the possibility of another use of chemical weapons cannot be ruled out. As many commentators have noted, the so-called Syrian "rebels" probably have access to some crude chemical weapons they could have got from al-Qaeda or other sources, and they will not be under any supervisorship by an international force. Similarly who knows what is in the hands of Hezbollah. Consequently, the bigger picture is to halt the supply of materials that make it possible for countries such as Syria or Iran to have chemical, biological and nuclear weapons and their delivery systems. As my article below suggests, we have done far less than enough to head off WMD threats. In Putin's smart reaction to Kerry's offer, take note that Putin did not deny that Syria has chemical weapons. Nor did he say they did not use them. He said it was time for them to give them up. So we can say that, as clumsily as it was done, the US has achieved some kind of partial deterrence. But to bring it home, a broader agreement is needed to really control the export of precursor materials and delivery systems and to make sure that whoever does make such exports, including from our own shores and the territories of our allies, pays a price –a high price. After all, that is what is meant by deterrence.]

It has received very little attention in the United States, but it is now clear that the British government authorized the sale of nerve gas precursor materials to Syria, and granted 5 export licenses to a British company authorizing the transactions. The London Daily Mail, in an exclusive story says these export licenses were issued between 2004 and 2010.

A 2012 license was also issued by the British government for the same precursor materials, but it is claimed by the UK government that the chemicals were not delivered.

The British government has, so far, refused to release the names of the two British companies supplying the material on the grounds of "client confidentiality." Likewise the government has refused to disclose the amount of the banned material sodium fluoride delivered to Syria. Furthermore the so-called end-user, a Syrian cosmetics company name is also being protected by the British government (supposing it exists at all).

Sodium fluoride is the key component of the nerve gas Sarin. Sarin, originally developed by Nazi chemists and industrialized by them in 1939 is also produced by other countries, including Russia (previously the Soviet Union).

One needs to recall that British companies supplied Saddam Hussein with chemical precursor materials in a similar manner. It is not known if Britain has also shipped chemical weapons precursor materials to other countries such as Iran. One would suppose that a cover story good for one could be used for all. It is a disgusting performance by the British establishment.

One of the issues that arise from these "discoveries" is either to accept that the British export licensing system is either incompetent or corrupt, or the UK government has covertly authorized its overseeing agencies to approve such export licenses. The fact that so far the UK government is resisting full disclosure and won't reveal either the names of the supplier companies, the name of the recipient company, or the volume of material exported, leads to serious suspicion of the behavior of the UK authorities.

It is beyond dispute that the Russians have supplied chemical weapons delivery systems to a number of countries including Iraq and Syria.

An excellent assessment of chemical weapons warheads in the Syrian arsenal which were used in the recent Sarin attack is provided by the Royal United Services Institute. RUSI is an independent institute originally founded by the Duke of Wellington in 1831.

Following the RUSI assessment, there is the suggestion that sometime after the fall of the Soviet Union, the Russian government stopped supplying the chemical precursor materials to Syria, maybe even the chemical warheads. If true it would help explain why the Syrians would go to the trouble of buying the precursors from other sources.

Looking beyond the Russian source of supply of rockets and rocket launching equipment, one can see in the RUSI video clear evidence that the launch heavy lifters and trucks are Western, not Russian in design.

The sale of chemical precursors is not limited to the UK. US firms have also sold sensitive materials, including chemicals to make cyanide and biological materials for WMD's. There is plenty of evidence that US authorities knew about all of this, and Wikileaks shows that "cables" were sent out to our allies pointing out these transactions. But it also clear that these "efforts" were not followed up by vigorous action by the US government and perhaps excepting the most recent 2012 transaction from the UK to Syria, US protestations, if that is what they can be called, were largely meaningless. At the end of the day there is a lot of hand wringing and complaining about weapons of mass destruction, but no real willingness to put a stop to them.

We are now seeing that countries such as Syria and Iran have no trouble getting hold of whatever they want for their WMD programs. A serious means of stopping future supplies is badly needed. This can be done if we are willing to put tough sanctions on suppliers, sanctions that cut them out of the free trade markets entirely. As most of the suppliers depend on trade, such an approach would change things for the better. To get there we need leadership. It has been lacking. The Syrian debacle triggered the need for a response because public opinion world wide was outraged. It needs to be similarly energized against the supplier companies and complicit governments.

SEP 01 2013

WHEN THEY WAKE FROM THE DEAD

When the little children, the mothers, aunts, uncles, grandparents and fathers who died in the Syrian Army's gas attack wake from the dead they will learn that they were killed by their government with help from Europe, Russia, Iran and other countries.

What kind of help?

What we know right now is that the British Government authorized the sale of nerve gas chemical precursors to Syria after the outbreak of the Syrian civil war. The licenses were for potassium fluoride and sodium fluoride.

Sarin, the nerve gas that killed them as they slept in their bedrooms or on the rooftops (where families often sleep during the hot months in the Middle East), was developed originally by Nazi Germany in 1939. Originally called T-144, the gas was later named after its inventors who were **S**chrader, **A**mbros, **R**udriger and van der **Lin**de. After the war the allies learned about Sarin and other nerve agents including Soman. The Russians industrialized it quickly and in 1946 the Stalin Prize, First Class, was awarded to M.I. Kabachnik for his work in building the requisite factories for production of the agent.

Sarin is an agent that is not long lasting, so stockpiles of Sarin can deteriorate. Iraq, which used Sarin against the Iranians and against the

Kurds (who were Iraqi citizens) during the Saddam period, produced substantial quantities of Sarin and other toxic agents. Learning from Soviet practice Iraq mixed nerve gas with other poisons. News reports suggest the Syrians are doing the same thing, and this may be because the Russians either directly, or through the Iranians, advised them to do so.

In the Iraq-Iran war there was very heavy use of chemical weapons, including Sarin, during the battle for the Fao (or al Faw) peninsula. Al Faw is located on the Iraq-Iran border along the Shatt al-Arab in the marshy area bordering the Persian Gulf. It is strategic because it controls traffic on the river including oil-laden ships and barges. The US role in this battle was to help Iraq in a variety of ways including advice on how to use chemical weapons and protect their own troops. At that time, Iran did not have nerve gas, but Iraq did. And Iraq used the gas in heavy amounts against the enemy. It is acknowledged that the US provided key satellite intelligence and military advisors to Saddam's Iraqi forces at the time, and tried to directly provide military atropine injectors to Iraq's army, disregarding the fact that the "enemy" did not have nerve gas. A license for 1.2 million "AtroPen" injectors was requested with the support of the State Department and elements in the Pentagon (including the Pentagon legal department). In the end, the license was blocked, but what is not known is whether alternative supplies were "facilitated" by the US government. Photos from after the battle should thousands of discarded syringes and pills coming from Europe, primarily Swiss pharmaceutical companies. What role Washington played in helping Iraq get these antidotes is not known.

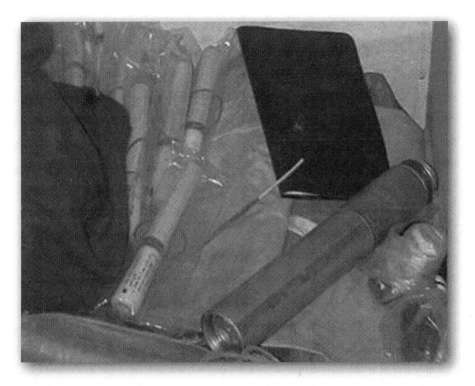

Chest containing atropine injectors reported by US Marines at An Nasariyah
(Image: Capt. NV Taylor/US Marines)

Atropine is an antidote to nerve gas because it frees constrictions in the lungs caused by nerve agents. If it is used within moments, it can save the life of a soldier or civilian.

Of course the children who died in Syria and their families certainly had no protection at all. Does the Syrian Army have atropine injectors, and if so where did they get them? And do they have chemical protective gear, and if so, from where?

These and a host of other questions about global culpability should be answered.

Syria is not an advanced industrial country, and neither is Iran. Both are backward and have to get their technology from "outside." So who is outside?

As the British case illustrates, the murdered children and their families when they awake from the dead should be told the truth. Who will tell them? Will it be arrogant governments who know very well that their deaths could have been prevented? Will it be the Russians or the Iranians who simply lie about what they have done? Will it be the Syrian regime that fired the Grad rockets filled with Sarin and other lethal gases?

AUG 23 2013

Reacting to Chemical Weapons & What to Do About Syria

By Stephen Bryen and Shoshana Bryen
From American Thinker

It is hard to look at the photographs. American newspapers are showing largely sanitized versions, so you're safe. But Twitter feeds and UK newspapers such as the *Daily Mail* don't hesitate to show the full horror. Hundreds of beautiful children, all dead, most of them wrapped in white shrouds, and their mothers, aunts, uncles, fathers, and grandmothers.

These people didn't die of gunshots or explosions; there is no blood. If you look at photos from the fighting in Cairo, blood is clearly seeping through the shrouds, evidence of external wounds. Not in Syria. The Syrians died from nerve gas — probably Sarin, a type of gas known to be in the Syrian arsenal.

Israel's Minister for Intelligence and Strategic Affairs Yuval Steinitz confirmed observers' worst fears. "According to our intelligence assessments, chemical weapons were used, and of course not for the first time," he told Israel Radio. The Europeans and the United States still want an "investigation," because they fear punishing the Assad government would make them party to the civil war on the side of an armed opposition that is, itself, unacceptable to the West. But destroying

Syria's Air Force and long-range artillery, and for that matter its known chemical stockpiles, would not be an act of war or an intervention in the Syrian civil war. It would be an operation to remove a threat of mass murder.

Dead is, of course, dead, and more than 100,000 people have been killed already, many in atrocious acts of horrific violence and through brazen war crimes by the Syrian government — including artillery barrages on town squares and hospitals. But chemical weapons have always triggered a different level of international horror. The 1899 and 1907 Hague Conventions banned them, as did the 1925 Geneva Convention, the 1972 Biological Weapons Convention, and the 1993 Chemical Weapons Convention. And yet they are produced and stockpiled by the most heinous regimes precisely because they are a terror weapon.

It is worth recalling the use of chemicals against Iraqi Kurds by Saddam Hussein. Between 25,000 and 250,000 Kurds were killed by the end of 1991, but the 3,000 dead in the chemical attack on Halabja are the indelible image of the Kurdish revolution. Saddam wanted the Kurds terrorized, and so they were. Terror would also serve the Syrian government.

Bashar Assad and his Iranian and Russian sponsors have reason to believe the West (meaning the US and the leading European countries) will not intervene in Syria. They are not alone. The remoteness of the chance of Western intervention drove Saudi intelligence chief Prince Bandar bin Sultan to visit Moscow in an unlikely and maybe desperate effort to reduce Russian support for Assad. According to an Arab diplomat, Putin "listened politely" and declined. Could the belief that they're immune to Western pressure explain the resort to nerve gas?

On the other hand, some experts think that the rebels, who were facing the bleak prospect of defeat, may have regained some strength. They captured a government air base and are again more effectively challenging the regime — including in the suburbs of Damascus. Could the belief that they're losing explain the government's resort to nerve gas?

The Russians have their own explanation. It was, they said, a "provocation," launched by the rebels themselves to justify Western intervention. From a technical perspective that argument fails. The rebels have no chemical weapons delivery systems, no aircraft, and very limited ability to withstand a nerve gas attack themselves.

Gases like Sarin are pernicious agents. A gas mask, even a chemical protective suit, may not be enough to protect a fighter even if suits were available. While there are some photos of rebels with gas masks, none have been seen in protective suits. And, of course, the population has neither. The only way to treat a nerve gas victim is with atropine injections, which must be quickly administered. US forces use encapsulated atropine injectors; in Israel atropine injectors, antibiotics (for biological weapons such as Anthrax) and gas masks are part of the civilian defense system. Not so elsewhere in the Middle East.

If the rebels were acting as agents provocateur, murdering their own people, you can be sure of two things: first, many rebels in the area would have died along with the population, so the mission would be doubly suicidal; and second, the surviving civilian population would surely try to kill any rebel they could lay their hands on.

It is long past time to punish the Syrian regime for the atrocities it has visited on its own people. Oddly enough, the American perhaps most opposed to military intervention in or above Syria, Chairman of the Joint Chiefs Martin Dempsey, may have made the case. In a letter to Congressman Elliot Engel, Dempsey said the American military is clearly capable of taking out the Syrian air force. He wouldn't do it because it would "offer no strategy for peace," he wrote. [The war] "is a deeply rooted, long-term conflict among multiple factions, and violent struggles for power will continue after Assad's rule ends. We should evaluate the effectiveness of limited military options in this context."

He is correct. Looking for a "strategy for peace" would be premature, but precisely in the context of "the effectiveness of limited military options," the destruction of the Syrian Air Force and its long-range artillery would teach a hard and effective lesson to the regime about what the civilized world considers behavior beyond the pale.

JUN 15 2013

Perilous Syria

The Obama administration decision to openly funnel arms to the Syria rebels is an escalation that has serious consequences for the United States and for the neighboring countries, particularly Israel, Jordan, Lebanon and Iraq. It also risks the credibility of the United States, because most of the outcomes that will result from US arms transfers undermine our regional and global policies.

Ostensibly, the United States is taking action on the grounds that the Syrian regime has used chemical weapons. There is proof that chemical weapons have been used, but mostly the culprits are the rebels and not the Syrian government. Even the UN's top experts think the rebels have used such weapons, albeit with poor results where they have managed to kill their own villagers and some of their own fighters.

So the claim put out belatedly by the administration is neither credible nor can it be proven empirically. It is not a Tonkin Gulf incident sufficient to trigger a US response. On top of that, since absolutely no US interest is directly threatened by the Syrian civil war, the administration's claim seems to create new risks, and not necessarily mitigate the situation.

Among Israel's two top allies that border on Syria, neither wants to see the civil war in Syria spill over, any more than it has already, onto their territory. The Israelis are worried, of course, by the take-over of the

Golan by Hezbollah, an Iranian-Syrian backed gang of Sh'ia terrorists whose armaments and training come from their sponsors. But the likely best bet for Israel, at the moment, is to wait out the civil war in Syria. Should Assad prevail he will re-position his forces on the Syrian side of the Golan heights. If he refuses, then the Israelis may do some of their own re-positioning.

For Jordan the problem is actually more serious. That is because all its "friends" –e.g., the US, Turkey, Saudi Arabia, and the emirates are using Jordanian territory to flow in arms to the rebels, many of whom are foreigners and Jihadists coming even from Europe, the US and Chechnya. They are probably also flowing through fighters, a very risky problem for Jordan's king, Abdullah.

Jordan's long term stability has been a question mark for a while, and too much involvement in Syrian matters could be a tipping point. The US could lose an ally, as can Israel, if mismanaged. Putting US troops on the Jordan-Syrian border, even in the form of a so-called exercise, is a provocation that will be noticed by the Iranians and their allies.

In the big picture, the civil war in Syria is a manifestation of religious and tribal divisions that will not easily go away. One outcome scenario if Assad and his Alawi supporters win will be revenge on the Sunni population and on the Kurds. Massacres of population are predictable.

On the other hand, the same is true if the rebels win. They will slaughter as many of Assad's people as possible and that includes the civilian population. In this culture as is already perfectly clear, there are no red lines or limitations on excess.

The US, Israel and Jordan in particular have an interest in getting Iran out of their backyard. It is very clear that if the Assad regime prevails, the Iranians will establish real bases in Syria across from Israel and Jordan, and once developed they will move nuclear weapons there as well. In that context, Iranian bases in Syria are akin to Soviet missiles in Cuba.

So what of the Russians? Russia has marines already positioned in Syria, is supplying weapons, and probably is directly supporting some Syrian assets (e.g., intelligence, missile deployments and operations, air power). Essentially this is what Russia did for its clients in the Middle East in the past. It echoes what the Soviet Union did in the early 1970's in Egypt that encouraged the Egyptians (and the Syrians) to make war on Israel in 1973.

At the same time, sharing Syria with the Iranians must make the Russians truly uncomfortable. The Iranians have been heavily involved in Syria providing troops, advisers, supplies, and training supported by an airlift operation that is continuous. They also pushed Hezbollah into the fight which has paid off handsomely for Assad.

The Russians have intimated that they could see a change in leadership in Syria, if handled by the Big Powers. But for any deal to work, the Iranians have to be expelled from the area. How to do this is a major challenge, but it may be the only way to avoid an escalation that will lead to widespread chaos and war. Iran has been allowed to become powerful even though it is still largely an untested state with significant flaws in its military capability (e.g., no real air force, no proven land army, and limited logistic ability if Iran's enemies decide to block their power projection capability). This leaves Iran vulnerable to heavy pressure, including military pressure —something the administration, which has focused on so-called engagement, has utterly failed to do. Yet, looked at objectively, the Russians and the US could find common ground here, if only they had the vision and clarity to make the effort.

JUN 7 2013

ALL SHOOK UP – NATIONAL SECURITY, THE PATRIOT ACT AND PRISM

The United States has been shaken up by the news of pervasive US government spying that touches millions of American citizens. The first swing of the bat was news that Verizon Business Services was providing on a daily basis a dump of all its land line and mobile metadata to the NSA as a result of a secret type of court order. While the Verizon story was a leak, it is easy to figure that all the other Verizon phone services, and their competitors such as AT&T, Sprint and T-Mobile (and the lesser players) are also coughing up their meta-data.

Just as the Verizon story was peaking, another story hit the wires, also originating from the London Guardian. This, much bigger story, said that pursuant to another court order, all the social media including VOIP favorites such as Skype were being mass downloaded by the government. All the stories about these channels being encrypted turn out to be only partly the truth. The encryption is not a problem, it seems, if you are inside the servers at Microsoft or Google or Amazon or any of the other players. And NSA, according to its PRISM program (which was revealed by the Guardian) was clearly inside the servers. Of course all the "biggies" immediately denied this: but the truth is that they are under a legal obligation to give such denials.

How does this come about? Public officials, to the extent they will tell, say that the Patriot Act is the authority under which they are authorized to conduct surveillance "suspected terrorists, those suspected of engaging in computer fraud or abuse, and agents of a foreign power who are engaged in clandestine activities." While terrorism is the explanation most often given, the mandate is much broader than that, and it is highly subjective.

In fact, the US government has made a decision that to effectively maintain coherence in government and protect national security; the full-blown Patriot Act is an essential component. We live in an age of rapidly proliferating Internet connectivity, social media, and communications globalization. In this exponentially growing sector, nation states survival may be threatened as never before.

Consider, first of all, the security of leaders in government and industry. They live in a fishbowl environment where their every move can be tracked and every sentence they write or speak intercepted. Not only, but the actions of leaders can open important information doors for cyber thieves by outlining connections such as relationships and alliances that can be exploited. On top of all this, leaders can be represented fraudulently by impostor, fakers and "mal-verts." This can lead to significant mistakes, errors, frauds and disasters.

Consider also the security of technology and the protection of intellectual property. There are credible studies that show that US technology is being stolen of huge value, estimated as some $300 billion annually. The US spends roughly $645 billion annually on defense, which includes all war spending and personnel costs. About $128 billion is spent on procurement each year. So the cyber thefts of defense designs are double what is spent on what is being purchased. When you add what is being sucked out of the private sector, it is clear that trying to prevent these crimes is, and must be, a priority if the country's prosperity is to continue, its social compact preserved, and its security safeguarded.

Finally physical threats to America and American citizens also is a major worry. The Patriot Act is concerned in the first instance with terrorism. There is broad agreement that the United States is engaged in what is called sometimes the "long war" against terrorism threats. It should not surprise that a significant part of the "long war" originates in radical Islam, which sees the United States as the Great Satan. Attacks on Americans, and American allies are considered a religious duty. Western values are off the table. Attacks on churches, synagogues, airlines, communities, public places, are part of the long war. And the long war is on the verge of getting far worse, not better. By setting a standard for viciousness and ferocity, the long war is being taken up outside Islam by other radicals and anarchists, right and left. Fascism is again starting to spread in Europe, and anarchism is rising again in America. Trying to get a handle on these threats and deal with the broadening threat is a critical duty of government. The Patriot Act sets the framework for this.

What we don't know is whether the Patriot Act is being used fairly and honorably. As it is set up today, there is no satisfactory way to prevent abuses, and it is fairly likely there have been more than some. If you can go looking for "foreign agents" and "spies" you have a free hand to use these means for intimidating people and for ruining reputations and careers. There have been enough examples in recent years to make us more than wonder how often this occurs.

So if it is agreed we need a Patriot Act, we should also put in place some independent safeguards. Without them, there is a great risk that the system will run a muck, out of control, sucking up information that will wind up being used nefariously. This can't be 100% prevented, but Congress and the Administration need to figure out a way to put serious controls in place to stop abuse in its tracks and punish those who do that.

The alternative could be public revulsion so great that the Patriot Act and the agencies it feeds will be changed significantly and our security the worse off.

JUN 6 2013

WILL CHINA STOP CYBER-ESPIONAGE? ABSOLUTELY NOT

With Rebecca Abrahams

No matter what President Obama and China's President Xi Jinping agree this week, China will not stop cyber espionage.

China may decide, as a result of the upcoming summit meeting, to crack down on hackers who operate independently, or who moonlight for profit in the hours they are not working for either China's government or China's military. That will be a bone to try and lower the tension that has been building between China and the US on the issue of cyber theft. But it won't really make a big difference.

There are, roughly speaking, five kinds of cyber crime.

The first is based on vicarious hacking by groups of computer geeks who want to show off their prowess and gain bragging rights for successfully attacking important institutions and organizations. The "thrill" involved is to show how smart they are, how brilliantly they can defeat the CIA or the Pentagon.

The second group grows out of the first but it has become ideological. Ideological hacking is hacking for a political purpose. Many of the ideological hackers are really anarchists in modern dress. This kind of hacking has been growing and is illustrated by phenomena such as Wikileaks and its leader Julian Asange, currently holed up in the Ecuadorian Embassy in London while wanted by Sweden where he has been charged with rape.

The third type of hacking is "For Profit." Information is stolen, bank accounts and money machines are pilfered, and sometimes blackmail is used. For Profit hacking is not always separable from ideological hacking or from vicarious hacking.

Fourth is cyber crime against individuals and political groups carried out by governments. Sometimes this is pursuant to law and follows a legal process, but not always (even in the US where phones can be tapped and computers can be invaded without a warrant or clearance by a court).

Fifth is cyber crime for national security reasons. This is a specialty of China. Recent information says that China is annually stealing $300 billion worth of national security information, much of which is weapons designs.

Why? There are essentially three reasons why China is doing this.

The first is that stealing the information is easy to do. There are hardly any credible barriers to scooping up defense information, government data, and the proprietary information of private companies.

The second reason is that there are not any consequences. This is crime without punishment. And because China owns a large part of the US Treasury, the enthusiasm by US government leaders to crack down is tempered by concern that our own economy would unravel if we push too hard. On top of that, a lot of our top industry people are making money on China.

And the third reason is that China cannot be a superpower without US technology. There is very little innovation in China, despite large investments, the presence of foreign companies, a strong electronics industry, and a huge number of Chinese nationals educated abroad (subsidizing plenty of American graduate schools of engineering, science and cyber studies).

Taken together this put the US in a bind. Lacking a credible strategy to confront the losses, the US defense posture is at risk thanks to the China thieves. And more and more companies will also feel the heat as China's clones of their products swamp the US market.

Meanwhile, one thing Xi Jinping will not do is allow China to be anything less than a superpower, so he must continue robbing the US blind. And he will.

Apr 27 2013

A Question About the Bomb Making Magazine

NBC has published an important article that says the Boston terrorists followed the bomb making advice of the al-Qaeda online magazine, ironically called Inspire.

Inspire Al Qaeda Magazine

The article, called "How to Make a Bomb in the Kitchen of Your Mom," outlines a scheme using pressure cookers, igniters, and shrapnel just as done by the Boston Marathon bombers.

But here is a question.

Since 2001 at least, the US government has been doing everything it can to destroy al-Qaeda. It is an open question whether the billions we have spent so far has done the job. It is true we got rid of Bin Laden and a bunch of his henchmen and operatives. But al-Qaeda remains a force in many places, including the Arabian Peninsula and north Africa, and in the Middle East as we now see (again) in Iraq and Syria.

There are many reasons why al-Qaeda persists –it appeals to a significant segment of Islamic radicals and so seems to have little problem recruiting replacements for the terrorists we have managed to kill or capture. Another reason is that some governments are protecting the al-Qaeda operation –you can guess who they are by remembering who was behind 9/11.

So we have a self-regenerating, government(s) protected organization wreaking havoc. And they publish a magazine on the web that tells their potential and actual recruits how to kill innocent people.

Why, then, does the United States with all its cyber fighting capability, and the billions we are spending on both defensive and "offensive" operations, not take down the al-Qaeda (and affiliates) web sites?

There is no reason for Inspire to be allowed to stay online. You can listen to all the excuses you want –such as they will just put up another site, we learn who goes to the site and it gives us counter terrorism leads, etc. Don't believe any of the muck. If it was at all true, the guys in Boston would long ago have been in jail. Even the Russians, with countless pleas to the FBI and CIA, could not get anything done.

The fact is we have really poor leadership in Washington, who don't act when they should, and can't get off their rear ends to come up with a strategy that gets much beyond sending in the drones.

Well you can't use drones in Boston, and you should not let al-Qaeda dominate in the public communications space. Surely someone in Washington can figure this out.

APR 11 2013

WHAT IS THE NORTH KOREAN GAME?
IT MAY BE UNIFICATION

North Korea is a deeply impoverished country where it is said that things are getting so bad that the Korean regime is having trouble even feeding the army.

The country also lacks energy supplies and, aside from some few arms sales and probable transfers of nuclear technology to Iran, there is no real other source of revenue.

The short term and long term prospects for the regime have reached the crisis stage.

In this light, why is North Korea threatening nuclear annihilation of South Korea, Japan and the United States?

One rather obvious explanation, but not necessarily the definitive one, is that such circuses help to keep the population totally focused on a dire, external threat, reducing pressure on the regime to deliver anything more than fighting the enemy. You may be starving, but it is their fault, not ours.

Even a captive people, half starved, sitting in the dark, and freezing, hardly will buy this kind of nonsense for very long. Either the enemy is "there" and you have to fight, or the whole thing is a ruse. All of this means that this policy has only a brief half life –either back off with the result of an inevitable and bloody revolution at home, or go to war and get bombed into a wasteland. Each result is more or less the same.

Another explanation is that this is the negotiating style of the regime. What do they want?

It is unlikely they want some oil, food and money because there is little chance they will get it, or get enough of it to matter and solve their problem. In fact, they are rather late, probably too late, if this is the objective.

Another, more plausible, explanation is that there is underway a Kabuki-like negotiation with South Korea. What could it be?

Basically it is a negotiation for unification in which North Korea brings two assets: people to provide cheap labor for South Korean factories which will make Korean factories even more commercially formidable; and nuclear weapons that will turn the peninsula into a nuclear nation with both the bombs and the delivery systems needed to challenge their neighbors and become something more than just another Asian sweat shop: a united Korea becomes a major power capable of taking on its rivals, that could include Japan, even China.

There is no doubt that South Korea covets reunification. This would buy a much larger nation with a big labor force; the cultural re-uniting of a divided people (as happened in Germany); free Korea from dependence on the United States, a kind of dependence that is not well trusted and, as American reliability elsewhere has made clear, is a big risk for a dependent nation, even a democratic one. Becoming a real independent nation, unified and dynamic, with nuclear power capability, is a tectonic shift in the region and globally. From such a vantage point Korea could properly define itself, create a truly integrated national identity, and exploit even more the resources it has, challenging a declining Japan and even challenging China, if China fractures or stumbles because of internal upheaval.

So one can suspect that sub rosa such negotiations could be going on. What deal would work? Probably the Kim dynasty would need to be liquidated because sustaining it is a deal breaker. The remaining elites could either be sent into retirement (many of them are quite old), paid off, or given prestigious (if meaningless) jobs.

What should we look for in this prospect? We should pay attention to any sign that Kim is faltering, or that there is some dissatisfaction with him or some part of his family, such as his pregnant wife. Any evidence that there is real pressure on the ruling dynasty will tell us that a deal is on the table, if not settled.

On the whole to pull something like this off must be done in a matter of weeks. When you light a short candle, it burns down fast. When it goes out, the game is over.

APR 07 2013

Is Kim Jong Un Working for the CIA?

Here is the question: either Kim Jong Un is a madman or he is working for the CIA?

In regard to the former, the popular view is that he is crazy as a loon, that he is living in a surrealistic world where the North Koreans think they can intimidate the United States, Japan and South Korea; threaten nuclear war, without any real consequences. Or he has come to believe, as his cronies probably have told him that the United States is readying war against North Korea, so his best bet is to threaten a nuclear strike. Hence the movement of a couple of mobile ballistic missiles to the sea coast, so that they can credibly claim they can hit something, maybe Japan, maybe Guam. His idea: stare down the Americans, show they are cowards, and get them to say they won't start a war against him.

The other theory is that Kim is working for the CIA. By setting up his ossified and repressive military for annihilation, he helps the CIA to solve a vexing problem –an aggressive Iran that threatens American interests in the Persian Gulf. Under this theory, Kim is being well paid and will be protected for causing an attack on North Korea that will result in the liquidation of key North Korean military assets –missiles and nuclear establishment, and factories that support the military. Well within the means of the US Air Force, there needs to be a suitable provocation and young Kim is working overtime to create the right pretext. In this scenario, no one can blame Obama for doing what he had to do, and doing it, shall we say, comprehensively. If Iran is denied rockets and nuclear know how, the regime in Tehran is toast. Without teeth it is an overextended regime that is close to bankrupt both financially and politically. Its influence will quickly decline as the Mullah-regime itself disintegrates. And, for its part, the administration can then try and stabilize around moderate Sunni Moslem rulers and, even possibly, start to introduce a kind of guided democracy to the region.

Not possible? Both theories are ludicrous? What is really happening is that the North Koreans have got themselves exercised to try and cover up deterioration at home, with starvation and lack of energy resources close to the top of their worry list. By raising the looming threat of the United States, the North Koreans are playing for an American bailout, shipping lots of food and money to the regime to keep them from being militarily crazy. And it seems to be working –the State Department is running about saying they want to restart the six power nuclear disarmament talks with North Korea –how much do you think that will cost?

If this is the poker being played, it is a hazardous game.

To begin with, moving missiles around and threatening nuclear annihilation, sending foreign embassies home, evacuating the North Korean embassy in London, all creates an impression Kim and company are not playing a bluff. How, for example, can we be sure they have not got a couple of nuclear warheads on the missiles they moved over to the coast to get the maximum range out of them?

For the US the issue boils down to a tough choice. A US surgical strike can easily knock out the threatening missiles and their command and control "system" (assuming there is one). The benefit of this is the nuclear threat is, as is said, OBE (Overcome By Events). The problem is the North Koreans will start to shell South Korea, putting Seoul at risk. So to do the job right, a big effort has to be made to neutralize the entire North Korean bombardment system, which is not easy since many of their guns are in hardened locations and are hard to destroy.

Alternatively, the US and South Korea can wait until the other shoe falls. But by then someone (who knows for sure who) may be hit by a nuclear weapon, albeit one with a low to moderate yield. When that happens the only possible result will be retaliation on North Korea with nuclear weapons.

In fact, the administration has made the decision, which is risky, to wait and see, to try and "lower" the rhetoric, which in any case has been amazingly soft, and to hold back on certain planned exercises to try and restore some calm. Under this theory, the North Koreans will climb down, things will stabilize, and life will go on as normal (however that is defined on either side of the DMZ).

We are in the retreat mode at present. But North Korea is a strange place. Usually simple minded and culturally reclusive dictatorships interpret retreat as weakness and up the ante. We will soon see if that is the case. If it is, fate may be tempted and whether Kim Jong Un is a CIA employee or not won't matter.

MAR 08 2013

THE COMING WAR AND CHEMICAL WEAPONS

[Editor's Note: This article was prepared on March 8th, 2013. On March 19, 2013 the first reports on the use of chemical weapons is being reported in Syria. Here is the information from Debka, which echoes other filings: "Extensive preparations by Syrian army units for launching chemical weapons against rebel forces have been sighted in the northern town of Homs, Western intelligence agencies told DEBKAfile's military sources Tuesday, March 19. Damascus paved the way for resorting to unconventional weaponry with an accusation run by the state news agency SANA Tuesday that Syrian rebels had fired a rocket containing chemical substances in the Khan al-Assad area of rural Aleppo, allegedly killing 15 people, mostly civilians. Rebels quickly denied the report and accused regime forces of 'firing a chemical weapon on a long-range SCUD, after which 20 people died of asphyxia and poisoning.' Neither of the accusations could immediately verified."]

According to reports coming out of the Middle East, the Syrian stockpile of chemical weapons has already been compromised and some of their supplies have fallen into rebel hands, including among the rebels the most radical al-Qaeda backed extremists. These extremists are said to operate in the Yarmouk valley area and in the Syrian side of the Golan Heights that borders Israel. The occasionally reliable Debka Report says that "the Islamist Martyrs of the Yarmouk, is now seen as tying in closely with the next plans of the Islamist militias of the Syrian rebel force, headed by Jabhat al-Nusra, which are to cement their grip on the Syrian

Golan, eastern Syria and the Upper Euphrates, where the important towns of Deir Azor and Abu Kemal are situated." This group is reported to have in hand Syrian chemical and biological agents.

Syria is known to have stocks of mustard gas, Tabun and Sarin, which are nerve gas, and according to some reports the even more lethal nerve agent called VX. Syria also is reported to have biological weapons. Syria has worked on: "anthrax, plague, tularemia, botulinum, smallpox, aflatoxin, cholera, ricin and camelpox, and has used Russian help in installing anthrax in missile warheads."

Biological weapons of one sort or another have been used throughout history, everything from throwing infected animals over the walls of towns under siege, to fouling water, to the use of Mycotoxins on innocent populations, as happened in Laos and Afghanistan. According to Global Security "Between 1974 and 1981, evidence suggested that the Soviet Union developed complex delivery systems for trichothecene Mycotoxins including aircraft spray tanks, aircraft-launched rockets, bombs (exploding cylinder), canisters, a Soviet hand-held weapon (DH-10), and booby traps. Aircrafts used to deliver the toxin included L-19s, AN-2s, T-28s, T-41s, MiG-21s and Soviet MI-24 helicopters. Soviet client states also reportedly used these sophisticated delivery systems." Given that both Syria and Iran are clients of Russia, and the fact that much of the weapons know-how came from Russia (although the manufacturing equipment was supplied mostly by Europe), the Syrians and, perhaps, the rebels also have Mycotoxins.

The full extent of the damage that can be caused by the spread of biological agents was shown when a secret Soviet-era anthrax production facility in Sverdlovsk leaked a deadly gas on April 2. 1979. There are different versions of the story and a lot of official lies, but probably more than 600 people died and thousands of animals, mainly sheep, were killed as the poison cloud went downwind some 75 miles. We now know, based on exploitation of cadaver tissues** that were preserved and were analyzed in recent years, that the Soviet-made Anthrax was actually a "cocktail" of different Anthrax seed stocks, one of which, at least, came from the United States. It is why, after 9/11 when Anthrax showed up in attacks in the US (in Florida, New York, New Jersey and Washington D.C.), the type was American and the belief was it came from Ft. Dietrich, where the Army has biological weapons labs. But, in fact, the Soviet-Russian Anthrax was made to look like it came from the US by using American feedstock, and Saddam Hussein was getting the same feedstock from the same place, namely from the US Department of Agriculture.

Nerve gas and mustard gas were used extensively by Iraq in the Iran-Iraq war, especially in the fighting in the Al-Faw peninsula. Again these agents were "cocktails" —making self-defense very difficult.

The last major attack of nerve gas, mustard gas and probably some toxins was against the Kurdish village of Halabja on March 16th, 1988. Around 3,500 villagers were killed outright, another 10,000 were casualties and there were many subsequent deaths, among them cancers, particularly colon cancer. The attack, carried out by the Iraqi Air Force and Army, ranks as the worlds most lethal use of chemical weapons and toxins. It also was an attack purely against a civilian population.

The problem with the spread of Syrian WMD in the form of its chemical and biological arsenal is that there is very little defense against them, and the only country that presently has a fighting chance to survive such an attack is Israel, because it has a chemical defense program.

In Israel there are a combination of defense strategies which include early warning, the use of "sealed rooms" during an attack, gas masks, Atropine injections and training and instruction on what to do ahead of an attack. Israel may also be providing antibiotics to deal with Anthrax.

Typically, Israeli preparations are based on relatively long range threats, primarily by missiles like the SCUD. This provides some warning time. The Israelis also have know how to clean up after an attack.

For Jordan and Lebanon there is no such program that amounts to a coherent and well organized effort to thwart any such attack through population defense. Ditto for Syria. So in case there is the use of these kinds of weapons, whether by the Syrian army, the rebels, or both, the victims will be largely in population centers, which could be devastated. The chance for more Halabjas is great.

As things now stand, there is no good answer to the coming war threat.

** PCR analysis of tissue samples from the 1979 Sverdlovsk anthrax victims: The presence of multiple *Bacillus anthracis* strains in different victims in Proceedings of the National Academy of Science of the United States, February 3, 1998.

***I want to dedicate this article to my uncle, Lou Bryen, the brother of my grandfather Jacob Bryen. Lou Bryen, a private in the US Army, was gassed in World War I on the western front, probably a victim of mustard gas and phosgene. He lived into his 70's, but long suffered because of damage to his lungs. When I was a boy, Lou told me stories of the Great War. He remembered they were ordered to put gas masks on the mules, before they put their own gas masks on. Lou, a real American Patriot who came from Czarist Russia as an immigrant, followed orders.

******AN ADDED NOTE**
In 2002 I wrote an article on Iraq's chemical weapons called Iraq's Threat. It was published by the National Review Online. It is reproduced below. The URL for the article is http://old.nationalreview.com/comment/comment-byren010302.shtml

Iraq's Threat
What we know about their biological and chemical weapons.
By Stephen Bryen. Mr. Bryen previously headed the Department of Defense's technology-security program.

January 3, 2002 9:20 a.m.

When US forces overpowered the Iraqi Army in the Gulf War in 1991 they found many valuable documents about Iraqi chemical and biological weapons. These captured documents, plus interviews with POWs, made it clear that Iraqi forces were well trained in the use of chemical agents such as Sarin, a nerve gas. But they had almost no guidance on how to handle or use biological weapons, although the documents support that such weapons were available. According to declassified Gulf War intelligence reports, Iraq had trained teams of chemical-weapons NCOs (non commissioned officers) on how to manage a chemical-warfare operation and how to decontaminate their own troops and equipment after their use against allied forces. But Iraqi Army NCOs were not given concrete guidance on biological-weapons use or safety precautions. Unlike US troops in the Gulf, Iraqi troops were never vaccinated against biological agents like anthrax. Yet, had Iraq used its chemical weapons it may have found its own troops affected by biological agents which, no doubt, would have killed as many Iraqi soldiers as alliance forces. After being hit by Iraqi chemical weapons during the Iran-Iraq war, Iran learned the dirty secret of Iraqi weapons: they tend to mix together various types of chemical agents with biological-warfare agents. An early choice was a Soviet-developed form of Mycotoxins (sometimes called "yellow rain"). Mycotoxins were used by the Soviet Union in Laos against Hmong tribesmen and, later in Afghanistan. Intelligence sources believe there was considerable cooperation, particularly in the 1980s and perhaps since, between Iraq and Russia's biological-warfare units. Some reports single out the Russian organization Biopreparat as being linked to Iraq. One of the "fingerprints" of Russian weapons is to mix many substances together. Adding Mycotoxins to a chemical-weapons "cocktail" is a trademark of the Soviet/Russian-weapons program which Iraq copied. Iraq's use of Mycotoxins combined with chemical agents was confirmed by Belgian scientists working on behalf of the United Nations. While Iraqi soldiers did not know what was in their bombs, NCO war prisoners told allied interviewers that they feared that if they used such weapons many of them would die just from contamination. Indeed, the fact that the Iranians found it very hard to get rid of the persistent CBW agents used by Iraq against them is a harbinger of what we are now experiencing trying to clean up a relatively small anthrax attack. The truth is nobody knows how to use biological weapons, or even the best way to protect themselves from them.

Russia, the US, and Britain have worked on vaccines to protect soldiers exposed to biological agents. During the Gulf War over 150,000 American soldiers were inoculated against anthrax. In the US, with the failure to adequately decontaminate post offices, America's homeland-defense agency has offered anthrax vaccine to US Senate workers and US Postal Service employees for post-anthrax exposure protection. It is not known if it really works — the offer is strictly an experiment and the vast majority of postal workers have turned down inoculation.

It is far from clear that anthrax inoculation works reliably, even to protect against initial infection. The success of the inoculation depends on the type of anthrax and how the anthrax was "engineered." The anthrax manufactured in the Soviet Union, for instance, was no simple germ agent. The stuff that leaked into the air at Sverdlovsk in 1979 contained at least four, and perhaps five, different strains of anthrax mixed together (including the Ames strain, the strain that was used by terrorists in the United States). At least one of the Russians killed by the Sverdlovsk anthrax leak, probably an employee of the Soviet weapons lab there, had received anthrax vaccine before exposure.

Recently, the Russians have said they have made progress on new vaccines and have offered them to the United States to combat the anthrax attack.

Dr. Philip Brachman, a pioneer in anthrax research, told the *Los Angeles Times* that the anthrax spores found in the US were so small that they could get in someone's lungs and, perhaps years later, fester into the anthrax disease. US Government officials concur with this assessment.

During the Gulf War there was concern about so-called "dusty agents." Dusty agents are very fine types of chemical or biological dust that can penetrate protective clothing and gas masks. In the Gulf War US intelligence was sure that Iraq had dusty chemical agents and may have had dusty biological agents.

Dusty agents remain a major problem, as the recent US terrorist attacks make clear. The US Army is searching for better gas-mask seals and improved protective clothing to protect troops against chem-bio attacks. (During the Gulf War troops were advised to put rain gear over their chem-bio protective suits to try and block dusty agents.)

Engineered anthrax in dusty form is an indiscriminate terror weapon. It has no sensible military use, and how it operates on a complex society is not well understood. When the Sverdlovsk leak occurred, the Soviet government ordered surface soil removed, buildings decontaminated on the outside as well as the inside, roads paved over, and dead bodies buried in coffins filled with caustic chemicals to kill remaining anthrax spores. That is how they dealt with a dusty agent.

Over the next few years the United States will be searching for ways to handle the anthrax threat, and threats from other biological weapons. But is that enough?

Countries that build biological weapons whose effects can't be controlled or even predicted are engaged in global terrorism. That is one reason why the US ended its offensive biological-warfare program years ago.

Countries with a demonstrated capability and willingness to use chem-bio weapons, and who continue to develop nastier forms of biological-terror weapons, are a potential threat to global survival. Iraq, from all the evidence available including recent defectors, is the world's leading threat.

JAN 31 2013

RUSSIA, IRAN AND SYRIA TAKE A BIG RISK AND COVER IT WITH THE BIG LIE

[**Author's Note, 3 Feb. 2013**: Since this article was written there have been many news stories on the air strikes against Syrian assets. The Syrians say there was no attack on any SA-17 missile convoy; instead they say that Israel hit the "research" facility and "killed civilians." Syrian rebel sources say that the Israelis blanked out the Syrian air defenses. Meanwhile the US has only confirmed the Israeli strike on the convoy and not on the research facility, and Israel has put out vague hints that it carried out actions because of threats to Israel's security. Syria has also put out a video of the strike on the compound. The video shows the destruction of a number of vehicles, trucks, an SA-17 launcher vehicle, and many cars. The video also shows the interior of a lab and an office. All the images either are the result of anti-personnel bombs or machine gun fire. None of these are the types of weapons Israel would use –if it wanted to destroy the facility it would have done so. Consequently, the thesis of the article below seems even stronger than when it was written, namely that Israel took out a convoy of SA-17's. The attack on the so-called research facility was probably done by the rebels and, not wanting to give them any credit, Syria blamed it on Israel when Israel conveniently destroyed the SA-17 convoy. This stand by Syria also deflects the argument that Syria was in direct violation of UN Resolutions in providing missiles to Hezbollah in Lebanon.]

Russia and Iran are unreservedly supporting the Syrian regime, providing weapons, military advice and advisers, and, insofar as Iran is concerned, military forces. On top of this, Iran's surrogate, Hezbollah, is providing direct military help to the regime's thugs, and are being used against resistance targets inside Syria.

In the midst of this mess, the Syrian regime has lost control of important areas of the country and, despite wanton killings, has failed to cow the uprising.

The Russians have put a few thousand troops offshore Syria, ostensibly to assist in evacuating Russian dependents. As a recent Russian "airlift" out of Lebanon showed, very few Russian dependents have taken up any offer to leave Syria. The Russian forces are there for one of two reasons —either to standby in case it is necessary to pull Syrian officials out of the country (Assad has already moved out of Damascus and is in helicopter range of the Russian ships), or to help the regime with its 2,000 marines stationed on these ships.

Meanwhile the status of Syria's weapons stockpiles has grown precarious, and most worrisome is its toxic chemical weapons, especially nerve gas. Some of these stockpiles are in range of the rebels, and the US, Israel and many other countries have gone public with concern about security for these WMDs.

On Wednesday, January 30th (or the night before), it was reported from Lebanon that Israel had flown a dozen or more sorties over Lebanese territory along the Syrian border. Additional reports, also coming from Lebanon and recently confirmed by the US, say that Israel attacked a convoy heading from Syria into Lebanon, bound for Hezbollah.

"Buk-M1-2 9A310M1-2" by .:Ajvol:. - Own work. Licensed under Public Domain via Wikimedia Commons - http://commons.wikimedia.org/wiki/File:Buk-M1-2_9A310M1-2.jpg#/media/File:Buk-M1-2_9A310M1-2.jpg

The flow of weapons through Syria to Hezbollah has been going on for a long time. It is how Hezbollah has acquired missiles it uses to bombard Israel.

But something obviously changed for the worse, in Israel's view. Either more advanced surface to surface missiles were being delivered to Hezbollah or advanced ground to air missiles (officially known as SA-17's and made only in Russia).

For quite a few months it has been getting clearer and clearer that the Iranians, probably with Russian backing, have been posturing to create a renewed conflict between Israel and Hezbollah.

Advanced missiles that could be equipped with chemical warheads, and advanced ground to air missiles, look to be part of what Hezbollah would need to initiate another war with Israel.

What purpose would a war with Israel have? There are two theories.

The first is that by getting Israel locked into a war with Hezbollah, a second front with Hamas and Gaza would open and the focus of attention would be on that conflict, deflecting any possible US-sponsored intervention in Syria.

The second theory is that not only is the Syrian regime under severe stress, but the Ahmadinejad government in Iran is also wobbling and could fall. Rumors are about, and one of them is that Ahmadinejad needs some kind of external "success" to head off his liquidation. Whacking Israel could be the kind of "triumph" he needs to stay in power and remain alive.

These two theories are not mutually exclusive. Even Russia, which is playing a double or triple game, could somehow benefit if they could salvage, or help salvage, the Syrian regime.

But the problem with all of this is that it is a gamble that is ruthless as it is dangerous. Given current circumstances, Israel might achieve a great deal if as a result it squashes Hezbollah and wipes out the Syrian Air Force in the bargain.

Today the Syrians, and the Russians, started screaming that Israel had attacked a chemical weapons precursor facility near Damascus. According to the Syrian "explanation", Israel's aircraft flew "under the radar" and successfully hit the facility killing a guard and a workman. The Russians made the extraordinary claim that Israel had violated UN resolutions and should be called to account.

It is impossible that Israeli aircraft can fly around Damascus without activating Syria's extensive missile defense network. This network, put there by the Russians and probably with Russian technicians and operators, would have responded and Syrian Air Force planes, busy killing innocent civilians, would have been scrambled. It never happened.

In fact only one airplane, well after the fact, a MIG 31, was flown toward Israel near the Golan Heights, but never crossed into Israeli territory. When it was "painted" by Israeli radar, the MIG turned right, flew to the coast, and headed home. It was just there, it seems, to try to make the fake Syrian-Russian story a little more real.

One could, playing on Shakespeare's Hamlet, say that "the Russians and the Syrians doth protest too much, methinks." In fact, sending a convoy loaded with military hardware to Hezbollah is a direct violation of UN Resolution 1701 (for what it is worth).

But the real matter is whether the Syrians, Iranians and Russians will continue to try and implement the confrontation strategy they started to execute in shipping advanced weapons to Hezbollah. Israel has made clear that it will respond to these provocations and that it is on alert. There won't be any surprise. And the Syrians must recognize that there is a tipping point in this strategy that it could result in the annihilation not only of their chemical stocks, but also their Air Force, command and control network, and other defenses. If a gaping hole is ripped through these assets, the Syrian regime will cease to exist.

JAN 20 2013

"Incapacitating" Agents and Hostage Taking Raids

News reports from Algeria tell us that the hostage siege at the Ain Amenas Gas Plant in the Sahara is now over, but the final list of casualties remains uncertain. So far we know that the operation resulted in the escape or release of some 685 Algerian workers and 107 foreigners. Current information says that 23 hostages are confirmed dead; another 25 bodies, presumed to be hostages, have so far been found in buildings. There are probably more deaths as a number of vehicles were struck by Algerian Air Force helicopters and destroyed, and these vehicles are said to have been carrying both hostages and terrorists. The Algerians report that "all" 32 terrorists were killed.

There has been serious criticism of the Algerian Army and Special Forces raid and claims they did a poor job resulting in an excess of civilian deaths. From information so far that is available, about 6% (six percent) of the hostages died during the operation. Possibly the number will rise, but it is unlikely to exceed 10%.

Is this a bad result or a good result?

In October, 2002, Chechen terrorists took over the Dubrovka theater in Moscow. There were some 850 hostages trapped in the theater and around 40 to 50 Chechen terrorists. The Russians tried to negotiate, over the course of a number of days, with the Chechens but no solution was found. Meanwhile the Chechens had executed a few of the hostages for various reasons.

On October 26 Russian Special Forces flooded the theater with a chemical agent, pumping it in through the ventilation system. Following this the Russian forces poured into the building and killed all the terrorists. Of the hostages 117 died as a result of the gas.

The incapacitating agent has never been officially identified but it is something called by the Russians **Kolokol-1**. Kolokol-1 is likely a morphine derivative that is aerosolized and based on fentanyl. The actual compound is 3-methylfentanyl.

In evaluating the Russian operation it can be seen that the number of civilian casualties was particularly high –roughly 15%. Many of the hostages, when freed, required urgent medical treatment. There is an antidote for Kolokol-1, but it must be administered quickly to work.

Poison gases intended to maim or kill are regarded as chemical agents and are banned under the Geneva Convention and the Chemical Weapons Convention. Kolokol-1 straddles the fence of legality, because while it is not intended to kill, it is a potent substance (1,000 times stronger than morphine) and, as the Moscow theater case shows, can be quite lethal.

Physically, the Moscow theater episode occurred in a closed building that was barricaded and filled with 40 or 50 heavily armed killers equipped with explosives, automatic weapons, grenades and RPG's. If the Russian Special Forces had operated in the same way as the Algerian forces, and attacked with conventional arms, it is likely that the death count may have been higher than it was because of the lack of space to pick out targets. Perhaps other weapons, such as stun grenades, may have helped; but it is unlikely to have been effective given the mass of people and the determination of the Chechens.

If comparisons are used, the Algerians did "better"(6% to 10% versus 15%) than the Russians. Of course, the physical space of operations was markedly different.

Just last month the US Consul in Turkey reported in a "secret" cable (which was leaked) that the Syrians used chemical weapons in Homs on December 23rd. The chemical weapon identified is called by the Syrians **Agent 15** and, in fact, it is a CX-level incapacitating agent that causes some temporary sickness and disorientation. The agent is probably 3-Quinuclidinyl benzilate, which is a compound related to atropine (which itself is an antidote for nerve gas). This compound is "controlled" under the Chemical Weapons Convention although Syria is not a signatory to the convention. States who signed the convention should have destroyed chemical weapons and weapons manufacturing by last year, but Level 2 materials are not actually required to be destroyed. (Level 2 or Schedule 2 chemicals supposedly have legitimate small-scale applications. Manufacture must be declared and there are restrictions on export to countries which are not CWC signatories.)

The issue of incapacitating agents is not resolved under the Convention and most countries have them, including the US. Probably for this reason the State Department was encouraged to not denounce the Syrian regime for using chemical weapons in Homs.

Would a more effective incapacitating agent have been better than the military assault carried out by the Algerians? It is far from clear, but it may be that more research into less lethal, but more effective, incapacitating agents that can work in open areas rapidly and effectively would make sense (especially if the lethal characteristics of such materials can be mitigated). Of course this means that chemically based incapacitating agents can be an important element in future counter terror operations. While there is no public discussion as yet, research in this area seems warranted and urgent.

No one should fault either the Russians or the Algerians for standing up to a terrorist attack and doing their best under extremely difficult circumstances. Perhaps in future they will have even better tools and such incidents will result in fewer casualties.

JAN 06 2013

AN E-Z PASS FOR GUNS?

Instead of new draconian gun laws of dubious effect, consider the ubiquitous E-Z pass.

Like millions of other Americans, I pay a small monthly fee for my handy E-Z Pass transponder. It gets me through toll booths on highways, bridges and tunnels quickly and efficiently; it crosses State lines without interruption. For the most part, the E-Z Pass billing system is accurate and gives you a helpful record of your travels.

The E-Z Pass is a passive sensor, actually a transceiver activated by a radio signal from the toll booth or toll lane. The transceiver operates at 915 MHz and transmits information at 500 kilobits per second. No battery or other power source is needed. The specific E-Z Pass technology is proprietary, but transceivers for other applications have already been built. Today, RFID (radio frequency identification) devices are inserted into credit cards, building passes, garage gate openers, and Metro fare cards, to name just a few applications.

Can this technology be applied to guns and how would it work?

Putting RFID sensors into manufactured guns and tagging them to the owner is in fact simpler than the E-Z Pass system, because the sensor can be embedded at the time of manufacture or, for guns already in circulation, can be added at a very small cost. Putting antennas around schools, colleges, hospitals, sports stadiums (for example) and public buildings is not complex. Linking the sensors to existing security systems also is reasonably straightforward and not expensive.

Consider this. A person with a gun approaches an elementary school. If the school perimeter contained RFID antennas, they could detect the gun, automatically lock down the school, and warn school personnel that there is a potential threat.

Consider this. At the entrance of the State Department there is a security check that includes an RFID antenna to find a gun. Even if the gun is hidden or the magnetometer cannot not find it, it is likely the RFID antenna will detect it.

Consider this. At the entrances to the Cherry Hill Mall in New Jersey, there are RFID antennas. If someone enters the mall with a gun, the security guards are immediately alerted. The detectors are linked to PTZ (pan tilt zoom) cameras that can track the likely gun holder.

RFID technology can buy a lot of protection. It can be implemented quickly in new guns and existing registered guns. It is low cost.

In fact an Italian company called Chiappa Firearms has already introduced RFID chips in all its new guns. While their press release is in Italian they say that the chips are virtually indestructible and that they can be read by remote detectors in microseconds.

Putting protection around schools, for example, compliments existing security systems and procedures and can be done quickly and probably within existing security and infrastructure budgets.

But isn't the problem illegal guns? Illegal guns are a major crime problem, but — as we just saw tragically in Newtown — *legal* guns are often the ones used in incidents such as school shootings, work places attacks, and shootings in public access places or events. For the most part, schools, colleges, malls, work places, and public buildings have only limited, or no defenses against legal or illegal guns, with the preponderance of crime they experience coming from legal guns.

Thirty years ago, I served as Deputy under Secretary of Defense for Trade and Security Policy, and Director of the Defense Technology Security Administration. Our offices became concerned with Glock pistols that were being made of synthetic polymers (a type of plastic). The problem was that the "plastic" Glock might not be recognized by metal detectors or X-Ray machines in airports or in secure buildings. The answer, which the Glock people accepted, was to add some metal powder to the plastic so the gun shape could be seen in an X-Ray machine and picked up by a metal detector.

The RFID tag is a modern evolution of the Glock idea, but with the advantage that it can provide early warning of danger.

In the coming months, the President and Congress are poised to consider new gun laws in response to the multi-victim tragedies of our recent past. Many of the ideas currently advanced sound draconian, may violate the Second Amendment, and are unlikely to reduce violence committed with legally registered weapons. An E-Z Pass-type solution wouldn't reduce the likelihood of a violent *attempt* being undertaken by a mentally unbalanced or otherwise disturbed person, but it could very well protect innocent people from victimhood.

DEC 05 2012

Syria and Gas Warfare

The US and the international community have voiced serious concern about the movement of some of the Syrian chemical warfare stockpile apparently in the direction of Aleppo, which is the seat of Alawite population and power in Syria. Like Damascus, Aleppo is under siege by Syrian rebels and the fighting is reportedly bitter. There is talk that the Syrian Army is beginning to disintegrate, that Damascus itself could soon fall to the rebels, and that countries in the Middle East, South America and elsewhere have informally offered asylum to Syrian President Bashar Assad and his family.

Whether Assad stays or leaves will not, in and of itself, resolve the Syrian security situation. The civil war is only the start of Syria's problems, not its end point. Unresolved is the situation of the Alawi population and its security, the Kurdish minority, and the Christians among others. While many thousands have already gone to Turkey, Jordan and Lebanon they represent only a fraction of the at-risk populations and the potential for retaliation again civilians, the military, government employees, business leaders, educators and thousands of others.

In this context, the Syrian situation is nothing like Egypt's, where there has been regime change, or even Libya where there are sharp, unresolved tribal differences. Syria is far more treacherous and there is very little an outside power can do to prevent attacks that will target diverse groups in the country.

The decision, apparently by the Syrian army, to collect chemical weapons needs to be understood in this context.

There are at least five, and perhaps more, chemical weapons storage facilities in Syria plus manufacturing facilities that were acquired with help from European countries and from Iran. It is highly unlikely that all the chemical weapons have been moved, or that all can be moved easily given current security conditions. News reports indicate that the Syrian army has grabbed artillery shells filled with Sarin, a highly toxic nerve agent. Sarin was used, with other chemical agents, by Saddam's Iraq in the ten year Iran-Iraq war in the 1980's. It played a big role in certain battlefield situations, especially the fighting on the Fao peninsula. But the most dramatic use of nerve gas was against the Kurdish population in the village of Halabja, on March 16, 1988.

Halabja was an attack using aircraft bombs filled with Sarin and other chemicals and helicopters to spray chemicals on a defenseless population. Sarin was one of the chemical agents, along with Tabun, another nerve agent. Also used were mustard gas, a blistering agent, and cyanide. Upwards of 5,000 civilians were killed outright in an attack that went on for some five hours; another 10,000 or more people became very ill as a result of the attack and many died later. There are also reports of cancers and other diseases caused by the WMD attack.

Halabja is a more likely "model" of what might happen in Syria if chemical weapons are used, because conventional rebel military targets hardly exist. The rebels tend to operate inside the population and in built up areas, not out in the open field. The battles are not territorial and strategic as much as they are psychological and, often, murderous. Add a chemical component to what has transpired so far and it is easy to see significant civilian casualties. Furthermore, it is likely the rebels will, at some point, get their hands on chemical weapons that were not in-gathered by a retreating Syrian army.

So far as is known, training, chemical protective gear, and nerve gas antidotes such as atropine, hardly exist in Syria. This means that any population concentration will pay a heavy price if chemical weapons are used.

Of course the United States and its friends and allies can demand that poison gas not be used. In a devolving, chaotic situation, the chance that these demands will have effect is difficult to say. Clearly holding Syria's leaders to account, both civilian and military, may help but no one can be sure if they will be persuaded. As more and more defections occur, the rise in angst inside Syria within the government and military may outweigh rationality.

Much of the capability that Syria has, that was in the hands of the Iraqis, and that is today in the hands of Iran, is a Western moral and political responsibility because the supply of manufacturing equipment, precursor material, and WMD know-how happened with little active intervention by governments, and sometimes on a complicit basis. If chemical weapons are used against populations, it will be a black mark on Europe and the others who supplied Syria just as the supply of nuclear know-how to Iran endangers world peace in an unprecedented way.

OIL AND THE CHANGING SHAPE
OF AMERICAN SECURITY

It will be a different world if the United States achieves energy independence. And now predictions are that this will happen sooner rather than later, probably by 2020. But becoming energy independent is starting to happen even now, and organizations will try and take advantage of large surpluses, especially natural gas.

Becoming energy independent has huge foreign policy and national defense implications.

Today the Great Risk Point (GRP) is the supply of oil through the Persian Gulf. An adversary could create havoc in the shipping lanes, blow up supply depots, or even set oil fields on fire.

GRP is such a big problem that the current administration is petrified that a rogue Iran will inflame the Gulf, and if not them, then al-Qaeda or the Muslim Brotherhood or their analogues. Take your pick. So the idea is to embrace them and try and redirect them away from precipitous action.

But an energy independent America no longer faces GRP. And there are developments that may also save Europe arising from oil discoveries from Israel, to Cyprus and probably to Greece that, if they can be moved quickly enough, can make up the difference from the Gulf. The money is starting to come into these alternatives and this is shifting the geopolitical stage.

OPEC will try and fight the trend by lowering energy prices. But lowering energy prices a lot means less money that can be used at home to buy off adversaries, especially the local kind. So if prices dip, this may already be starting to happen, revolution rises. The trouble in Bahrain is a harbinger, not an oddity.

The US, depending on the timing of all this, is in fat city. But the loser are not only the Gulf States (including Iran), but also the outliers who do not have enough oil of their own. China could get into staggering trouble if oil supplies are interrupted. It's the same for Japan, Korea and many others. And Europe –already heading for its own self-made depression- could collapse. Euro-socialism will go, but what will remain could be a fierce civil war in Europe between have's and have not's, and between ethnic groups such as Euro-Arabs, Gypsies, Jews –some new suspects, some the usual ones.

US foreign policy is built around defense of the Persian Gulf and safeguarding the flow of oil. The first Gulf war started for the United States when Saddam's Army crossed into Saudi territory. Then the threat was clear and unambiguous. The second Gulf war also was alarm about Saddam's intentions and his ability to blackmail the region thanks to arsenals of chemical and biological agents. (How much he had, what happened to it, remains a matter of dispute, but policy makers believed he had WMD, which is all that is really important.)

But as local oil replaces imported oil, and natural gas replaces diesel and, eventually gasoline, we enter a period of enhanced ambiguity, not clarity. Voices will ask why the US should make the supply of oil safe for Europe, or safe for China? Others will explain that we cannot roll-back revolution in the region that we lack credibility to do that, and a political upheaval is not easy to solve with military force, especially the diminished forces we now have. As we learned in Iraq and Afghanistan, the war costs probably exceed our ability to pay, at least for the next five to ten years.

Certainly there will be renewed emphasis on the southern Mediterranean, and NATO may try and strengthen its role in protecting the emerging supplies of oil. But to do that Israel will have to become either a de facto or de jure member of NATO, and the Euro-politics of that are really formidable. Other solutions may have to be found, such as new localized collective security agreements. These are in the future, but not very far.

Meanwhile we are on the precipice of a huge transformation. American domestic and foreign policy may never be the same.

APR 09 2012

Exporting Spy Technology to Iran

Eighteen years ago, led by the United States, the Coordinating Committee on Multilateral Export Controls, otherwise known as COCOM, was closed down, ostensibly because the Cold War was over and COCOM was not needed anymore.

COCOM included all the NATO countries plus Japan. It ran an embargo against the sale of advanced technology to the Soviet Union, Warsaw Pact countries, and China. While COCOM never included certain countries such as Cuba and North Korea, the participants generally observed the embargo on a wider basis. For that reason key enabling technologies were not sold to places like Syria, Iraq or Iran, or at least they were not supposed to.

During the mid to late 1980's the United States led an effort, largely successful, to more formally include certain high risk countries such as Iran, Iraq, Syria, Libya as formally embargoed.

COCOM controlled goods and technology for military use, and it also set limits on what was called "dual use" technology that could contribute significantly to military applications or intelligence gathering.

There was great pressure from exporters, with the collapse of the Soviet Union, to abandon COCOM and the Clinton Administration obliged them.

Unfortunately this was a big mistake, because it left the field wide open for the export of sensitive technologies to "thug" nations –that is, countries that routinely and ruthlessly suppressed dissent and engaged in aggressive operations against their neighbors.

While a supposed export control system was put in place theoretically to deal with the residue of COCOM's activities, known as the Wasenaar Arrangement, this was more of a fiction than anything else, a pretend solution to a looming problem.

Now 18 years after COCOM's closure, we are starting to learn some of the consequences. The Guardian, a liberal UK newspaper, now is reporting that the UK is exporting advanced surveillance equipment to "countries run by repressive regimes…" Among them are Iran and Syria. According to the Guardian, some 30 UK companies were exporting such equipment, with the tacit (and perhaps also official) backing of the UK government that ardently promotes exports.

But it is not only UK companies involved in this kind of activity. According to the same newspaper, 50 or more US companies were doing the same, followed by German and Israeli companies exporting spy technology.

In response, the European council banned the sale of surveillance equipment to the Iranian government. But the ban is a fraud, as the same companies are selling to Iranian commercial companies who then re-sell it to the Iranian government.

What is being sold? Technology to spy on cellular phones that not only steals data from mobile phones, but also allows the "thug" regimes to turn the phones on and listen in on conversations at will. The Iranian customer is MTN Irancell.

Along with the cellular Spyphone technology, sales are booming in Internet spying technology, so emails, Facebook, Twitter and all other social media are not only under surveillance, but can be altered and changed to suit repressive regimes.

Why is there such enthusiasm to sell goods and technology for spying to proven repressive governments and even to terrorist organizations. No one has bothered to find out, but greed is certainly one of the motivations.

Meanwhile those who are fighting for freedom are paying a terrible price.

And we should remember that these same repressive regimes and terrorist organizations can do to us, what they can do to their own citizens using our own technology against us.

FEB 12 2012

THE SWARMING BOAT PROBLEM – WHAT DOES IT MEAN?

The US Navy has been concerned for some time about the threat of "swarming" boats. This threat is seen as very strong where American warships go through narrow passageways like the Strait of Hormuz, or around important anchorages, as for example near key oil ports. The swarming boat thesis is that terrorist, whether directly or indirectly state sponsored (i.e., Hezbollah, al-Qaeda) will load up a number of small boats with high explosives and drive them toward US warships at relatively high speed. These boats, which just need a couple of high powered outboard motors, can move very fast. Because they are made out of fiberglass and do not protrude far above the waterline, they are hard to see, hard to catch on radar, and hard to shoot at because they expose very little surface.

A swarming boat attack can be a suicide attack, or it can be an attack where the boat driver jumps out at the last minute. Or, in a more sophisticated version, the swarming boats can be remote controlled.

Swarming boats can be launched from shore at night, or they can be dropped into the water from old transport ships or empty, obsolete oil tankers.

Multiple boats coming at a US Naval ships present a problem, because it is unlikely that the ship's missiles can hit these targets. This leaves only the guns on the ship to do the job.

American ships today are significantly under-gunned. During the 80's Pentagon planners were focused on "big" naval threats like the Soviet Union. Ships needed missiles to fire, guns were thought to be obsolete.

Most US warships have a CIWS gun (pronounced Sea-Wiz). This is a 20mm Gatling gun that was put on ships to take on any enemy missile that got through past the missile defense on the ship. CIWS fires a lot of rounds very rapidly, but it also runs out of ammunition just as fast. It is a short range gun, but probably will not be very effective against multiple swarming boats coming in from different angles of attack. CIWS was only used once in 1991 against an Iraqi Silkworm missile. It missed its target but managed to hit one of its nearby sister ships. Another CIWS, belonging to the Japanese Navy, shot down a US A-6 Intruder aircraft, when it was supposed to hit a target drone towed by the A-6.

The US Navy had a program to integrate the CIWS gun with the Oto Melara 76mm Compact 75 on US frigates. The project, called Swarmbuster, does not seem to have been completed. The Compact 75 is a long range 3 inch gun that is effective in the counter-ship counter-boat role. It also has ammunition with sufficient burst to blow a swarming boat out of the water. Improved versions of the Oto gun fire 100 rounds per minute or better. It can use the same sensor as the CIWS gun.

The US Navy is right to be worried about the swarming boat problem. On the other hand, the Navy is not very well prepared to deal with the threat, particularly if the enemy strikes at night. One wonders why, despite the depth of concern and the years the Navy has had to deal with the threat, very little (if anything) has been done to build proper countermeasures.

February 7 2012

Can the US Navy Cope With Iranian Mines?

Well, we don't have any minesweepers...

By Stephen Bryen and Shoshana Bryen
Courtesy PJ Media

The USS Ponce, a lightly armed and slow-moving amphibious transport dock built in 1970, is about to be upgraded by the US Navy. According to The Washington Post, it will become a forward staging base aimed at Iran.

Official Navy Photo

Navy specifications published in Federal Business Opportunities indicate that the refurbished ship will carry 370 personnel, plus four video teleconferencing centers each capable of holding 25 staff and an operations center of 20. It will be loaded with 10,000 gallons of extra fuel for helicopters, and store weapons and ammunition. The ship itself has only a couple of small guns — a CIWS Phalanx gun (with an old and ineffective sensor) and a machine gun — neither of which can challenge an incoming missile.

Why anyone would want to float nearly 400 people and a gazillion gallons of flammable liquid on an indefensible bucket in the world's most hostile waterway is unclear, but three possibilities exist: staging SEAL attacks; meeting "local" surface threats; and minesweeping. The Obama administration denies the first, and the Ponce is optimal for none. Under the Navy's specs, the Ponce is optimal only for becoming a very large fireball.

Aggressive-class minesweeper, USS Constant (Official Photo)

The Navy proposal includes adding cranes to raise and lower riverine command boats and 4 Zodiac RIBs (Rubber Inflatable Boats) which are typically used for SEAL-type missions – hence the belief that the Ponce will become a platform for SEAL missions. But SEAL missions, at least in theory, are surprise affairs that catch the target unawares. Any mission launched from an old, slow boat like the Ponce would be instantly known.

It could be that the SEALS will be used to go after local surface threats, which are anticipated mainly to be heavily armed Iranian fast patrol boats attacking oil tankers. The theory is that the SEALS would chase the patrol boats or, if necessary, capture them. This requires both capability and political will.

The Iranian fast patrol boats are well armed and numerous. Would the SEALS be authorized to fire warning shots or to take other aggressive action against them? It is one thing to rush out to meet what looks like a fishing boat but might be a vessel with al-Qaeda operatives or other terrorists, or a vessel stuffed with explosives like the one that hit the USS Cole; it is another to pick a fight with a warship.

In 2007, two RIBs manned by 15 British sailors and Marines dispatched from the British frigate HMS Cornwall were challenged by the crews of two Iranian fast patrol boats. The British did not resist. They were taken captive and held for 13 days before the Iranian government released them. Had the British fired on the Iranians, it is not clear that they would have survived to be captured.

Would American RIB boats or crews do better or fare better?

In addition, the Ponce is not the Cornwall; the Iranians weren't about to take on a serious fighting ship. But in our case, the Seals would also have to protect the Ponce, which is ill-equipped to defend itself. But RIB boats cannot do both missions. Iranian patrol ships are equipped with Chinese C-802 anti-ship missiles and torpedoes that could make short, explosive work of the Ponce and its crew.

So, if it isn't a launch ship for covert action and it isn't a response to local surface threats, what about anti-mine operations? The likely mission for the Ponce would be responding to Iran's threat to mine the Strait of Hormuz and prevent oil tankers from passing through the Gulf.

The Navy probably plans to use the four MH-53 helicopters supported from the Ponce flight deck in counter-mine operations. Unfortunately, the MH-53 is old and has an aging mine sweeping capability. It will be hard pressed to do the job, and if it fails, there will be oil tankers burning in the vital and narrow Strait.

DEC 22 2011

Patriots for Tehran

The shipment of 69 Patriot missiles seized in a Finnish port was not going to South Korea. I am sure their final destination was Iran, and that the seizure is the tip of the iceberg of a huge espionage operation.

Tehran badly needs air defenses to protect against US and Israeli aircraft and cruise missiles that might attack Tehran's nuclear and missile sites. The Russian air defense system is not yet in place, and it lacks sufficient coverage to meet Iranian needs. Already feeling pressure because of significant and multiple clandestine attacks on critical missile and nuclear facilities, Iran is expecting all out war, and soon.

The Patriot may not be too good against Scud missiles, but it is an excellent air defense system that can kill jet fighters and bombers and cruise missiles. Iran does not have a competent air force and cannot challenge any western air force. So its only defense against air attack is ground launched missile interceptors. The Patriot is the best system for that purpose.

The MS Thor Liberty, a British-flagged vessel, was carrying the Patriot missiles and tons of propellant for the missiles. Not found (yet) are the radars and command and control system for the missiles. Maybe they are on the MS Thor Liberty, or maybe they were shipped separately. But it is nearly certain they would have been stolen as well as the missiles and propellant.

South Korea does have Patriot missiles, but whether the missiles they have are the same as those found on the MS Thor is not now known. What is known is that South Korea, if it wanted to buy these missiles legally, would have had to ask the Germans (where the missiles came from) to ask the US for permission. This, in turn, because of the sensitivity of the shipment and the fact that these missiles are also controlled under the Missile Technology Control Regime (MCTR) would need Congressional approval. It is unlikely the South Koreans would need propellant, as they already probably make their own.

It is reported that Finland says that there were legitimate arms export documents with the Patriots on the MS Thor. Why then would the shipment be declared as "fireworks"? If such documents exist they have probably been forged or obtained through illegal means. No German export official would issue documents of this kind without the government's approval, and there is no reason to believe that the German government would authorize such a transfer without American approval. American law says that arms exports need to be shipped in US flagged ships.

I spent almost eight years as the head of the Defense Technology Security Administration in the Pentagon. My team went after what we called techno-bandits around the globe. Some of them were smuggling arms to the Soviet Union, others to Iraq and other Middle Eastern locations. I am convinced the end user here was Iran, who would get the missiles and the technical help from China.

SUMMER 2012

IRAN GETS SPY AND NUCLEAR TECHNOLOGY DESPITE EMBARGO

Courtesy InFocus Quarterly

Although Iran is at the top of the list of countries hostile to the West, and although the United States and its allies claim to be embargoing technology in an effort to slow Iran's nuclear program, the regime is still getting its hands on both nuclear-related technology and spy technology from the West. The embargo on Iran and export controls have failed because these controls are poorly enforced and the United States lacks leadership willing to crackdown on this dangerous trade.

Iran's Nuclear Program: A Product of the West
A centrifuge is a complex piece of machinery that requires special materials available only from a limited number of sources. The centrifuge is needed to enrich uranium, and enriched uranium (90 percent or more U-235) is needed for nuclear weapons. The original goal of the West was to keep centrifuge technology out of the hands of the Iranians. Today there are more than 9,000 centrifuges spinning in Iranian facilities and more on the way.

Pakistan obtained its centrifuge technology from Europe, the design coming from Urenco, which is owned in equal parts by Ultra-Centrifuge Nederland NV (owned by the Government of the Netherlands), Uranit GmbH (owned equally by German energy companies E.ON and RWE), and Enrichment Holdings Ltd (owned by the Government of the United Kingdom and managed by the Shareholder Executive). Urenco operates in Europe and in the United States; its centrifuge designs are all based on the work of Gernot Zippe, an Austrian-German mechanical engineer.

Pakistani nuclear scientist A.Q. Khan has taken credit for stealing the centrifuge design from Urenco while he was an employee. He also takes credit for spreading the technology around the world with the apparent blessing and support of the Government of Pakistan. Iran was one of the beneficiaries.

The Zippe centrifuge has been changed and improved over time, and Iran has taken great advantage of those improvements. It is unknown precisely how these improvements reached Iran, but the continuous leakage of technology from Europe in related sectors suggests that Europe's nuclear technology continues to spread far and wide. The most important centrifuge upgrades in Iran required specialized materials including carbon fiber tubes, composites, maraging steel, and gas bearings. Maraging steel and the carbon fiber tubes that make up the rotor of the centrifuge are spun at very high speeds and operate for long periods of time. Stability of speed is very important, and centrifuge cascades require reliable, filtered power controllers, and sophisticated electronics.

The electronic controller and controller software for the centrifuges, known as the model S7-300, was designed by the German engineering firm Siemens as was its software package, Simatic Step 7. The frequency converter drives that work with the S7-300 are based on a design that comes from the Vacon company of Finland.

The Siemens S7-300 is distributed in Iran by a company named Pcsromo. Investigators think they are only doing final assembly work and that the circuit boards, software, and other components are imported. Pcsromo announces its relationship with Siemens unequivocally: "We can offer very attractive prices for Siemens S7 series PLC and I/O Modules, ranging from S7-200, S7-300 to S7-400. We are currently supplying Siemens S5 and S7 parts to USA, Europe, South-East

Asia, India, Pakistan, Middle East and etc. Please contact us for more details." Its website says that Pcsromo is linked to a number of companies including Siemens, PCS Automation, Allen Bradley, Mitsubishi, Toshiba, and others.

At least some of the frequency converters were supplied by a small Iranian company called Fararo Paya. As in the case of the controllers, it is not clear they are manufactured in Iran. According to the Institute for Science and International Security (ISIS), "It is unlikely that Fararo Paya makes frequency converters from scratch for Iran's enrichment plants. It likely either makes them from major subcomponents acquired abroad or purchases them intact from overseas suppliers. The latter is difficult to accomplish successfully since frequency converters with a range of 600-2,000 Hz are considered nuclear-related dual-use goods controlled for export by Nuclear Suppliers Group (NSG) guidelines."

The international embargo on Iran is supposed to be working, but clearly the Iranian nuclear program continues to expand as Iran puts more centrifuges on line. This means that the supply of components to Iran from Western countries continues. The so-called embargo has failed to work because Western governments are not enforcing it.

Both the Siemens controller/controller software and the Vacon/Fararo Paya frequency converters were directly targeted by the Stuxnet worm, which changed the spin rate of the centrifuges so they were unable to separate U-235. Someone knew precisely the equipment used by the Iranians, if not where it came from. Reportedly the same equipment was set up at Israel's Dimona nuclear facility and Stuxnet was test-driven to ensure its functionality.

Spying on the Iranian People
Not only is the Iranian nuclear program flourishing thanks to Western technology, but its effort to suppress dissent and smash political opposition is also receiving help from European and American companies.

Consider the International Mobile Subscriber Identity (IMSI) "catcher." In Iran, as in Europe and in the US (AT&T and T-Mobile), the IMSI systems authenticate users and allow one GSM-type mobile phone to talk to another using the standard built in encryption chip known as the A5. The A5 offers a moderate degree of security to users, which the IMSI "catcher" is designed to circumvent. The "catcher" is essentially a police-run mobile phone tower that pretends to authenticate the user's phone but in fact turns the encryption off, opening the network to instant police spying. IMSI catchers can be installed just about anywhere and thus offer a convenient way for police and secret services to listen in.

IMSI catchers have been sold to Iran and, according to the group Privacy International, once the Iranian state has unimpeded access to a targeted cell phone, not only are the police and security forces listening to "live" phone conversations, but they also can put malware on the user's phone so that the phone can be tracked and all its messages and emails read, and its off-line conversations heard.

Privacy International says some 30 UK companies and at least 50 US companies have been exporting surveillance technology to Iran (and to Syria). While the EU and the US have recently "banned" the sale of such equipment to Iran and Syria, the ban is largely meaningless because it only targets sales directly to the Iranian and Syrian governments; so-called B-to-B sales (business to business) are not blocked. In the US case, the equipment is believed to be exported to a middle country and then re-exported to Iran and Syria.

Spyphone software is a huge problem for the Iranian dissident movement, as it allows authorities to steal data from a smartphone, listen in on "live" phone–to-phone conversations, turn on a phone's microphone and camera even if the user thinks the phone is turned off, and much more. Spyphone software is sold freely without any export license in the US and Europe. Once planted on a phone, it is very hard to discover and even more difficult to erase.

A wide range of surveillance technology from reputable companies is flowing to the Iranian regime. Technologies to monitor personal computers and tablets, to listen in on Skype calls, and to do cluster analysis to link together dissidents, along with face recognition and other video surveillance systems helps the regime keep a finger on dissent in the country.

Stopping Iran Late in the Game
Perhaps the best hope to stop Iran from acquiring nuclear weapons and threatening, if not using, them against Israel or Saudi Arabia (two potential targets) is regime change. If the Iranian regime could be replaced with a more moderate government, one that does not want to annihilate Israel, there is reasonable hope that the nuclear program would be shut down.

Unfortunately the spyware and surveillance equipment pouring into Iran are making it hard for dissidents to operate. Many people complain that they, or their friends and colleagues, have been arrested by the regime after being tracked by Iranian internal security. Some say lives have already been lost because calls, SMS messages, and location data have fallen into the hands of the police and security services.

The lack of enforcement of export controls is what led the US and Israel to try cyber attacks against Iran's nuclear infrastructure with tools such as the Stuxnet worm and the Flame virus. Cyber warfare is, as the name says, a form of warfare. A cyber attack against a military-type target requires a great deal of expense and effort, as well as coordination with industry.

Was there coordination with industry in the case of Stuxnet? It is difficult to say with certainty. It is true that Siemens eventually offered a solution to their clients that was widely propagated, and at least one high ranking Iranian general accused Siemens of being complicit in helping design the Stuxnet attack. Meanwhile other companies jumped in offering ways to clean the Stuxnet worm although it seems the worm actually only had an impact on the Iranian centrifuges and did little or nothing to machines performing other industrial functions.

Because the US and Israel denied any involvement in Stuxnet, it appears that both governments kept quiet, meaning that some of the fixes got out perhaps too quickly. Nevertheless, in recent weeks the Obama administration, through leaks, claimed cooperation with Israel on both Stuxnet and Flame.

In fact, some firms, such as Kaspersky Labs, which focuses on building anti-virus software, provided assistance to Iran and continue to do so now. As Eugene Kaspersky said on June 14, "Being a global company with a primary mission to care about our customers' security, we state officially that we will fight any cyber weapons irrespective of the country of origin and any attempts to force us to 'collaborate.' We consider any compromise on this score to be incompatible with our ethical and professional principles."

While Kaspersky is a Moscow-based company, it does business in the United States, providing the US with a lot of leverage. Thus the US has a big stick in the closet but there is no sign that the White House is even contemplating using it.

Likewise, the US government, its allies and friends, also need to understand that supplying surveillance technology is self-defeating and risks the lives of those who are challenging the harsh and reckless Iranian regime. Surveillance technology including intercept systems should be strongly controlled by listing the technology under munitions laws. This would help a great deal in creating some discipline in this uncontrolled area.

There are two main types of export control laws in the United States and Europe—export regulations on dual-use products and items controlled as munitions. Armament laws (the US uses the International Traffic and Arms Regulations—ITAR) are far tougher than dual-use export controls. Surveillance equipment should be put under the ITAR and similar regulations in Europe, Japan, and elsewhere (including Israel). Not only would ITAR controls stop much of the export of surveillance equipment directly to rogue regimes, it would require exporters to certify the end user of its products and impose strong penalties on the originating company—penalties that can include an export ban, fines, and even criminal prosecution. In essence the exporting company is made responsible.

Supporting the Opposition

There was no excuse for Western complicity in Pakistan obtaining nuclear weapons just as there is no excuse today in regard to Iran's nuclear plans. The US has shown minimal leadership so far, and the results are abysmal. While serious damage has been done, there are still chances to hinder the Iranian nuclear program and give regime opponents a chance to operate more effectively.

NOVEMBER 12 2012

WHY DID AL-QAEDA TARGET AMBASSADOR STEVENS?

Was he murdered for reasons other than being an American on 9/11?
By Stephen Bryen and Shoshana Bryen

Courtesy PJ Media

Most of the questions related to the Benghazi debacle are about the mechanics, both offensive and defensive. What did the White House know and when? What assets were available to the military? Did someone order a stand down, and if so, who? Why was "the video" blamed long after the administration knew the truth — and didn't the administration know the truth from the beginning? If it didn't, why didn't it?

All reasonable questions, but a generally unasked one deserves attention: "Why did al-Qaeda want to kill Ambassador Chris Stevens?"

The ambassador had good relations with some of the most extreme Libyan militias, including those with al-Qaeda ties. Did he upset them with something he did, or didn't do? Was the White House fully apprised of his connections and dealings with the militias? Was he killed because of something the administration told him to start doing or to stop doing?

There are things we know and things upon which we must speculate, including the entry of surface-to-air missiles to the Levant.

Emerging from the chaos is a dim understanding that the US was operating a clandestine arms operation from the CIA post that was loosely — and incorrectly — described as a "consulate." Before and during the revolution, Ambassador Stevens had helped arm the anti-Gaddafi militias, including the Libyan Islamic Fighting Group (LIF), whose leader Abdulhakim Belhadj later became the head of the Tripoli Military Council.

The LIF's Abdel-Hakim al-Hasidi told an Italian newspaper in 2011 (later reported in the British Telegraph) that he had fought the "foreign invasion" in Afghanistan. Captured in Pakistan, al-Hasidi was handed over to the US and returned to Libya, where he was released from prison in 2008. Speaking of the Libyan revolution, he said:

Members of al-Qaeda are also good Muslims and are fighting against the invader.

Belhadj met with Free Syrian Army representatives in October 2011 to offer Libyan support for ousting Assad. Throughout 2011 and 2012, ships traversed the Mediterranean from Benghazi to Syria and Lebanon with arms for the Syrian rebels. Turkish and Jordanian intelligence services were doing most of the "vetting" of rebel groups; in July 2010, the Washington Post reported that the CIA had no operatives on the ground and only a few at border posts even as weapons were entering Syria. Said a US official, addressing the question of even non-lethal aid:

We've got to figure out who is over there first, and we don't really know that.

In August, a report by Tony Cartalucci, a supporter of the Syrian nationalist opposition, detailed the extent of Libyan and al-Qaeda involvement in Syria, calling it a "foreign invasion." In November, the Washington Post noted a $20 million contribution by the Libyan government to the Syrian National Council — of which the Muslim Brotherhood is a member.

Ambassador Stevens would have known all of that; he was the go-to man. He didn't seem to have a problem with it, so why did they want to kill him?

DEC 16 2011

America's Shift in International Security Strategy

Declining defense budgets, regional upheavals and – most important – a change in the American energy picture will alter America's international priorities and the role that has been ours since World War II. The White House, the State Department and the Defense Department have all failed to come to grips with the realities of the 21st Century.

For 65 years, American foreign and defense policy has been constructed along the following lines:

- Nuclear deterrence
- NATO
- Safeguarding the supply of oil
- Protecting the sea lines of communication
- Stopping terrorism

The first two were born in the post-war/Cold War period, but since the collapse of the Soviet Union, safeguarding the oil supply has been the top defense priority and the first objective of American diplomacy. Terrorism, particularly when it is related to oil policy, is another priority, although the US allowed itself to be diverted into a nation-building venture in Afghanistan that has no readily discernible strategic importance.

The Middle East and Persian Gulf

American power is intimately linked to the ability of US forces to protect not only the transit of oil but also the bigger oil-producing countries. So, unlike Afghanistan, the Iraq war was related to our priorities. The 21-year venture was an attempt to stop the destabilization of the Persian Gulf and Middle East, which supplies oil to Europe and Asia as well as the United States. The United States entered the first Gulf War only when American policy makers were convinced that Saudi Arabia was at risk from Saddam's forces. We would not have gone to war just to help Kuwait.

We have left Iraq now because it has been suitably beaten down and "converted" for the time being to a democratic-like country, a Persian Gulf anomaly.

Meanwhile, the rest of the Middle East has become a boiling cauldron of Islamic radicalism. The US has lost its clients in Egypt and Lebanon and will soon be evicted from most of the other Arab and North African countries. Even Turkey, a NATO ally, has a pro-Islamic government and once the Brotherhood takes control of Syria, which seems likely, Turkey will shift even further to the Islamic side.

Notwithstanding the rhetorical embrace of these changes by America's current leaders, the truth is the US is in big trouble in the region. Iran is on the brink of nuclear capability, has built alliances with China, North Korea and Russia, and will soon be able to do what Saddam dreamed of: directly threaten the US and US-friendly forces and regimes.

The US seems reconciled to the inevitability of a nuclear Iran, and its passivity is a spur to the Iranians to enlarge their hostile posture and speed up their programs.

Saudi Arabia is also in trouble. It has for decades accommodated its Islamic radicals by supporting their activities outside the Kingdom. Bin Laden, after all, was one of its boys and he was supported by the ruling families for ideological and practical reasons. Unfortunately for Bin Laden, his attack on the United States put him and al-Qaeda at war with America. This not only assured his future annihilation, but severely weakened the Saudi ability to maneuver – allowing Iran to gain the upper hand in the Gulf.

As with any other vacuum, a geopolitical vacuum is quickly filled. The Iranians are filling this one with little or no resistance.

The Iranians are working overtime to convince the Saudi ruling families that if they want to survive they have to align with Tehran. The Iranians are so zealous they are already talking about shutting down the Straits of Hormuz, through which most of the Gulf oil flows, and – if attacked – creating global havoc. These boasts, though currently unrealistic, reveal their ambition and intention, and though they may have jumped too quickly, the Saudi regime already believes it cannot count on the US any more. It is predictable that once the Iranians demonstrate nuclear weapons, Saudi Arabia will concede position to the Ayatollahs.

Iraq under Saddam was the major counterbalance to an assertive Iran. For nearly ten years, the two countries fought a nasty, bloody and costly war, preventing either from doing much damage elsewhere. Iraq today, however, is a country without power, without deterrence, without a credible army, navy or air force – for which it can thank the United States. The US made itself responsible for Iraq's security in 2003, but was not a substitute for Iraq's Arab influence in the region; and now the US is gone. It is not surprising that Iraq's leaders today are doing their best to work with the Iranians, and it will not be a surprise in the future if Iraq's hostility to the US grows commensurately. Sales of American hardware will not make Iraq a friend of ours in the face of Iranian opposition.

Saudi Arabia has military hardware but won't use it on its own and it isn't clear that it could if it wanted to. Even the reliability of Saudi Arabia's armed forces is suspect. When the Iranians get tired of making offers to the Saudis to get in line, they will try harder to undermine the

Saudi leadership. A future of upheaval and destabilization is more certain than continued stability.

America's interests are being swept aside by Islamic radicalism and revolution. American ability to protect the oil producing countries and the transit of oil is rapidly diminishing, but the United States appears confused or timid or uncomfortable with its role as regional protector.

Even the US Navy will be hard pressed to do much. America's only "ace" is its aircraft carriers because of their air power assets. But the Iranian threat to oil shipping comes from shore-based missiles supplied by China and quiet diesel electric submarines supplied by Russia. The Iranians have been building up such a capability, and have transferred sea skimming missiles to Hezbollah and others. In a closed environment like the Gulf, with clear choke points, the ability to cause havoc gives the Iranians and their surrogates a leg up, especially if the US declines to attack Iran.

It is not unnoticed by the Iranians (and the Syrians), that despite major cross-border provocation against American forces in Iraq, the United States strictly restrained itself and never retaliated, even at the height of the Iraq war. Iran has also seen that provocations in Afghanistan have not resulted in American push back.

It is, of course, possible that the Iranians will be ambitious and foolish enough to trigger a real confrontation with the United States. After all, Bin Laden attacked the United States and temporarily rode the crest of his "accomplishment." An overt Iranian attack somewhere could change the calculus, but if the Iranians keep going the way they have been, and if US policy is to pursue only a diplomatic solution, then America's role as the protector of oil suppliers and supply lines will be gone.

Energy – for America and for Europe
In this context, there are some trends in the world's energy supply picture that affect US foreign and defense policy.

America's dependence on foreign oil is declining, and declining fairly rapidly. New energy sources – particularly natural gas, which is an expanding domestic resource – are increasingly available and will continue to come on line. In the next decade, it is likely that American cars will be multi-fuel capable – that is, they will be able to run on gasoline or diesel, but also on natural gas. Once Detroit and Japan decide to manufacture multi-fuel vehicles, America will have little or no incentive to worry about oil supplies from the Persian Gulf. A key indicator is that the big oil companies are rapidly becoming big natural gas companies. Their business is automobiles and trucks, not power plants or home heating.

It is more than interesting – indeed, it is downright intriguing – that America's energy companies are making the shift to North America at precisely the time the American government's ability to control events in the Middle East and Persian Gulf is declining.

The change has implications for European security. One pillar of American foreign policy has been NATO, but the collective security system was focused on the now-defunct USSR and Warsaw Pact. Both European and American policy makers and military leaders hold onto NATO, but it is hard to argue the relevance of European-based collective security.

Furthermore, NATO has been an American armed and financed security umbrella over Europe. With collapsing budgets in the US it is hard to see how the US can sustain the NATO welfare system and the idea that European countries will pay for their own security in future is risible – until it is faced with its own energy requirements.

The US will not protect European oil supplies. If European countries want oil from Libya, Europe will have to provide the security framework. As Europe has almost no ability to operate in the Persian Gulf, getting oil from that area will be fraught with uncertainty.

The Europeans have allowed themselves to become more dependent on Russia and specifically on Gazprom for energy supplies with respect to natural gas, but that is an inadequate long-term source.

There is an emerging shift in natural gas to supplies from Greece, Cyprus and Israel (with the possibility that Turkey could also be a supplier depending on Turkish policies). This means the Eastern Mediterranean will once again be a critical security zone for Europe – particularly in the face of the upheaval across North Africa and the increasing role of Hezbollah in Lebanon. The Greek, Italian and French navies will play the critical role in holding this area secure. Bases in Greece, Cyprus and Italy (particularly southern Italy and Sicily) will be vital.

A new security system will be needed and it is unlikely to be NATO – both for lack of US funding and because Turkey, as a NATO member, can veto any coordinated NATO action. In its current posture Turkey is unlikely to approve security measures that include security for Israeli energy in the Mediterranean or Cyprus where it sponsors an unrecognized occupation in a part of Nicosia and in Famagusta.

It is too early to tell if the Europeans are capable of fitting together an alternative system for the Mediterranean. Italy, France and Greece, as well as Israel, either have or will soon have the naval assets needed although some (especially Israel) will need to dramatically grow their navies, which now, along with their traditional and counter-terrorism roles will need to protect oil installations and pipelines. The three European states, plus Cyprus and Israel, will also need to find a way to work together without political distractions that undermine their common security interest.

The US probably will play a role too, although America's allies in the Mediterranean understand that America's reluctance to challenge Iran is a harbinger of a different course and the US Navy seemingly has lost direction in terms of its mission. The punch-less Littoral Combat Ship, for example, seems a poor choice for such missions because it lacks long range guns and it has only defensive missiles on board. By contract, the new class of Italian-French frigates (FREMM) is exactly the right size and with the right firepower to protect oil and natural gas offshore assets and pipelines.

Conclusion

These changes have many implications. One is that the US will need to reset and refocus, with an emphasis more on the Pacific, where China presents a significant and growing security challenge. Other countries, especially India, will have to pick up the slack as far as south Asian security goes, and also balance China. The US will have to offer India much more technology than previously, and real security cooperation. Afghanistan will become a memory, and not a good one.

With a diminished oil security role, and an increasingly non-relevant NATO, major decisions will need to be made about America's defense posture. The role of special operating forces and counter-insurgency operations (COIN) will slow as classic strategic defense capabilities gain emphasis. The Marines have already begun to reconfigure themselves for more traditional missions; others will follow.

America's future priorities will look like this

- Nuclear deterrence
- Strategic defense focused on the Pacific
- Support for European security focused on the Mediterranean
- Counter terrorism focused on the US and the Americas

JUL 27 2011

Sharing our Defense Budget with China

Our defense budget is doing double duty – for our military and for China's. China has access to every manufacturing and technological tool it needs. Today's restrictions on Western technology transfer to China have all but ceased to exist. If the Chinese wants the latest supercomputers, or the most up to date machine tools, or advanced coating technologies, or hot section technology for fighter jet engines, they can buy it. The US government technology security program is flat lined, dead, kaput, worthless. A total failure.

What China doesn't buy, it steals. Every time the US government finances a technology – a new missile seeker, a new engine composite – China gets the plans free by tapping the computers of the manufacturing company. It is not a secret and no one can claim – actually, no one does claim – that even technology we want to control is secure.

So China has access to everything it needs and is sharing freely in the massive investment the United States has made in technology by sucking every bit of information about these programs out of our computer systems and networks. Innovations such as cloud computing are only going to make things worse.

It wasn't always this way.

In 1984, by authority of the Secretary of Defense, DOD issued the Directive "International Transfers of Technology, Goods, Services, and Munitions," to announce, "It shall be DOD policy to treat defense-related technology as a valuable, limited national security resource, to be husbanded and invested in pursuit of national security objectives."

The challenge was the exploitation of Western technology by the Soviet Union in the midst of an unprecedented build up of Soviet military power. There was no way that the United States and its NATO allies could afford to match Soviet arms on a one to one basis. The Russians were sinking well over 25% of their GDP into armaments, while the US was in the low single digits, and our allies were below 3%.

So the US exploited its high technology to gain a qualitative, as oppose to a quantitative, edge on the Soviets. Much of the qualitative edge derived from computer technology and microelectronics.

Computers made it possible to design defense products in a new way, where platforms and components were modeled using CAD-CAM and other tools, and manufacturing was done by robotic machine tools using sophisticated multi-axis machine controllers. The famous silent propellers of America's submarine force were made possible by horizontal, multi-axis controllers manufacturing highly sophisticated shaped blades that could minimize noise and cavitation. Fighter aircraft wings and fuselages were designed in computer wind tunnels and fighter planes optimized so that computers could fly the new generation of planes that, without them, would not fly at all.

Microelectronics made possible very small computers that could be integrated into missiles and smart munitions.

Understood that their only way forward was to steal as much technology as possible from the West and try to copy the computer and microelectronic capabilities of the United States. The Soviet Union created "Directorate T" in the KGB whose job it was, along with military intelligence (the GRU), to penetrate Western companies and steal whatever they could.

They tried – but ultimately failed, presaging the collapse of the USSR and the end of the Cold War. But the "old" idea of technology security remains of vital interest. Only the targets and the perpetrator have changed.

In the 1980's we were facing the Russian military buildup. Today we are watching the Chinese vastly expand their military abilities. There is a smug notion in Washington that China is decades away from "challenging" the United States, so we do not have to worry – yet.

This, of course, is not far different from the ludicrous predictions the CIA made about the Soviet Union in the 1970's. Russia, the theory went, was weak, although it had nuclear weapons. So if the US was smart it would engage Russia, negotiate arms control agreements, and open serious trade relations that would help dampen the enthusiasm for Communism. SALT agreements, detente, and major trade deals that pumped more technology into the Soviet Union were born of the theory. Not only did it not change the arms policy of the Soviet Union, the Russians jammed more and more resources into the military and churned out weapons of increasing capability.

China approaches its arms buildup differently, but its objectives are equally clear. It, too, is using espionage to steal whatever it can, as the Pentagon and the CIA know full well but cannot say. China is exploiting the Internet to rob the Pentagon, America's defense industry and our high technology industry, of just about everything.

And the United States has no plan.

The Pentagon's cyber security proposals are 20 years too late and much too weak. Classified networks have been compromised, contractors ripped off and valuable technologies stolen. This means trillions (not just billions) of taxpayer-funded R&D dollars have been squandered. Ultimately it means that China can be a credible military superpower much faster than the Washington geniuses say.

Compounding the problem is that we have spent so much domestically and on foreign wars, that major new programs for defense are already being delayed or canceled. Add to that the growing absurdity of our defense priorities, which are focused on tin-pot dictators and small wars rather than strategic defense.

In 1984 the Defense Department and the administration defined the threat and marshaled resources against it. The reverse is the case today.

After this report was written McAfee published an extensive report on cyber spying under the title "Revealed Operating Shady Rat." A "Rat" in this case is a Remote Access Tool and not the sort of animal one sets traps to destroy. McAfee's Vice President for threat research, Dmitri Alperovich says the following:

> "What we have witnessed over the past five to six years has been nothing short of a historically unprecedented transfer of wealth," he writes, "closely guarded national secrets (including from classified government networks), source code, bug databases, e-mail archives, negotiation plans and exploration details for new oil and gas field auctions, document stores, legal contracts, [Supervisory Control and Data Acquisition] configurations, design schematics and much more has 'fallen off the truck' of numerous, mostly Western companies and disappeared in the ever-growing electronic archives of dogged adversaries."

Cyber Security
PART 2

MARCH 2015

Encryption is Only Half the Story

There is growing enthusiasm and interest in encryption for smartphones and tablets in order to protect privacy. But encryption is only half the story, and probably not the most important half. What really matters is platform security.

A smartphone is a powerful computer and communications tool harnessed to a number of radios that link to the outside world. Those radio links can be compromised fairly easily. People worry about how they can keep their phone calls secure and private and are looking at alternatives such as secure phone APPS.

A secure phone APP encrypts the connection between one phone and another. In some cases the encryption works in a phone to phone scheme; in others the encryption and connections are managed by a server. Either scheme can deliver some security for phone calls. In elaborate set ups with servers, they can try and protect emails and text messages. While encryption folks promise a lot, there are two main pitfalls to using encryption that are not so well understood.

The first pitfall is that a determined adversary, such as a competitor or enemy or government agency, can bypass your encryption without too much effort. That is to say, any of these intruders can install spyware on your phone. Spyware can record your conversation or transmit it no matter if you are using encryption or not. That's because your microphone and cameras are accessible to programs that might be secretly running on your phone being put there by the intruder. In these circumstances you may think that you are protected, but you are not and your risk is even greater since you are unlikely to be cautious and circumspect in what you say on your phone.

The second pitfall is that the platform's vulnerability will be there with encryption installed, meaning that offline conversations can be "overheard" by an intruder without you knowing it. This kind of malware is generally sophisticated and difficult to detect, making matters worse. Think about it: you are in a meeting in your office and every word is being recorded secretly and will be sent over the internet to an intruder without you knowing it. This can give a spy or competitor a tremendous amount of sensitive information. He can use it for commercial advantage, or to bribe you or your colleagues, or sell it to other parties.

Encryption does not help against either Pitfall #1 or Pitfall #2.

Some people think the best thing to do is to turn off one's phone when serious conversations take place. To be sure, there are few people who actually do this, because they are always waiting for some phone call or text message to arrive. They "need" the information fix that the smartphone promises to give them on a minute by minute basis.

Even worse, turning off a phone does not really mean that it is safe. There are good quality spyware tools that can turn your phone back on without you knowing it. The screen won't illuminate, but the phone's microphones will be on and the phone can record and stream out information. One tip off that the phone might be so infected is that it seems oddly warm, even hot when you pick it up.

Are there solutions that can protect a phone's platform and avoid the two pitfalls?

JAN 06 2015

Will the Stingray End Up at the Supreme Court?

The Stingray is a device that can track cell phones in real time. It is a type of IMSI catcher. IMSI, the International Mobile Subscriber Identity, is built into all cellular phones. The IMSI number is broadcast by a phone when it connects to any cellular tower. An IMSI catcher pretends to be a cellphone tower, "catches" the IMSI broadcast, and then can act as a relay to a legitimate cellular phone tower, meaning that everything that is broadcast across the IMSI catcher can be heard or intercepted.

There are many IMSI catcher devices on the market. Some of them are "active" intercepts and others operate passively. Stingray is the product used by the FBI and law enforcement. Its capabilities are kept secret from the public.

All cellular phones encrypt the connection between the phone and the cellular tower. Thus for an IMSI catcher to be any good, it has to break the encryption or defeat it one way or another.

Essentially there are two ways of getting rid of the encryption: Knowing the algorithms used by the phone companies and how the key is composed or finding a means to turn off the encryption. Both are feasible strategies and it is likely that Stingray employs both strategies and perhaps others.

The IMSI catcher is a tool for law enforcement, for intelligence agencies, and for criminals. Other than Stingray, many of these devices can be bought online. And the US government also supplies such devices to friendly foreign countries and foreign entities.

The heart of the FBI case is that it can use the Stingray because the public has "no reasonable expectation of privacy" when using a mobile phone. This argument is not generally accepted, and nine states, including Virginia and Maryland, require a law enforcement agency to get a warrant if the agency wants to use a Stingray device, or to agree in advance on the protection of information gleaned from cellular phones that are not part of a current law enforcement investigation.

The expectation of privacy issue was first brought out in Smith vs. Maryland (1979). In that case law enforcement used a "pen register" to record the time, duration and phone numbers called from a phone line belonging to a suspect. The Supreme Court said that the pen register (an electro-mechanical device) did not record actual phone calls and that use of a pen register did not rise to a violation of either the First or the Fourth Amendments (e.g., Freedom of Speech, Illegal Searches and Seizures). In an earlier case, Katz vs. U.S., the Court held that warrantless wiretaps were unconstitutional searches and seizures because the public had a reasonable expectation of privacy. Katz was decided in 1967, before the cellular phone era.

The FBI is not relying entirely on its argument that the public has no reasonable expectation of privacy when using a cellular phone. It also argues there are urgent circumstances, such as preventing the commission of a crime or stopping a terrorist, where a warrantless wiretap of a cell phone is justified. To my mind, law enforcement has to have the ability to make an informed judgment there is an imminent risk, and law enforcement should be able to move against these threats. The same idea is what was behind the War Powers Act, which recognized that the President as Commander in Chief needed flexibility to protect American national security. Law enforcement needs the same flexibility.

The question is whether one should hang that argument on the idea that the public lacks a reasonable expectation of privacy when using mobile devices. It seems to me the stronger case is the ability to respond to a concrete threat.

And therein lies the rub, to quote the Bard. Law enforcement has to take a risk when it uses the argument of dire necessity to justify acting without a warrant. In other words, law enforcement will need to defend those decisions before an impartial court if challenged. Law enforcement cannot, willy-nilly run around setting up fake cell towers just to suck up as much information as it can. Right now, except in those states where there are laws on the books, the standards for law enforcement operations when it applies to IMSI catchers, are far from settled. That is why, short of specific legislation, the use of Stingrays may end up in the Supreme Court.

DEC 18 2014

WHEN THERE IS NO PRICE TO BE PAID THE HACKERS WIN

If there is one salient fact that emerges from the now infamous Sony hack it is that the bad guys won. The bad guys won because there they paid no price for the damage inflicted. In the Sony case the hackers are outside and beyond the law, so their backers and sponsors are encouraged to cause even more damage in future. To stop cyber attacks, particularly those sponsored by foreign governments, we need to respond to attacks now.

Sony is a movie company, a major cog in the entertainment industry. Whether Sony rises or falls has little or nothing to do with national security. There are plenty of other entertainment companies that can fill the gap if Sony drops out, something that Sony surely understands.

But the sort of intimidation attack suffered by Sony is non trivial, and presages similar attempts that surely will come by hostile actors to intimidate our government. The Russians have used such attacks against at least three former Soviet Republics (Lithuania, Georgia and Ukraine), electronically hacking telecommunications, and banking, government and military organizations. Newspapers have also been attacked by foreign hackers, signaling displeasure over certain stories. The North Koreans have also pummeled South Korea with cyber attacks, destroying hard drives and shutting down banking operations.

One South Korean bank was out of commission for more than two weeks.

Despite precautions, cyber attackers can often stay one step ahead of protection mechanisms. Sony, of course, had little in the way of cyber security protections, making it an easy soft target for hackers. But even better protected systems can be penetrated.

Liran Tancman CEO of CyActive in Israel, quoted in the Times of Israel, says "Cyber-security is, for the most part, reactive, not proactive. A company will spend hundreds of thousands or millions of dollars to secure themselves against a major malware variant, fighting off a specific attack." But hackers can often get around better protected organizations. "All they have to do is insert some changes in their malware code, and they are in the clear. For $150, a cyber-criminal can hire a hacker to do $25 million of damage, and then do it again a few months later, making very minor changes to their malware code."

In the wake of the Sony attack, former Republican Speaker of the House and presidential candidate Newt Gingrich says that we have lost our first cyber war. Commenting on Twitter, Gingrich said "it wasn't the hackers who won, it was the terrorists and almost certainly the North Korean dictatorship, this was an act of war."

Gingrich begs the question: if a serious cyber attack is an act of war, how should America respond?

The Pentagon has set up Plan X supposedly to respond to cyber attacks by launching cyber assaults of its own as retaliatory strikes. But nothing like that has happened. Russian, Chinese, North Korean, Iranian and Syrian hackers –all government backed– continue to operate unabated. Is there a threshold that remains to be crossed, and when it is will the Pentagon launch a massive retaliatory cyber attack on the perpetrators, namely the governments that sponsor the hacks? Plan X is a nice idea, but it is a wasted effort unless it is used.

Hacking is a cheap crime to commit unless there are costly consequences.

It is a bad idea to wait around until a massive cyber attack leads to costly consequences such as paralyzing our government and military, creating a run-away chain reaction cascade at a nuclear power plant, or wrecking our banking system.

A prudent policy is to start striking back when we are hit the first time, not the last time. Only in that way can limits be set and warnings understood. If the United States answered even one of the Chinese-Russian-Iranian-North Korean-Syrian attacks by a strong meaningful response, the bad guys would get the message. Then the hackers would lose.

DEC 05 2014

THE DAY THE CRITICAL INFRASTRUCTURE GOES UP IN SMOKE

It is virtually certain now that the critical infrastructure of the United States will, in whole or in part, crash in the next few years, if not sooner. What is the critical infrastructure and how does any of this matter to you?

There are different ways that critical infrastructure can be understood. The Department of Homeland Security breaks it down into "sectors" that include the information technology sector, energy sector, communications, health care and public health, commercial facilities and transportation systems. To this we can add government and military operation and law enforcement as sectors of prime importance if any of the "sectors" collapses.

Consider the following simplistic scenario. A number of nuclear and conventional power plants stop functioning, creating a grid crisis that cascades, and leaving major cities without electrical power. Some facilities, those with natural gas generators, may function; but most services will shut down, factories will close, and law enforcement which certainly will include National Guard deployments will be under pressure to prevent lawlessness and panic. Gas stations will not be able to pump gas, so after a few days most cars won't run. Traffic signals will be out. Trains won't run and planes won't fly. Some radio may stay operating, but as people's phone batteries run down, communications will be more difficult. Even worse, food stores will run out of supplies and can only operate in daylight hours and without cash registers, lighting or refrigeration. Government services will also stop and government employees won't be able to go to work or be paid. Services like Medicare and Social Security will be suspended. Financial services will halt; the stock market will be suspended and for all intents and purposes crashed. No one will get a paycheck and the value of the dollar will plummet. Inflation will soar, just as it did in the Weimar Republic.

Why would a crisis like this happen? There is a natural cause scenario, where an overloaded and badly managed power grid just disintegrates taking with it all the services described above and a lot more we have left out. There are different points of view as to whether a natural cause scenario will happen, or even if a natural causes scenario could be recognized.

The emerging scenario is a successful cyber attack that brings down the power grid. This type of attack could happen so swiftly and cause so much physical damage that understanding what happened and figuring out how to bring the grid back on line is a non-trivial problem.

Our government is focused on attacks on the critical infrastructure from China, or Russia or Iran. A real attack is a form of war, and one would expect that a state actor would not sponsor such an attack unless there was a parallel conflict, or at least a series of events leading up to a military confrontation.

But are these expectations realistic? The recent Sony attack, which many are still trying to understand, may have been caused by collaboration between North Korea and Iran. North Korea had a score to settle with Sony Pictures because of a film with an unfriendly portrayal of the North Korean dictator. As North Korea and Iran are closely collaborating on nuclear weapons and missiles, it makes sense to think that if the North Korean dictator asked for Iran's help to attack Sony that could have been easily arranged. While North Korea's capabilities in cyber are suspect, Iran is well advanced thanks to help the Iranians have gotten from Western European companies anxious to cash in. Companies such as Siemens have also transferred critical SCADA technology to Iran, so the Iranians have all the tools they need to attack power grids, refineries, manufacturing centers and transport systems.

As a matter of fact, because it is difficult to pinpoint who is behind a cyber attacks on the critical infrastructure, it is mostly guesswork to assign blame. For example, if Russia actually attacked the American power grid (perhaps because President Putin was tired of hearing lectures from the Obama administration) can we be sure it was the Russians and not some other state or non-state actor? In today's crazy world, non-state actors often are employed by governments (including our own) to hack someone's network or system; and we also know that many intelligence agencies collaborate so that what might be illegal in one jurisdiction can be done in a place where taking such an action is not against the law.

An equally big problem is how one can respond to a cyber attack on the critical infrastructure. Supposing there is some reasonable certainty about the source of attack, how does one respond? Attack the other state's critical infrastructure –tit for tat? It is not clear we yet have the capability to do that. The Russians, who inherited the systems built in the old Soviet Union, always kept their power systems, communications networks and government systems secret. Moreover, many of the systems the Russians have are built with separate government and military hook ups and are redundant; furthermore a good many of them are buried underground.

This leaves the US in the unenviable position of needing to take some other kind of action to respond to a critical infrastructure attack. Whether we can truly take a military risk is an open question. Military escalation with a well-armed nuclear power is very risky, as the famous Cuban Missile Crisis illustrates.

In short, the problem is asymmetric and difficult. While the Pentagon has put in place Plan X to be able to respond to cyber attacks, no one knows whether Plan X is much more than smoke and mirrors.

A key question is if you have limited options to respond to a successful attack on the critical infrastructure, can you find a way to protect the critical infrastructure from attack or at least mitigate damages should such an attack occur.

When Russia got the atomic bomb and the Cold War was in full swing, we had Civil Defense. Some readers may remember being taught to duck under a desk at school, or line up in areas thought to be more resistant to bomb blasts. Many Americans built and equipped and stocked bomb shelters. Some folks went so far as to buy cabins deep in the countryside in order to survive.

A Civil Defense program invites the notion that the threat is great enough to warrant taking defensive measures.

We have not done that to protect the critical infrastructure. Despite a lot of exhortatory legislation supposedly pushing the idea of protecting the critical infrastructure, doing that has mostly been left to the private sector owners of major critical infrastructure elements. It is not that they have not tried to put some security around their systems. But individual companies cannot compete against dedicated, well funded foreign government assaults. While the US government could try and fill the gap, the record to date on providing real help is spotty. A lead agency, the FBI, has created something called InfraGard, a public private partnership, but every time a business or infrastructure player asks for help, they get blank stares and an unwillingness to share intelligence or practical solutions. The same holds true for the Defense Department, the NSA, and the Department of Homeland Security —not really helpful.

Part of the problem is institutional. Some of these agencies are poorly equipped to provide solutions when most of the time they are trying to break into someone else's network. Some of it is a lack of leadership: lots of talk and not much else. And some of it is because of the dependency that has developed on commercial computer products and technology, most of which is ill suited to security.

The result of these multiple conundrums is that the United States is ill prepared to deal with any threat to our critical infrastructure, has no clear way to respond to attacks, and has no solutions that really help defend what we have. Are we to wait until the mostly inevitable happens and we are without light and power, fuel, food and medical support? Do we really want to risk urban riots, disease and upheaval?

The answer should be self evident.

Thus the question is what we should do. It makes no sense to continue to "study" the problem: we need to solve the problem.

I have proposed a kind of Manhattan Project for Critical Infrastructure Security. The idea is to create a large team of the best experts available, with suitable policy leadership and substantial funding on the order (for starters) of $2 billion. The goal: build secure America-only computer network systems for the critical infrastructure from the ground up. There are some problems that will be very challenging, for example how to use computer hardware that is manufactured in China and in other places where malware and Trojans can be built in at the point of manufacture. There are other problems, how to manage authentication and encryption so that no part of any critical infrastructure network lacks encryption. This means very strong encryption that needs to be available to American critical infrastructure elements and that is constantly tested against external threat. But all these problems can be solved if there is a real will to do it.

I used the funding number of $2 billion because that is what the Manhattan Project to develop the atomic bomb cost originally (in 1945 dollars). Today $2 billion is a drop in the bucket and may not be enough. But it is, as they say, a good start.

The Manhattan Project should be run by the best and the brightest and not by any government agency. Government can have a seat on the board, but not management of the Project. The program must be authorized by Congress; must be non-partisan, open only to US citizens with security clearances, and run in secret. Critical infrastructure organizations and entities need to be vetted and made ready to accept and support a classified program. Administratively this is a big project, but just as the original Manhattan Project ultimately employed tens of thousands of people, so too would this project involve thousands organized entirely on a need to know basis.

If we wait much longer we will be sitting in the dark or worse.

---

*The Army part of the Manhattan Project was known as the Manhattan District. The British counterpart organization codename was Tube Alloys.

DEC 01 2014

Is Hollywood Going Back to Flip Phones?

Hollywood stars, producers and writers are so worried by hacks at Sony and the compromise of "selfie" nude photos; many are saying they are going back to Flip Phones to protect themselves. Are Flip Phones safer than today's smartphones?

A Flip Phone is called a "Feature Phone" in the trade. It is not a "smart" phone, but it can do some of the things a smartphone can do. For example a typical Flip Phone can receive email, SMS (text) messages, send photos, keep a calendar and use Bluetooth. The big difference is in the Operating System and the fact that Feature Phones typically don't use high speed data connections such as 3G or 4G or WiFi.

STEPHEN D. BRYEN

By Twburger (Own work) [GFDL (http://www.gnu.org/copyleft/fdl.html) or CC BY-SA 3.0 (http://creativecommons.org/licenses/by-sa/3.0)], via Wikimedia Commons

Feature Phones also don't have operating systems like iPhone, Android or Windows, although some of them might have cut down versions of these systems. Mostly they have semi-programmable software sets that support the phone's functions.

But Flip Phones are certainly not "safer" than smartphones.

For example, Flip Phones have GPS chips and your location can be tracked on a Flip just as well as you can be tracked on a smartphone.

And SMS, Email and pictures can be easily intercepted by government organizations as well as by hackers.

There is even pretty good spyware that can be installed on some Flip Phones.

What Feature Phones or Flips generally don't have is much access to social media such as Facebook which needs a data connection. Nor can you use programs like Skype for communications. But you can access the Internet, although the connection is very slow.

If the Hollywood types can live without high quality nudie photos and the social media, maybe the Flip Phone will work for them. But it won't make them much more secure.

Just like smartphones, communications on a Flip or Feature Phone are just as vulnerable to intercept as they are on a smartphone. In fact, maybe even more so because you can't put your own encryption on a Flip or Feature Phone and many Flip Phones have only rudimentary scrambling that can easily be turned off by any hacker.

The truth is there is neither much protection nor much future in Flip Phones, which is why they are increasingly losing market share.

The big problem for everyone is that as far as smartphones and Flip Phones are concerned is that we are living in the "Wild West" in the sense that there are few security standards, lots of spaghetti code, too much foreign manufacturing and tampering, and a home government that exploits all these vulnerabilities meaning that our government is compromised and won't do much to help the average citizen, or even the above average citizen (assuming such a citizen exists). This leaves American business at risk and it violates most of the freedoms we are supposed to enjoy. Folks in Hollywood are rightfully offended, but the big picture is even more challenging.

NOV 21 2014

Saving the Critical Infrastructure

I have been writing about cyber security for many years. I believe I have some credibility in this field. I headed and ran the Defense Department's program for technology security as the Director of the Defense Technology Security Administration and as a Deputy under Secretary of Defense. I also started and ran two cyber security companies, one in the 1990's called SECOM which was the world's first secure chat program, and currently (as a founder and Board Chairman) Ziklag Systems which markets secure mobile smartphones. Over the years I have been increasingly concerned about the vulnerability of our critical infrastructure and the risk to America. My concern has escalated along with growing and successful cyber intrusions into our power, energy, transportation and government grids and networks. And I have found it shocking that no one seems to know what to do about the menace.

Somehow our leaders in the administration and Congress, even Admiral Mike Rogers who heads NSA and the US Cyber Command, all of whom clearly understand the threat and risk, seem clueless on how to fix the problem.

Meanwhile China, Russia, Iran, Syria and plenty of rogue operations are increasing the pressure on us by attacking our computer networks. Nothing is safe. Not our defense Command and Control systems, our missile defenses, our energy grid, our refineries, our nuclear power plants, not even our telecommunications, transportation, water supply or health care systems are secure.

The reason for that is easy to see. All our computer networks rely on computer operating systems hardware and software that has been distributed all over the world. Since almost everything about those systems is public, it is easy for attackers with sufficient resources to take them apart. It should surprise no one that virtually all of our hardware is made in China, introducing a massive vulnerability into our critical infrastructure.

Add to this tremendous weakness the problem of SCADA systems. SCADA is the supervisory control and data acquisition system used by nuclear and conventional power plants, heating and cooling systems, manufacturing centers, refineries and lots of other automated systems. There are only two or three SCADA systems in the market with wide acceptance, and they are used worldwide. Once again, both the hardware and software for SCADA is accessible to foreign regimes and terrorists as well as other rogue actors. It is the SCADA that was the center of the attack on Iran's uranium enrichment centrifuges where the US and Israel hoped to slow Iran's acquisition of an atomic bomb. What was done with the Stuxnet worm to damage Iran's nuclear program likewise can happen to us.

Patching computer operating systems and fixing SCADA software won't work. This is proven empirically by the growing frequency of successful attacks on critical infrastructure systems,. If patches worked, they would save us from attack. But the plain fact is that they may help a little but not enough to stop a determined and resourceful adversary.

China, one of the countries known to be tampering with our critical infrastructure and helping to finance its growth by stealing defense designs and technology from our leading companies is already taking steps to keep us out of their networks by producing their own computer operating systems they won't share with us. We should take a clue from China. For critical infrastructure security we need secure operating systems and a new secure SCADA that replaces all the commercial equipment and software we have been using.

Changing over to a government proprietary secure system is a vital step in locking down our networks and management systems. It requires a bold and determined initiative by the US government, and it needs to be accompanied by security measures that are well drawn and deeply monitored to provide an additional layer of protection.

Above all we need a policy based on "Win Win" not on hopes and fictions we can make what we have work. It is foolish to wait for the worst to happen, as it surely will.

NOV 06 2014

US Policy and Cyber Attacks: A Byte for a Byte

Col. Todd Wood, commander of 1st Stryker Brigade Combat Team, 25th Infantry Division, gives Gen. Keith Alexander, director of the NSA, an operational update at Forward Operating Base Masum Ghar in southern Kandahar Province, Afghanistan. *Photo: US Army/Sgt. Michael Blalack, 1/25 SBCT Public Affairs.*

The Pentagon put in place Plan X to deal with cyber attacks. Apparently Plan X creates the mechanism for the Pentagon to counter attack against a cyber intruder. Unfortunately, the rules of engagement for Plan X are classified. As a result, Plan X is perfectly useless.

DHS reports there is a Trojan horse malware lurking in America's critical infrastructure computers that could cause an economic catastrophe. It comes from Russia. But are we doing anything about it? You bet! DHS issued a Memo on November 6, 2014! The threat has been there since 2011!

The United States needs an explicit, public plan to deal with cyber attacks on the critical infrastructure of the United States. The critical infrastructure includes banking and finance, government, defense plants, energy, communications and health and safety systems. All of them have been attacked by outside powers, the most reckless attacks from China and Russia. But Plan X does not seem to have been activated. This should tell us that Plan X is not the answer to the problem that threatens our national security.

To the degree we have any policy, it seems it is to sit on our hands and watch as our defense secrets are stolen, our technology compromised and our commercial, transportation, energy and banking systems threatened. Do we want to watch attacks on nuclear power plants when the result could be another Three Mile Island or Chernobyl?

The policy we have is purposefully defeatist and highly dangerous. The idea that Secretary of State Kerry would go off to talk to the Chinese and ask them to be nice about cyber attacks is absurd on its face and demeaning to the United States. The time to talk to the Chinese is after we slap down a cyber intrusion that came from Beijing.

The policy I advocate is a byte for a byte. It is biblical. If you mess with our power plants, we can mess with yours. If you strike at our banking system, we will hobble your banking system.

This message should go out to the Chinese, Russians, Iranians and anyone else who thinks they can attack us without penalty.

If we had a policy we would put it openly on the table: We will not tolerate attacks on our critical infrastructure. If you are so brazen as to do it anyway, we will respond in kind and more.

The word in Washington is that no one wants to confront China because, after all, they are sort of paying our bills these days. If that is the sum of our foreign policy we are dead ducks. When we talk about national security, we cannot turn the other cheek.

Clearly the United States is in a great position to win any cyber confrontation. We have the talent pool and much better capability than any of our potential adversaries. This won't always be the case: even the Pentagon is taking notice that our edge is slip slip sliding away.

The new Congress should demand a tough policy of retaliation for cyber attacks. Happily the new Congress is closer in tune with the outlook of the American people. Appeasement is not an answer to cyber attacks anymore than it is an answer to military invasions.

OCT 25 2014

TIME TO DUMP MICROSOFT AND GOOGLE

It is time for the US government, critical infrastructure components, the military and important businesses to dump Microsoft and Google*. The products of these two companies, and many others, built primarily for entertainment have no place in sensitive government and business operations. All of them represent a time bomb whose chain reaction has already started. The constant hacking and intrusion of these systems is robbing the American taxpayer blind and undermining national security.

Our government has long been two-faced about the vulnerabilities of popular operating systems, open source software and the total lack of security that dominates America's software industry. That's because NSA and other intelligence organizations in the US government take advantage of the stunning weakness of these platforms for spying. So, while the government opines about hacking and foreign governments, it is busily at work spending billions of dollars to spy on anyone and everything.

I am not at all against government spying. It keeps me and my family safe. It is important and if we decide to curtail it we may pay too high a price enabling terrorists and foreign regimes to bring harm to our country.

My problem is that the two faced approach has blocked any chance to put real security in place for critical computer networks providing essential services, and it has left our military vulnerable to hacking. Today we know that our energy companies, banks, transportation systems, even our health care delivery has been heavily assaulted from within and without, by foreign and domestic hackers. Key defense programs have been compromised and billions of dollars worth of data stolen. Important stealth combat systems have been stolen.

America is a rich country, one of the richest in the world. But can we afford the losses we are taking? Because of the two faced approach, we do not have accurate reporting on how much has gone out the window, but it is a lot. Our government will not own up to the true danger so long as its spying trumps security at home.

Risks are multiplied by the fact that almost all our computer hardware comes from China. Certainly American companies make some of it although production is abroad, but none of that really matters. The opportunity to slip micro code into mobile phone and computer platforms is there and plain to see. But our government offers no guidance on this sore subject, and in fact continually encourages production outside our borders.

Surely at some point in the not so near future tragedy will strike. Someone will penetrate a nuclear power plant and generate a Three Mile Island type disaster; or Amtrak will end up with trains on the same track heading in opposite directions; or the power grid will go out as it did on overload in 2003; or Air Force One's elaborate systems could cause a crash landing. There are plenty more dire scenarios.

The Chinese have got sick and tired of NSA and GCHQ. Thus China is investing in new hardware for its government and military systems and a Chinese operating system without Google and Microsoft. In a few years China will be better protected than America. Maybe we should pay attention. What the Chinese are doing is not just a curiosity.

It is a serious investment that may give them more secure systems than we have.

We waste billions each year trying to graft security onto open, public computer systems and networks that were never build to be secure. Thousands of software engineers from all over the world work for America's software companies. Computer technology has become so globalized that trying to manage production and keep any semblance of security is strictly impossible. Recent bugs found in open source software widely used in all computer systems came from Germany. It could just as well come from France, the UK, India, Israel, Singapore or China. It seems everyone is playing in this field and there is zero auditing of the final products. The rush is to get to market. It can be patched later! But as we know, once vulnerability is introduced, it lives on. The myriad systems that use these products can't possibly track the known bugs; and the unknown holes in the system rise to the surface at an increasingly fast tempo.

No one can, or needs to, fix the globalized software and hardware industry. What is needed is a trusted solution that is available only to qualified government, military and critical industries that is build on rigorous, tested security standards and on hardware that is strictly controlled in the United States. Building a secure system is costly, but the investment is far less than what is going out the window today and certainly less than the risk exposure we currently have.

Some would say that a trusted solution will not stay up with the times and will become a costly and useless artifact. There are two answers to this complaint. A security system has a limited purpose and is not like commercial systems with features more geared to entertainment than productivity. Moreover, a security based system should not be divorced from the real world. If important communications, processing or data management solutions are important and attractive, nothing would prevent these from being adapted to a security-based system.

I am far from optimistic our government will throw out Microsoft and Google and all the Chinese hardware it has bought. But without a new way of protecting ourselves we will pay dearly for our government's short sighted approach to protecting its citizens.

---

*Silicon Valley companies, especially Google, have very close ties to the Obama administration. Google reportedly is invited to many White House meetings.

OCT 10 2014

HACKING BACK AND THE CYBER BALANCE OF POWER

The Washington Post carried a front page article on October 10th "Hacked Firms Quietly Talk about Fighting Fire with Fire" about growing corporate anger over successive cyber attacks. The new theme: go on the offensive. Hack back!

They are not alone. The Pentagon has set up a secretive unit called Plan X which is supposed to fight back against hacking. Its "rules of engagement" are classified, and nobody really knows if Plan X is operational or pie in the sky.

But how would "hacking back" work? The corporate approach, as reported in the Post, seems to be that one can attack the hackers, send them bogus information, as a way of closing them down. Would this work?

Most of the really bad hacking, attacks on government computers and networks and on America's critical infrastructure is foreign government sponsored. The latest banking attacks are thought to be Russian-sponsored, Putin's reaction to American-led sanctions because of the Ukraine crisis. And the Senate Armed Services Committee has found that American defense companies are being systematically looted by China through cyber espionage.

Well-financed foreign governments do not directly launch attacks on American companies or our government and military. They would be foolish to do so, especially since they have plenty of other options. The Russians and Chinese have cadres of hackers who can operate on their behalf. Occasionally these state-sponsored "independent" hackers make a few extra dollars by stealing credit cards and emptying bank accounts. Sure you can hack them back, but they will just get another computer and do it again. Living abroad they are beyond American law enforcement. The FBI may want to investigate; one can expect few results.

Then there is the problem of recognizing that a hack has occurred. A study by Verizon which was done with the cooperation of many businesses, security firms and government experts points out that it often takes a long time to uncover an intrusion. If you don't know you have been ripped off you may in the end find your coffers empty when it is too late.

The level of angst circulating in business and government circles caused by huge financial losses from cyber intrusions (one study says $300 billion per year goes out America's cyber "pipeline") suggests we are rapidly reaching a tipping point. The security model we are trying to apply is a failure.

In fact as I have pointed out elsewhere, the security model we have cannot work for the simple reason that it is impossible to protect computer networks when the networks, fixed and mobile platforms, and transmission equipment are composed of open-source computer code and foreign sourced hardware, predominantly manufactured in China. The time has come for the government to realize we cannot protect America's resources or critical systems such as telecommunications, energy, health care and banking if they are running on foreign produced equipment and globalized software.

And there is more.

It makes no sense to go after hackers who are employed by foreign governments. If we want to be serious when our banks are attacked or our nuclear power plants are damaged we have to respond in kind. This is the ancient rule of warfare. We need to establish a cyber balance of power. To do so, we have to act like a grown up superpower that is no longer willing to be picked on by hackers and intruders ad nauseam. It is doubtful the Pentagon's Plan X rules of engagement allow it to attack the other guy's critical infrastructure, but maybe they should. If the White House is timid maybe Congress can put some backbone into our leadership.

Successive administrations have kicked the ball down the hall on cyber security. Leaders have bought into the idea that there is some nice solution just around the corner and all we needed to do is to be more rigorous, spend more money, and apply the right security safeguards. If anything, as spending on security has increased, so have cyber attacks.

There is no empirical evidence that more spending has produced anything approaching a cure. While it may get them off the hook by throwing more dollars at the problem, a more serious and comprehensive approach is needed and soon. That approach is tit for tat for those attacking us, and weaning our computer networks and communications systems off weak, compromised software and Chinese-made hardware. We would not give our soldiers rifles made in China? Why do we run our nuclear power plants and government computers on Chinese supplied parts?

The partying going on in Beijing and Moscow will go on until we get serious. We are still buying the beer.

SEP 15 2014

Losing the Cyber War: How to Get Out of the Box and Win

The United States is losing the cyber war. Despite hugely increased expenditures on cyber security, every day the situation worsens and we continue to fall behind. As I write there is no government or military website that has not been hacked and vital information stolen. It is not just the government —banks, health care systems, financial transactions, credit card data, identity theft, social security numbers, legal briefs, strategy documents, corporate secrets, intellectual property —the list is nearly endless.

When you are in a war you look for metrics to understand just how well you are doing and what the conflict outcome will be. An Army general surveys the battlefield, estimates his resources, evaluates his technology, and decides on his strategy. If the general believes he will lose the war, he tells his political leaders and waits for guidance.

There are four possible outcomes in a war: fight to win; fight to a stalemate of some kind; negotiate with the enemy; surrender.

Looking at the current state of affairs in the ongoing cyber war, we can reach some conclusions.

Firstly, right now we cannot fight to win because we do not have either the troops or the technology to win. No one has figured out a satisfactory offensive strategy other than to convert cyber war into a traditional war. This is impractical and no one is really willing to go down this path (other than to threaten some sort of offensive cyber warfare).

Secondly, there is no stalemate in cyber warfare available to the United States. One of the most serious potential threats, China, is too important economically and politically to be seriously challenged. Beyond China there are plenty of other cyber war makers, as in Russia, Iran, Syria and even hackers embedded in countries around the world. While the US and some of our friends have tried to prosecute some hackers, the triumphs are few and far between. None of the threats are under sufficient pressure to stop hacking; in fact they are more emboldened than ever.

Thirdly, there is no one to negotiate with today. Attempts have been made to talk to the Chinese; they deny everything and blame the US for spying on them.

This leaves the surrender option, but unlike territorial war, there is no one to surrender to so we face the prospect of going on losing. Our critical infrastructure is exposed, our government is losing control of its systems, and our military is watching as its command and control and its vital technology spills out through the back end of its networked systems or through its industrial partners.

Throwing more money at "the problem" is not a panacea. Our government, military, and critical infrastructure cannot continue running around like chickens with their heads cut off. That is the sum of what is happening today.

The entire infrastructure of information technology is based on mostly an open architecture approach to computer systems and network infrastructure. That is conducive to a fairly rapid spiral development of new commercial technology. Unfortunately, the commercial approach downside is that security plays second or third fiddle to the push for bagging commercial dollars from investors and customers alike.

It is very well known that spending money on security does not "produce" anything, so putting money and resources into security systems is resented by investors and corporations, even by individual users who often chafe under security restrictions and operational limitations.

The commercial computer space is heavily tilted toward entertainment and not to business or industry, No where has the entertainment element enjoyed more success than in mobile devices such as smartphones and tablets; for the most part there is not even a pretense of security in these systems.

We have to recognize that the entertainment function of computer systems and networks, mobile and fixed, is a fact of life. Where we go wrong is to use the same operating systems and network support for entertainment as we do for government, business, and the military. Adding to that, the same underbelly developmental system, a global collection of non-vetted persons and risky manufacturing locations, adds to the conundrum.

A great indicator of the collective mindset today is shifting everything over to so-called cloud systems, even where we don't have the slightest idea of how these clouds are managed or how easily they can be compromised. The Pentagon, which obviously knows better, is today endorsing cloud systems that are big risk, just as they are supporting mobile platforms that have been hacked to death.

It is time to break free from the open source globalized approach when it comes to government, military and critical infrastructure mobile and fixed computers and networks. Instead of wasting billions on hopeless security "solutions" while we continue to fall behind in the cyber war battle, is senseless, wasteful, frustrating and demonstrates bad leadership and hopeless management. Let's stop.

What we need a an American secure operating system and an American secure network environment built in a trusted environment by reliable people in safe manufacturing locations. Not in China. Not offshore. Here.

The talent to do this surely exists; it is just being wasted today on "other" projects.

A Strategic Plan would look like this:

1. Replace all critical infrastructure operating systems and networks with a US developed secure operating system in three to five years.
2. Assure that connectivity outside of the secure environment is carried out separately from vital secure computing.
3. Impose the massive use of encryption and truly protected authentication on the new secure operating system.
4. Make sure all OS and Secure Network users are properly cleared and vetted.
5. Put in place a compartmentalization system based on need to know and create a series of decentralized and regulated security centers to make sure the thresholds on need to know and a permission based environment are carefully maintained.
6. Do not use any equipment made outside the United States in the critical infrastructure.
7. Create a T&E center to check all hardware, firmware, software with independent auditors and engineers.
8. Create a Red Team to constantly try and break the system, point out vulnerabilities, and fix them immediately. The Red Team should be large and heavily incentivized to find problems.
9. Never, ever, share the US system with anyone outside the US. Make sure that the technology is controlled fully by the US government. And design the system so that if a piece is lost, it can be deactivated remotely and never be useful to an adversary or enemy.
10. Make sure the intellectual property, the technology developers, the Red Teams, and the system of compartmentalization are secret.

Clearly we cannot continue to run our country when there is global knowledge parity of computer systems, hardware and software we use and where most of our critical products are produced outside the US, especially in China. Nor can we sit around and wait for the inevitable collapse of our military command and control, electrical grid, transportation network, banking services or our health care system.

The above proposal sets a direction for a solution. We can win the cyber war.

SEP 05 2014

Give Me $46 Billion and I Will Build a Safe Computer System

With Rebecca Abrahams

ABI Research estimates that cyber security spending on the critical infrastructure was $46 billion last year. The largest part of these dollars was spent in the United States.

Meanwhile, in the United States, Federal government agencies have stepped up their efforts to improve cyber security protection. The Pentagon is tripling its staffing of cyber security professionals even while critical defense programs are being cancelled or curtailed. By 2016, the Pentagon should have 6,000 cyber professionals at work. In a boastful speech describing the Defense Department's investment in cyber, Defense Secretary Hagel says they are on the way to building "a modern cyber force." To back up his words, the Pentagon announced last June that by 2018 the Pentagon planned to spend $23 billion on cyber security.

The Defense Department also created a United States Cyber Command (originated in 2009) which is located at Ft. Meade, Maryland, the home of the National Security Agency. The Cyber Command (officially USCYBERCOM) is headed by a Navy Admiral, Michael S. Rogers, and is subordinate to the US Strategic Command. Strategic Command involves space operations (such as military satellites), information operations (such as information warfare), missile defense, global command

and control, intelligence, surveillance, and reconnaissance, global strike and strategic deterrence (the United States nuclear arsenal), and combating weapons of mass destruction. Thus USCYBERCOM is part of the Defense Department's most sensitive organization that includes control over America's strategic nuclear missiles.

But despite this massive spending and the hiring of thousands of security professionals, the United States has thus far failed to protect government agencies, the rest of the critical infrastructure of the United States, regular businesses, and personal security. Despite the billions sunk into the effort each year, none of the investment has stopped the Russians, the Chinese, the Iranians, the Syrians, or the tens of thousands of hackers from pounding America's computer networks. To date there have been massive hits against government computer systems, health care systems, banking and finance, power companies including nuclear facilities and energy companies, and defense companies. Vast amounts of information have been stolen, overwritten or mutilated by hackers. Today no one can be sure whether our communications are safe, whether the lights will stay on, whether our early warning systems will function. Instead of curtailing the threat, every evidence points to its escalating out of control.

Has anyone bothered to ask why this is so? Now, our leaders, bureaucrats and their academic and industry advisers keep telling us they need to spend more, and like Pavlov's dogs, when the bell rings, they appropriate more money to fight the threat.

If you have a spare $46 billion lying around there is an answer to computer security. But the answer will not be found in any Federal government plan. All of them are, like Hans Brinker, trying to stick their finger in the leaking dyke.

The reason is easy to discern. All computers, including all mobile devices, operate on open systems that were developed by countless software engineers worldwide. The computer industry and its allied software development is a global industry that is totally insecure. You don't know who writes the code, the level of competency, the degree of security training, the level of auditing and internal testing for vulnerabilities, or whether some of the engineers are owned by foreign intelligence services or are promoting various ideological causes. Even in the United States, major companies such as Microsoft, Apple, or Google are run by nameless developers who come from a plethora of places (including lots of foreigners). These companies have no ability to properly vet their employees, nor do they have any real incentive to do so.

What makes matters even worse is that we have grown a security industry, already embedded in government and in corporate America that feeds off the vast amounts of money being thrown at the computer hacking problem. To be frank, these folks have a vested interest in insecurity, because insecurity fuels their budgets. And even if the majority of them are sincere and want to help, their efforts will always fail.

The brilliant Pentagon, which is supposed to know what it is doing in cyber matters, has hired Amazon to provide "cloud" services for Pentagon information and data. The Pentagon has also cleared Samsung (a Korean company), Apple (an American company) and Blackberry (a Canadian company) to provide mobile phones for top Pentagon employees. These Pentagon decisions are intellectually defective and demonstrate that throwing billions of dollars at a problem may only compound the issue. Who clears the people at Samsung, or Blackberry, Apple or Amazon? A lot of folks in Hollywood right now, who stupidly "trusted" Apple's cloud service, now find their naked bodies (and more) posted on the Internet.

The truth of the matter is that public systems and "open source" software are the real danger. Give us $46 billion and we can fix the problem, at least for the Pentagon and the critical infrastructure by building a truly secure, totally encrypted system that is self contained and invulnerable to hacking. To be safe you must eliminate all open source, public systems for government and critical business enterprises.

Right now you cannot buy a safe operating system because no one has invested in one. That investment is absolutely necessary for our survival and our security, not to mention the protection of our freedom and democracy. Open source public systems will always trample on human rights. They are sources of constant abuse by our enemies.

Let's face it. The US government made a huge mistake when it decided to rely on public systems for critical communications and data storage. When you think that almost all the hardware is made in China and the folks producing these systems are everywhere around the world, you can see the enormity of the security disaster before us..

Given the destabilizing events around the world, the risks to American vital defense systems and critical infrastructure are reaching the tipping point. It is urgent for our leaders to recognize the nature of the threat and implement a radical change in our computer networks and systems. The Pentagon, DARPA, CYBERCOM, NSA and everyone else involved have a responsibility to figure it out and not just play dumb.

AUG 31 2014

Is China's New Computer Operating System a Threat?

With Rebecca Abrahams

China has announced it will introduce a new computer operating system in October to replace Windows. Already deeply embarrassed and unhappy over alleged spying on its computers by the US Government, China has vowed to take action.

Its first step was to stop government agencies from using Microsoft's most recent Windows 8 on their machines. But its latest project, to replace Windows altogether puts China into a new category as challenging US dominance in the ultra-sensitive computer operating system league. Controlling computers today is part and parcel of political power, and China understands this. That's why China is not only replacing Windows, but it wants to get rid of Apple's iOS and Google's Android too.

China has three related opportunities and can be expected to exploit all of them. The first involves better controlling China's domestic computers and mobile devices by regulating through the operating system what users can, or cannot, do. China is likely to achieve this through a strongly controlled computer software registration system managed not by Microsoft, Google or Apple but by the Chinese government.

China will gain many benefits. It will have tens of millions of users virtually on launch, and it will control all access by being able to directly regulate software and applications that run on its approved operating system. Likewise, China will likely build in some sort of encryption system linking computers to the Internet, which will create problems for any outside organization to penetrate. And China will stimulate development of domestic software alternatives to Western software products. China will also gain vast experience in how to manage an operating system evolution, how to fix vulnerabilities, how to add features, and how to support software in the field. This will grow a domestic industry that will rapidly mature and will benefit the Chinese state.

Beyond its domestic market, China will be able to look to introducing its software in the global market. China can find a number of opportunities to spread its operating system in many parts of the world. For example, it could potentially challenge both Microsoft and Android computer laptop platforms by offering a cheaper and stronger operating system to users. Price is a big factor in low end laptops and net books. China controls most computers manufacturing today. Put an operating system on top, especially one that is open enough to support popular software and social networking products and China could well have a winner. Of course, China's commercial OS will be different from the one it promotes internally, but this can easily be handled especially if registration and OS downloads are managed by a location-sensitive server.

A third an even bigger opportunity for China is to team with a non-American foreign company to offer an "independent" operating system to customers. This may prove to be attractive to a European partner because the Europeans are quite unhappy with American spying, and they have far less concern, if any, about China than America has. There are plenty of large European companies who are, in the IT world, always playing second fiddle to the US Here is a great chance for them to get ahead. And they can do it on the cheap, since the software investment will be heavily China's operational and financial responsibility.

Where does this leave US companies? Certainly China will emerge as a heavy weight challenger to the likes of Microsoft, Google and Apple. But it is not just US companies that matter here. The loss of control over where operating systems come from could pose a security challenge for America's intelligence agencies that will be formidable and hard to overcome. While that is still in the future, it would be foolish not to prepare ourselves for the problems on the road ahead.

JUL 08 2014

Deep Panda: Chinese Leaders Want to Reap the Benefits of Cyber Spying But They Will End Up Depressed

China shifted its focus from spying on the countries around China to spying on Iraq according to cyber experts who follow Chinese hacking. Called "Deep Panda" it appears China's leaders were trying to figure out what the United States was going to do about the Iraqi situation after ISIS seized over a third of Iraqi territory. To get answers, the Chinese Deep Panda folks targeted the top strategic think tanks in Washington to try and get answers.

"IS insurgents, Anbar Province, Iraq" by Islamic State (IS) - http://securityobserver.org/the-islamic-states-road-to-becoming-a-caliphate/. Via Wikipedia

It has long been the case that China's "official" hackers targeted US government organizations and institutions. But focusing on Think Tanks is something that is, apparently new. (See http://www.zdnet.com/article/china-reveals-existence-of-cyber-warfare-hacking-teams/)

One presumes that the Chinese wanted to read the emails, texts and opinion pieces of the experts to try and estimate America's strategic posture to Iraq. While we don't know the Think Tanks the Chinese targeted, it is likely they chose the ones they feel are most closely aligned with the current administration because their experts would have close ties to Obama's National Security Council, Pentagon, CIA, State Department and, possibly, to other "insiders" who use the Think Tanks as sounding boards.

Foreign governments with representation in Washington generally devote a lot of effort to gleaning policy information, and it is easier for them to talk to outsiders in Think Tanks then to get appointments with actual decision makers. China, like Russia, and all the friendlier countries (UK, Japan, Israel and many others) collect information and send it home.

But China opted for collecting information by hacking, than by meeting Think Tank specialists. Why?

By relying on a secret operation to steal information China's leaders probably thought they might find out much more than Think Tank specialists were willing to tell them. China is not in good odor today, even with the liberal Think Tanks that support Obama. That is because China is a growing power and increasingly a threat to American interests, of course. But the bigger reason is that China's increasingly poor track record on human rights and freedom is offensive both to liberal and conservative thinkers in Washington. If a Chinese official, even one who approaches a Think Tank as ostensibly independent academic, seeking information is likely to find himself or herself accosted about complaints of China's behavior against dissidents and minorities. From China's perspective, this means low productivity in garnering needed information. Thus there is good reason to believe that China needs to steal information because it cannot get it through "normal" channels.

China almost certainly has been following the contacts of Think Tank experts with administration officials for years. China maintains a sophisticated cyber-hacking capability with all the latest technology. The incorrigible sloppiness of Americans toward their own security is certainly well known to the Chinese, and it goes without saying they exploit it. The blabbermouths on cellphones, Twitter, Facebook, LinkedIn and everywhere else not only provides timely information on specific policy subjects to the Chinese, but they can very easily connect the dots and figure out who is connected to whom and which relationships are the most productive ones to follow. A Think Tank leader, therefore, will be known by much more than what he or she says; the Chinese will know his best connections, his reliability as a source, and his influence in decision making circles. The rapid shift of operational hacking resources to find out about Iraq, therefore, was quite easy for the Chinese, because they already previously mapped the network and only needed to probe more deeply and urgently to get answers to specific questions they had.

China is a relatively big industrial player in Iraq. Iraq is China's fifth-largest overseas oil supplier, behind top producer Saudi Arabia, and China as an imported oil consumer is larger than the United States. Unlike the United States, however, China has no military capability of any significance in the Middle East and cannot assure either the stability of oil-supplying regimes nor can they protect the sea lines of communication (SLOC) that bring the oil to China's refineries. Ironically, while China is in the midst of a significant military build up challenging US interests in Asia, China is depending entirely on the US for its vital oil supplies. While Americans don't recognize it, a big part of our defense budget directly benefits China in this way while, at the same time, China is assiduously stealing American defense secrets in an unparalleled, brazen manner.

While China could live without Iraq's oil, and can afford even to lose the $3 billion or so it has invested in Iraqi oil projects, the main Chinese interest is the risk that an out of control Iraq will lead to a general political collapse even beyond Iraq's borders. A blow up in Saudi Arabia, for example, would create chaos in China and might well spell the end of China's neo-Communist government.

This is the same threat that, naturally, concerns the US and its European allies. But, if the Chinese have been listening carefully, as they have, they won't be very happy with what they are hearing through their hacking channels. Right now any effective military response by the United States seems rather unlikely, and it is complicated even further by the foolish moves by the administration to try and use the Iranians and Syrians as proxies (along with Hezbollah) to bail them out of the ISIS onslaught. All this moronic move will achieve is to further frighten Saudi Arabia and push them into ISIS's outstretched but wicked arms.

In short, China's leaders have good reason to be depressed. America is not coming to their rescue on a white horse. And China has made almost all the wrong bets in the Middle East.

JUN 26 2014

Is the Supreme Court Cellphone Decision a Bad Decision?

The Supreme Court decision on cellphones, Riley versus California may seem like an open and shut case because the Court unanimously found that when a person is arrested a cellphone may not be searched without a warrant. But the seemingly unanimous decision may have more fissures and cracks than most people think, and it is far from certain that in the long run that the much touted "victory" for privacy will, in fact, be sustained either by the Court itself or by Congress and State legislatures.

The essence of Riley versus California, and a companion case, US versus Brima Wurie, is that an arresting officer or officers cannot search a person's cellular phone without obtaining a warrant. Riley was stopped by a police officer driving with expired number tags. When stopped the officer found that Riley also had a suspended driver's license. The car was impounded and searched and guns were found hidden under the car's hood. A search of the cell phone turned up a connection between Riley and a street gang and photographs of Riley standing in front of a car that was involved in a shooting a few weeks earlier. Riley was charged, among other things with attempted murder and was convicted with a 15 years to life sentence. His appeal was based on the fact that the search of his cell phone violated his Fourth Amendment rights.

Wurie was picked up in a routine surveillance where the arresting officer thought that a drug sale was taking place. Wurie had two cell phones that were searched and this led to a location and photos. The search of the location, an apartment, yielded crack cocaine, weapons and drug paraphernalia. Wurie was convicted of distributing drugs. The search of the apartment was covered by an appropriate warrant. Wurie got 262 months in prison but appealed that the information improperly taken from his cell phones should have been suppressed.

The Court needed to consider whether, in fact, the Constitutional rights of the two litigants were violated. In the Riley case, the decision by the Supreme Court probably frees Riley from a 15 year to life sentence. In the case of Wurie, he could not be convicted of selling drugs because of lack of proof and would need to be released.

It follows, therefore, that the Supreme Court decision in these two cases has a profound impact on law enforcement, and even though the Court reached a unanimous decision, there are a host of problems embedded in the decision, including the danger to society of releasing criminals from jail.

The Court did not say that cellphones cannot be searched. What the Court said is that you need a warrant, in most (but not all) cases before a phone can be searched.

Warrants are issued based on probable cause. The arresting officer or his superiors needs to convince a judge to issue a warrant. Warrant requests are rarely denied, although a judge may try and narrow the scope of the warrant in certain ways or ask questions before a warrant is issued. In a Texas case last year Federal Magistrate Judge Stephen Smith in Houston denied a request by the FBI to remotely hack a computer by planting spy software on it. His action did not completely block the FBI, but it created legal a problem because the Judge wanted to know how to supervise the collecting of information obtained in this way to make sure it was pertinent to a case said to involve alleged bank fraud and identity theft. Among other things the FBI wanted to remotely control the computer's webcam.

The Supreme Court, in its unanimous decision, also recognized that there were circumstances when a warrant might not be needed at all when a phone was seized. For example, the Court noted that if there could be information on a phone that would warn officers of impending danger from associates of the person arrested, the phone could be searched. This "concession" is a mess for law enforcement. If they search phones without a warrant feeling there is an impending danger and find nothing, are they guilty of an illegal search? What is to be done with evidence they may find of criminal activity, but not anything threatening of law enforcement officers? What if the threat was to the public –e.g., a terrorist attack or other plot against either individuals or groups or sensitive locations? Must the officers abandon this information? And finally, if they find evidence of criminal activity but not of impending threat to the officers, have they conducted an illegal search and must they abandon any prosecution based on such evidence?

In respect to certain categories of crime, murder, terrorism, kidnapping, rape –the Court needs to revisit its decision. When serious threats are involved, law enforcement should not have to wait for a warrant. This, it seems, is what Justice Samuel Alito was trying to get at in partially concurring with the other Supreme Court Justices in deciding these cases. There is little doubt that Justice Alito was uncomfortable and he urged (State) legislatures to enact legislation that draws reasonable distinctions "based on categories of information or perhaps other variables" because, as he says, cell phones pose "new and difficult enforcement problems." Justice Alito warns against "using the blunt instrument of the Fourth Amendment" in deciding these matters and points out that the Supreme Court "is poorly positioned to understand and evaluate" these matters.

Justice Alito, unfortunately, did not follow through his logic and reach suitable conclusions that properly protect our society. In fact, one can argue that the unanimous decision of the Supreme Court may create immense risks by creating confusion within law enforcement and in the courts which undermines civil protection and homeland security.

The truth is that the Supreme Court's decision in these cases leads to less safety for citizens, even though its intent was to protect privacy. The Courts need to recognize that there is a difference between privacy and criminality, and the level and type of threat needs to be part of any Court decision. At the end of the day, these Supreme Court decisions, universally hailed as a good thing, are probably the reverse.

May 26 2014

Your Camera is On, Beware!

With Rebecca Abrahams

Facebook says that it will be turning on your microphone on your smartphone –for what reason, we have no idea but can guess. Turning on cameras and microphones is becoming a huge problem.

Szymon Sidor is a Polish-born software engineering genius currently working for Dropbox as an intern –before that he served two internships with Google working on Google Chrome ⁎ and Google Analytics⁎. Now he is working on his PhD at MIT and he writes a blog called "Snacks for Your Mind." Sidor's latest "snack" is a demonstration of how the cameras on your Android⁎ smartphone can be turned on without you knowing it, and sequential photos sent to a third party over the Internet. Along with the photos, data on your location is displayed in the intercept so you can be easily tracked. All this happens without any awareness by the phone user –the screen can either be turned off or on, it does not matter. Szymon has gotten around the Android requirement to display any photo preview on the screen by reducing the preview to only one pixel, which you won't notice even when your screen is on. On top of this, his solution has gone around Android's notification that an APP is running, so you cannot even check to see if this brilliant piece of software "mal-engineering" is running.

Spying through cameras on smartphones and webcams on computers and laptops, as well as tablets, today is widespread. GCHQ, Britain's

NSA, ran a program called "Optic Nerve." Optic Nerve scanned live on line webcam chats on Yahoo and probably other chat services between 2008 and 2012. Many of these images were very personal ones, and could be used to either embarrass or blackmail users. Reports in the UK say that NSA engineers helped GCHQ develop the Optic Nerve program. Many have either claimed or speculated that one way the NSA and other US spy agencies got around the prohibition of spying on Americans was to let a third party do it for them. A recent case involving a US law firm representing Indonesian interests was bugged by the Australia Australian Signals Directorate. Special intelligence cooperation occurs under the "Five Eyes" program. The cooperating countries are the US, U.K., Australia, New Zealand and Canada.

News reports, based on the leaks of NSA information by Edward Snowden, say that GCHQ stored millions of images gleaned from its webcam surveillance. These images can be retrieved in various ways, including the use of advanced face recognition systems, so seemingly unrelated video chats from different computers and with different names or web addresses, can be linked together. Obviously, when used correctly and legally, this is an important counter-terrorism tool. But when it is used as a political tool to harass to blackmail people, the consequences are different and corrosive. A problem the US government still has, new legislation notwithstanding, is how to assure the proper use of information that can be very personal and completely unrelated to any counter terrorism or criminal activity.

It is not only the NSA or GCHQ that can spy on webcams. Marcus Thomas, a former assistant director of the FBI's Operational Technology Division in Quantico, Virginia, told the Washington Post that the FBI could spy on anyone's webcam without turning on the camera's indicator light. While not all webcams have indicator lights, and many laptops do not have them at all, the indicator light is a nice security feature that tells you when the camera is active. Webcam spying is part of a suite of so-called Remote Access Tools or RATS. Thomas told the Post that the FBI has had these tools for years but uses "Rattingly" (the webcam spying tool) sparingly.

But camera spying is not at all limited to governments or official spy agencies and organizations. It is so widespread today that it has even spread to schools. Just this year Lower Merion Township, a classy suburb of Philadelphia, settled a lawsuit brought by two students paying them $610,000 in compensation. The crime? The school provided 2,300 MacBooks to their students and installed spy software on them that snapped pictures of the students. Photos of the students included snaps of them at home, in bed, sometimes partially clothed. In one case the school claimed a student was "popping" pills: in fact he was eating candy.

"Sextortion" is a growing problem. What is Sextortion? Sextortion is the secret control of webcams or smartphone cameras to run extortion rackets against people. A major case gained notoriety in California where a now-20 year old Jared Abrahams " illegally hacked into the laptops of several young women in the US and abroad, then took control of their webcams in order to film and photograph them while they undressed" according to the FBI. The scam included web cam pictures of Miss Teen USA Cassidy Wolf, who was a classmate of Abrahams. "Abrahams threatened to post the images to the victim's social media accounts unless the women provided additional nude photos/videos or obeyed his commands during a five-minute Skype session" Abrahams was convicted and got an 18 month jail sentence. In another case, a Glendale California man was sentenced to five years in federal prison Monday after pleading guilty in a sextortion case that targeted hundreds of women. Interpol announced the arrest of 58 persons in the Philippines for sextortion, including one case where a17-year-old victim committed suicide in July last year following blackmailing by the group. In fact, "The scale of these sextortion networks is massive, and run with just one goal in mind: to make money regardless of the terrible emotional damage they inflict on their victims," says Sanjay Virmani, director of the Interpol Digital Crime Center.

Webcams and phone cams are also an important source for corporate spying. This works in two ways: companies and organizations spying on their own employees, and competitors and thieves spying on corporations. By being able to activate either a webcam or microphone on a PC, laptop or smartphone, intruders can listen in on sensitive meetings and conversations and even know where the meetings are held, who attended, and everything about what was discussed.

There are plenty of vendors selling spy software, some designed for "professional" business use and marketed as a way to track employees, such as a product for employee monitoring made by InterGuard. Such spying falls into a gray legal area, but once it goes onto a mobile device such as a smartphone or tablet it clearly intrudes on privacy outside of the work space. Even so, this is an unsettled area in US law. It is of course illegal to record a conversation without getting the permission of the person or persons being recorded, but keep in mind even web conferencing software allows for proceedings to be recorded and no permission is asked. These days there are hundreds of spying products to choose from, and the best of them facilitate surreptitious webcam and mobile cam spying.

Corporate spying can facilitate "insider" trading, where the "insider" is sitting outside but has privileged access to your webcam or mobile camera and microphone. No one knows the extent of financial manipulation and computer and smartphone spying going on that facilitates insider trading, stock exchange manipulation, and trading of sensitive investment and competitive information.

It is legal to sell spy software, just illegal to use it without permission outside the workplace, unless it is used to spy by parents on their minor children. Even this "permission" is fraught with difficulty, since other kids who are not related to the parents may well be captured while the parents spy on their children.

In short, there is an epidemic of webcam and smartphone camera monitoring and spying and such spying affects everyone. Our laws have a long way to go to catch up to the reality of this powerful attack on personal privacy.

What can you do? One "solution" often proposed is to cover up the webcam on your PC or laptop. This does stop the camera, but does nothing about the microphone, but it is a partial answer providing you remember to do it religiously. But with the number of devices in homes and offices, it is not simple to manage. And tablets and smartphones often have two cameras, one in front and one on the back. Covering both is awkward and probably unrealistic.

A second solution is to get positive control over cameras and microphones so malware and intruders can't switch them on. One product for Android is MobileOPSEC. It makes sure the cameras and microphones are turned off and nothing can be recorded. This solution trumps Szymon Sidor's brilliant Android hack, and other RAT tools that try to control your device.

Most important of all is to realize that the world is seething with snoops, provocateurs and criminals. No one, neither school children, teenagers, adults, corporate tycoons or government officials can escape them or live in this world unnoticed.

APR 24 2014

Verizon Blockbuster Data Breach Report is Bad News for Organizations

With Rebecca Abrahams

Verizon has published a blockbuster report on Internet "data breaches" which has garnered major headlines because it fingers Eastern Europe (primarily Russia) as a greater source of attacks than those from East Asia, primarily China. Prepared with the cooperation of 50 companies in different parts of the world, the Verizon study classifies "data breaches" into different categories –but the two most important stand out visibly from all the others. These are "point of sale" attacks and "cyber espionage" attacks.

A point of sale attack is one of the ways, but not the only way, to steal money. Point of sales attacks are most common in the retail industry (think Target), with the largest number in hotels, motels and the food service industry.

A cyber espionage attack is an attempt to steal valuable proprietary information, defense and government secrets, or significant information on individuals connected with these organizations and industries. The data is rather interesting in that the biggest victims of cyber espionage are manufacturing companies, professional groups and companies (including law firms, accounting and tax related organizations, computer systems design companies and services, and scientific research organizations), and mining companies (most importantly oil and gas industries).

One of the unfortunate problems with the Verizon Report, is that it has aggregated important categories using broad North American Industry Classification System (NAICS) codes. Trying to understand who was targeted and why is, at best, guesswork.

A second major difficulty is that the Verizon Report can only provide data on actual reports made by the targets or victims of data breaches. Actually, we do not know how many organizations, both government and private sector, actually report an incident; in fact there is good reason to believe that wherever possible the tendency in both sectors either is not to report an incident, or to minimize the impact on its business or operations. If, for example, a company were to reveal that a critical technology it owns was stolen, its share price would collapse. If a bank reported its central computers have been hit by thieves, people will move their money to a safer locale. If the Defense Department reported that its secret stealth technology was stolen (in fact, it has been, as can be seen in Chinese versions of the F-35 Joint Strike Fighter), it might face Congressional hearings or even budget reductions. For all these reasons we can be certain that the Verizon Data is missing big chunks of important information. We can also be sure that Congress has been asleep at the wheel.

A related problem is the linkage between government spying and criminals. There is no spy agency in the world that works in a vacuum. Spy agencies, in and of themselves, are not centers of technology excellence. They are centers for spying, and they buy the technology, know how, and help they need from outside companies and individuals in order to get the job done.

In some countries it has been often alleged that there is a close tie between criminals and spy organizations. For example, Russian intelligence has been accused of working with the Russian Mafia (for example, see William F. Jasper, "Russian Mafia: Organized Crime Is Big Business for the KGB" The New American Magazine, 12 (4) (February 19, 1996) and intelligence services in other countries are often linked in some manner to criminals or criminal organizations. Added to this is the problem that once trained as a spy, there is the potential for the same individual to freelance, often to steal money or engage in forms of extortion.

Spy agencies around the world, including the US, also use private companies, organizations and individuals to do things they would rather not be caught doing themselves. This means anything and everything from stealing personal information, leaking to newspapers, to crashing companies, disrupting banking or commerce –even to waging war. So long as spy agencies operate this way, criminality will increase even more. Of course this subject is well outside of the Verizon Report on Data Breaches, but it is more than worth pondering the consequences.

One highlight of the Verizon Report is how quickly cyber attacks are recognized and dealt with. Here the news is generally bad. For the cases which the Verizon team reviewed, 47% of the intrusions were not discovered "for months" and 68% of them were discovered by outsiders, not by the organization or company. While in most cases the intrusion could be fixed in hours or days, it almost doesn't matter if everything has already gone out the door.

Thus, thanks to the Verizon Report we know that that it takes far too long to recognize that a business or organization has suffered a cyber attack. In today's world, where it is getting easier and easier to exploit organizations through the web, often originating in mobile devices (phone and tablets), the problem of detecting a breach and fixing it is growing worse, instead of improving.

Unfortunately rather than seeing an improvement in cyber security, the threat continues to increase and, with it, the risk to our economy and to national security.

Apr 19 2014

Facebook's "Nearby Friends" is a Really, Really Bad Idea

With Rebecca Abrahams

Facebook has introduced a new feature for its mobile users allowing them to share their location with friends. It is an "opt in" feature, meaning you don't have to sign up for it. So on the surface it seems to be a useful tool for people to use. Isn't that right?

Actually, the new Facebook "feature" is pretty dangerous. It is sending your location information on a continuing basis into a network run by Facebook. Among the problems: your GPS is always on if you use this APP, meaning you can be followed by hackers, intruders or government agencies more or less at will. And Facebook itself, which is not a secure system, also can be targeted by the same folks.

Facebook has also revealed that it plans to share your Nearby Friends data with advertisers. It is far from clear if the opt in feature matters in collecting and sharing this information.

Social media are sometimes lots of fun, but they also leak a lot of personal information about your life, your relationships, your preferences, and your comings and goings which you may not want in untrusted hands. People who use these APPS seem to be oblivious to the risks.

Yet, on a daily basis, we read about people being hounded and abused through social media. There are many cases of such abuse, and it has led to suicides in the US and elsewhere.

People also forget that smartphones, tablets and PC's are high risk devices –with the mobile smartphone leading the pack as the worst of the worst. Why? Because the smartphone has few, if any, safeguards against hackers. There are no firewalls or security barriers; anti-virus and other tools tend not to work on smartphone platforms, and marketing and advertising people in cahoots with telephone carriers are using the platforms as a way to access your information and influence you to buy products, vote for candidates, or convince you to support some opinion or another.

We are at an early stage of exploiting the marketing features of the smartphone. But, if I know where you are, what you ate and at what restaurant, whether you are in your car or on foot, where you work and where you live I have in my hands some really potent information that I can, and certainly will, exploit to the fullest. Maybe it is just a nuisance when advertisers barge into your life. But it has far greater consequences –a haven for crooks, criminals and psychos.

Recently an iPhone update turned on the Bluetooth feature in all of the latest iPhone models. Why? Because Apple is now in the business of helping store owners flash messages to clients in the stores in proximity to a local Bluetooth transmitter. The reason: to push advertising. Say you are looking at a bicycle for your kid in a big outlet store. All of the sudden you get a "recommendation" on your smartphone: your kid will like a certain bike and it is safer than others. Would you pay attention? Most likely "yes." That is what Apple and the store owners are shooting for.

But at the same time, now your Bluetooth is on all the time, just like the WiFi that is on all the time if you opt in with Facebook. Not only will this suck your battery dry, provide critical information on your location and on your behavior, but it also leaves your phone wide open to hackers.

Nothing on the horizon is going to stop the exploitation of personal privacy now in high gear in our country. Our courts have stepped aside and, in fact, condoned our government ripping off our phone's metadata; forget about the Fourth Amendment to the Constitution. Google has announced that it not only scans all your emails, but in face you grant it a world-wide license automatically when you send anything, especially any attachment, through their Gmail system. Now Facebook wants to make sure that you keep your GPS humming so your location can be tracked all the time.

The gradual and sometimes voluntary surrender of personal privacy is increasingly dangerous not only for personal security, but in the end, to the preservation of our rights and freedom. The latest Facebook "feature" is a step in the wrong direction.

Apr 11 2014

Intelligence Agencies are Happy as Clams Thanks to Heartbleed "Bug"

The Heartbleed "bug" which has affected millions of computer systems and countless hardware devices ranging from telephones, to video conferencing systems, to routers and firewalls –was the result of work done by a German software developer named Robin Seggelmann. Seggelmann says it was a coding error that caused Heartbleed, and the error was not "caught" by an auditor inside the Open SSL Project. Open SSL is the security code that is widely used by industry to support encrypted connections on the Web, and to manage encryption on everything from wireless telephones to Cisco routers.

At the time of this writing, we do not know the full "team" who produces the Open SSL software.

The Open SSL Project works on a voluntary basis. Its headquarters is in Maryland but, according to their own description, the participants are on three continents and cover 15 time zones. If there are "rules" regarding membership in the Open SSL project, they are not transparent to the outsider.

The theory behind Open SSL is that if you gather together the "best" community of programmers to tackle a hard problem, you will get the best result that benefits everyone. Underlying is a sort of philosophical notion that people in the "community" join together out of good will, and everything they contribute will be based on pure altruism. The Open SSL project is, by far, not the only community based programming project.

In his interview with the London-based Telegraph newspaper, Seggelmann admits "it was possible that the US National Security Agency (NSA) and other intelligence agencies had used the flaw over the past two years to spy on citizens."

There is no reason to suppose that intelligence organizations would not have discovered the bug in their routine scanning of the Internet.*** Today the Internet carries much more than data traffic; it is increasingly how telecommunications are managed. The fact that we now know that some of the top VOIP (Voice Over Internet Protocol) telephone systems made by Cisco are infected with the "Bug" makes this crystal clear. You can add to this a large number of Cisco routers (the world's most popular router system), video conferencing systems, multiple servers used to manage communications traffic, and even firewalls that protect internal networks.

While a good deal of focus has been put on the NSA, thanks mainly to the leaks and revelations coming from Edward Snowden, the truth is that intelligence agencies around the world try to spy on just about everything they can. The British, French, Germans, Italians, Russians, Chinese, Israelis, Iranians and many others have built massive capabilities. It would be foolish to think they are not taking advantage of damaged encryption systems such as Open SSL.

In short, there is big possibility that, aside from causing untold computer damage, people may have lost their lives because of the Open SSL "Bug." Say you were an Iranian dissident and you send what you thought was a secret message to your compatriots. The knock on the door comes, and the Iranian government arrests you and accuses you of being an Israeli spy. You know the rest.

There is also clearly a link between some foreign intelligence organizations and general criminal activity. Anytime money is involved in spying, as is the case with the Open SSL breach (which affects credit card transactions, banking and other forms of trading information), some intelligence agencies and their criminal colleagues exploit the opening to make money, lots of money. For years we have been watching the Russian mafia carry out these exploits and attack banks in the US and elsewhere in the world. How much they have stolen is anyone's guess, because banks don't like to let on about their security failures.

A critical question is why anyone would rely on a misty group of international volunteers for security? Keep in mind that one of the sponsors of the Open SSL is the US Department of Homeland Security! (Whoever in DHS supported this endeavor ought to find work elsewhere.)

An additional problem today is that the agencies we rely on domestically for security, NSA and NIST (the National Institute for Standards and Technology) have, themselves, been caught bugging security codes so they could exploit computers and communications globally, including the PC's, tablets and phones of Americans. NSA's and NIST's bugging activity has compromised them fatally.

Today in the United States we lack an independent security agency that can provide guidance on security for Americans, public and private. Thanks to NSA and NIST the US government has thoroughly bugged itself, as well as everyone else. A critical task for Congress, aside from investigating the various NSA escapades, is to come up with a new, independent government organization that supports security for Americans. The Agency should have nothing to do with spying and should be prevented by law from cooperating with spy agencies.

APR 03 2014

Sometime Privacy Rules Lead to Murder - The Fort Hood Case

The shooting at Fort Hood could have been prevented. The shooter, 34 year old Ivan Lopez, a soldier who spent around three months in Iraq, was under treatment for severe mental distress. He was receiving anti-depressant drugs and other medications. While his full medical record remains secret, the information about his illness and the fact he was being evaluated for PTSD (although his minimal combat experience suggests that was not his problem) tells us this was a solider that had a problem that should not have been left alone. But he was.

Under Army procedures, as I understand them, someone being treated by the doctors with severe mental health issues, other than being hospitalized would normally be recommended for a Medical Board review. It is not clear that Lopez was recommended for a medical board, but even if he was it takes a considerable time to convene such a board and then gather all the evidence and information needed to reach a determination. Meanwhile the subject continues his or her service in the Army.

That is clearly an operational loophole that is unacceptable. To let someone loose who is having difficulty coping with normal life issues is to put a walking time bomb on the street and among fellow soldiers and personnel on a military base. It is even worse in real operations.

The loophole largely exists because of medical privacy rules, which apply not only to the military but in the society at large. But in the Army, which operates in a certain proscribed space, it seems especially unacceptable to have someone on the loose with so severe a condition as Specialist Lopez.

We can't blame the doctors here, because the problem is clearly a big hole in the system. Lopez met all the criteria of a big risk, but coping with that risk is terribly limited by privacy restrictions and lack of alternative procedures.

It does not end there. Specialist Lopez was able to go to a gun store and buy a Smith and Wesson .45 caliber handgun. He also was able to buy many ammunition clips for the weapon, which he may have bought at the store where he purchased the weapon, or elsewhere.

Under current rules, the gun store is obliged to check out the applicant and to ask him to declare whether or whether not he was recently hospitalized. Other than that and a police check, if the purchaser is clear of the law, he gets the gun. The information about his mental condition is not used in any way in checking him out, mostly because the privacy rules disallow it.

This is a big flaw. Someone with depression and paranoia often will play out his imagining by buying a weapon to confront those he fears are threats. If there is no way to prevent that from happening, there will be more Ft. Hoods in future, and more gun crimes committed by people with severe mental illness.

It would make sense that a database of people under strong medication for mental illness should not be allowed to purchase guns. This information could be held by the police or FBI and used in background checks when guns are purchased. Today that is not the case.

So, our concern with privacy has some deadly loopholes that need fixing.

Our thoughts and prayers go out to those who lost loved ones at Ft. Hood, and to those who were wounded we hope for a speedy recovery. We salute the female military policewoman who confronted Lopez. She is a brave woman who, by doing her job, saved many lives. She is a hero.

Most of all, it is time to reassess how we handle the severely mentally ill and guns, and it is time to modify our privacy rules to protect the public and our military forces.

JAN 09 2014

Have You Been Guccifer'd? Better Give it Some Thought

With Rebecca Abrahams

Have you been Guccifer'd? For those who don't follow the news, Guccifer is a hacker that attacks celebrities, government leaders, top business people and anyone else that suits Guccifer's fancy.

The list of victims is huge. Colin Powell, Air Force Secretary James Roche, Robert Redford, Leonardo DiCaprio, Jim Nance, Tina Brown, Whoopi Goldberg, Steve Martin, Sidney Blumenthal, Warren Beatty and plenty of others. Guccifer steals credit card information, emails, documents, passwords and cell phone numbers. Guccifer got hold of sensitive emails sent to then Secretary of State Hillary Clinton by former Bill Clinton aide Sidney Blumenthal on the attacks on the US mission in Benghazi.

Those emails, while not revealing who was the "most sensitive" source described in the emails, discussed cooperation between the Libyan government and the Muslim Brotherhood and other Islamist elements and included unverified intelligence that the funding for the attack on Benghazi allegedly came from Saudi financiers, possibly linked to al-Qaeda. It is not clear how or from whom Blumenthal got the information raised in his emails to Secretary Clinton, or why he was using a public email account to communicate with the Secretary of State. Certainly he should have known the risk.

In another scoop by Guccifer, emails shared by Colin Powell and a much younger, attractive Romanian diplomatic official, went viral. The Guccifer leak of the Powell/Corina Cretu's (the lady's name) emails not only appeared to be personally damaging to Powell, married for some 50 years, but it also left on the table the question of a top public official having a personal involvement with someone answerable to a foreign government. Powell insists there was no affair with Ms. Cretu.

So who is Guccifer and what is the game? Right now no one knows who Guccifer is, or if there is one Guccifer or more. But his game seems to be to cause maximum embarrassment to as many people as possible, especially folks who are household names thanks to their celebrity status.

Doesn't that mean that everyone else who is not a celebrity is off Guccifer's hacking hook?

Not exactly.

To begin with, while you may think that on the long list of Guccifer victims there is no one you know, chances are that you are still linked as a second or third party. If you use LinkedIn, take a look at how many folks are directly linked to your network, and how many more are connected as a result. The connections multiply much faster than rabbits. This matters because Guccifer collects information from a celebrity's circle of friends and friends of friends, so your personal information has a strong chance to be in Guccifer's hands.

The bottom line is that, other than leaking the juicy stuff he collects to the press, which is an avid consumer of dirt, we don't know what Guccifer does with the rest of what he collects through hacking.

He pleads poverty when talking to journalists — saying he cannot even afford a Smartphone. But that seems like just a cover story for what could be a big business –selling information about credit cards including passwords, tipping off competitors to business deals or stock transactions, learning about government secrets and trading them to the highest bidder, or giving your personal information to someone who can blackmail you.

The fact of the matter is that Guccifer is good at hacking, and it is hard to believe he is just sitting on mountains of potentially profitable hacked data. After all, Guccifer is not NSA and Guccifer's mission certainly does not include protecting any of us. We won't rule out that Guccifer is in it for the thrill and not for profit. But does that seem likely?

The message for everyone is that even if you do not think you are a target of a hacker, don't be too sure. Whether it is your credit card, your family, your business, or your opinions, all of them and more are certainly at risk from hacking. You need to start thinking about protecting your electronic communications, correspondence, transactions and voice communications. Below are some suggestions:

1. For more secure email, consider Hushmail. It is encrypted and so far as we know user passwords are secure
2. For secure communications for business or the enterprise consider an encrypted phone system such as FortressFone* or Blackphone.
3. For document security consider TrueCrypt.

---

*The author is Chairman of the Board of FortressFone Technologies.

DEC 24 2013

Is Knox the Answer to Android Security?

Samsung is offering a special version of its Samsung 4 Galaxy smartphone called Knox. Knox is targeted on the high end financial, business and government communities. Does Knox solve the problem of smartphone insecurity and significantly reduce risk for its users?

What is Knox: Knox is a partitioned mobile platform running two operating systems, one for personal use and one for enterprise use —the enterprise (private) side being within a "container."

There are other Knox-like partitioned mobile platforms either in the market or entering the market coming from other vendors such as LG, Blackberry, etc. None of them have been around long enough to know how well they are engineered in relationship to multiple Android vulnerabilities and OS/Kernel weaknesses.

The Knox container has its own separate home screen, launcher, applications and widgets. All the data and applications stored in the container are said to be isolated. It is claimed that no application or process inside the container can interact or communicate with any process outside of it and vice-versa.

All files within the container are encrypted using the Advanced Encryption Standard (AES) cipher algorithm with a 256-bit key.

Knox features are (1) Customizable Secure Boot, (2) TrustZone-based Integrity Measurement Architecture (TIMA), and (3) Security Enhancements for Android. Secure boot, the company claims, is the Knox-enabled device's first line of defense, ensuring that only verified and authorized software can run on the device bootup. TIMA monitors the kernel.

Knox depends on the user to carefully delineate use between partitions. Knox does not protect the public partition. Knox runs an APP store for the private side that provides safe APPS for Knox.

Problems with Knox
In the past two months there have been reports of vulnerabilities and flaws in the Knox system.

The latest report comes from the Ben Gurion University Cyber Security Laboratory in Israel. There two researchers Mordechai Guri and Dudu Mimran (the Security Laboratory Chief Technical Officer) claim that a hacker can easily intercept any data on the secure side of the Knox platform. The researchers also believe that professional hackers could actually modify the Knox platform, effectively compromising it by planting malware or spyware on the platform. In response a Samsung spokesperson said "Rest assured the core Knox architecture cannot be compromised or infiltrated by such malware."

Until now, no one has explained how spyware, planted on the public side of the Knox platform, won't seriously compromise the Knox user.

Researchers should look into two security problems that arise in a dual platform device.

The first problem is what happens if spyware is planted on the public side of the smartphone. This is the "open" platform that is generally unprotected. Spyware, or what is called a spy phone, can intercept literally any conversation and any transaction (email, text, video and photo) on the public side of the smartphone. Professional spy phones can activate a phone's microphones and cameras without the knowledge of the user and even if the phone is switched off. Since among the data normally targeted by spy phones are calendars, the intruder knows when to activate the spy phone. When the intruder does this, either he can immediately stream the information secretly back to his web address, or alternatively he can store it in a hidden folder and stream it back later. In short, the user remains entirely vulnerable on the public side to spy phones and other malware.

The second problem revolves around the question of the use of hardware on Knox. A smartphone consists of numerous sensors and transmitting systems including cameras, microphones, Bluetooth, WIFI, voice and data radios, etc. When a Knox user is booted up on the private side of the phone, are the sensors and radios fully and securely controlled by the Knox platform? If not, then a spy phone or other malware on the public side can take information from these same sensors being used on the private side of the platform. This would facilitate spying on the private side as well as on the public side of the platform.

APPS for the private side of the Knox platform are controlled through a store run by Samsung. Experience with attempts to block malware on Android platforms by auditing APPS in places such as Google Store, have been less than successful. One anti-virus company reported this past summer that some 1,200 APPS on the Google store over a 7 month period were malware. And these are the easy ones to detect. Really sophisticated malware is often embedded in legitimate programs. Because of the plethora of APPS available today, and the diversity of sources (APP production is truly a global enterprise), finding the "bad" ones is a challenge. If we learned anything from anti-virus software, the "bad" stuff is usually found after many computers are already infected. When you think of the small universe of enterprise and government users of a product like Samsung, the risk is exponential if a "bad" APP or "bad" modified APP infects the smartphone.

No one really knows if Samsung will be any more successful than Google in protecting APPS, yet this protection is critical under the Knox scheme. If history shows us anything, one should not be optimistic or confident in the result.

Conclusion

The Knox system is an effort at a serious security system for an Android platform. Other companies, such as LG and Blackberry, are working on improving Android platform security.

DEC 07 2013

BITCOINS, PRIVACY AND DEMOCRACY

[**Update March 1, 2014**: The AP reported today as follows: "The Mt. Gox Bitcoin exchange in Tokyo filed for bankruptcy protection Friday and its chief executive said 850,000 Bitcoins, worth several hundred million dollars, are unaccounted for." This follows the mysterious end of the British Bitcoin exchange which seems to have stopped functioning. Bitcoin investors have no recourse.]

[**Earlier Update**: Norway and China say that Bitcoins are not a legal currency. In addition, now the largest Bitcoin exchange in China will no longer allow customers to use the Yuan to buy Bitcoins because of pressure from the Chinese government and from the Central Bank of China. The Wall Street Journal says that Bitcoins have lost half their value in the past few weeks.]

While the Bitcoin may be a "virtual currency" its main characteristic is that it is a non-state currency. In this connection, the Bitcoin shares some characteristics with gold, silver, diamonds and other fairly portable commodities that can be used for exchange. The difference is that while gold and silver are often manipulated by governments who hoard these materials, Bitcoins are not, so far at least, under any government control.

Bitcoins appear on the scene at an unusual moment in time. The currencies of democratic countries are in decline and significant value has been lost over the last decade or two. This has happened because governments, who issue these currencies, have been spending far more than they have in income and have used methods such as "quantitative easing" to temporarily keep them solvent. Quantitative easing is just a semi-sophisticated way of printing more money.

Complicating the picture is the unique situation involving the Euro, which is the European currency that replaced the national currencies of France, Germany, Spain, Italy, Greece, Portugal, Luxembourg, Austria, Finland, the Republic of Ireland, Belgium, and the Netherlands in 2002. The Euro temporarily "solved" the currency problem in the weaker European countries (e.g., Italy, Greece, Portugal, Spain etc.) by putting in place a strong currency dominated by Germany and by European banking and lending institutions and organizations. Weaker states, without the ability to print more of their own currency, still were able to keep spending by floating loans to cover some of their deficits. Today these countries, foremost among them Greece and Spain, face the precipice because the lenders now want fiscal discipline in exchange for loan relief. The social, economic and political costs of the previous ten year Euro-ride are spawning a deep reaction including the rise of neo-fascist, sometimes violent, political groups.

The Bitcoin, which works through networks of computers and uses encryption, was designed to get around state-run currencies and to avoid state demands, especially taxation. Transactions in Bitcoins are anonymous and it is said to be nearly impossible to discover who owns Bitcoins and how many Bitcoins are held by Bitcoin buyers, many of whom are investor-speculators.

Most certainly there will be political problems with Bitcoins as nation states fight to get some control over Bitcoins. China has banned its financial institutions from handling Bitcoin transactions, the first major move to regulate Bitcoins which is becoming popular with Chinese entrepreneurs seeking to get out from under the control of the Communist state. For Chinese Bitcoin investors, the Bitcoin represents portability and anonymity, both of which are in short supply on the mainland.

A big question for Bitcoins is its privacy claim. Experts who have looked at the algorithms and computer methodology see the structure of the Bitcoin system as credible and technically strong; but modern computers and networks are incredibly weak in security, meaning that big government probably has the ability to penetrate the Bitcoin system and the capability to disrupt or pervert the Bitcoin network.

Inherently the Bitcoin system is not based on any democratic standard. One could say that it is an anarchistic system, but if this is true as it may seem, it is anarchism with a hidden hand. The problem is the identity and location of the hidden hand is not known to the players (investors, buyers, miners etc.), and some claim it may not matter as the currency has a life of its own that goes beyond the significance of any hidden hand. On this latter point, the jury is still out because the system is dark, and therefore non-discoverable except to powerful players with resources for intervention, such as governments or large criminal organizations.

Privacy is an important issue these days as the protected space of most modern democracies has been deeply compromised by electronic surveillance and manipulation of personal and institutional information. The problem is extreme in the US because the "checks and balances" system no longer is functional in protecting privacy, as the establishment simply preserves its wealth and prestige by stealing from the broader population. "Checking" institutions, such as the Congress and the courts, including the Supreme Court, are enmeshed in the establishment and despite some ineffective and worthless inquiries, generally have supported the surveillance system. To some degree the Bitcoin popularity is a reaction to the surveillance state.

A possible outcome of all this is that states will find a way, either overtly or covertly, to control the Bitcoin or blow it out of the water. The rise of the Bitcoin is only a symptom of a much bigger and unresolved problem, which is how freedom and privacy can be sustained against oppressive governments that were once democratic.

OCT 29 2013

GIFTS FROM MOSCOW TURN OUT TO BE SPY DEVICES

The Kremlin, host to the G-20 summit this past September, gave out "freebees" to the guests consisting of USB Memory Sticks and phone and tablet chargers.

A suspicious attendee asked the German Security Services (BND) to check the devices. The BND experts found that both the memory stick and the hand-out phone charger contained a Trojan horse that linked information on the devices back to the Russians, presumably the Russian secret services.

The news was broken in the Italian newspaper La Stampa and in Corriere della Sera.

A modern USB port has four wires –two of them are for charging and two others are for data exchange. Since the Trojans were hidden in the memory chip of the charger and the USB stick, it was a simple matter to move these hidden files, which are Trojan horses, into the mobile phone, laptop or tablet of the users.

This is a trick that was already done by the Chinese which deeply affected US forces in Iraq and Afghanistan. The Chinese uses the flood it and watch approach, not too different to what NSA has been doing scooping up millions of phone logs. Essentially the Chinese put the bugs in every USB flash memory stick it manufactured (which is virtually all of them) so everyone would be infected. Then using supercomputers, generously provided by the United States, the Chinese had the luxury of search files and information on millions of mobile devices, laptops and desktops seeking out specific persons or critical information.

The same thing happened in Korea where Army personnel charged their mobile devices on sensitive networked computers. The Trojans that got onto their mobile devices in various ways, instantly migrated onto classified computers and the data became available to the intruders, presumably the Chinese.

There are a lot of malicious phone chargers around, as reported recently by Forbes.

So what can you do?

Here are some rules to follow:

1. Never charge your phone on your PC or on anyone else's PC (including laptops and tablets with USB ports). Either you could inadvertently put malware on your PC (and onto the network that it may be connected to as well), but it also can result in malware being transferred to your mobile device.
2. Use only the charger provided to you by the product manufacturer.
3. Keep the charger with you –don't leave it sitting around. It is easy for a malefactor to switch it out with a bugged device. You will never know. This can happen easily in a foreign hotel.
4. Consider buying a charging cable that does NOT have data lines in it. These are far safer. Keep it safe and away from others. Another alternative: by a security adapter for your USB connection.
5. All memory sticks are risky and suspect. Consider investing in a US made secure memory stick. Keep it on your person.

6. Never charge your phone, tablet or laptop at a public place such as an airport or a train station or at a free charging station unless you have put in place a locking device in your connecting cable.

OCT 24 2013

HOW DID THEY HACK MERKEL'S PHONE?

They didn't tell us, and we did not ask, out of being polite we can assure you. But we can certainly guess how it was done.

There are both internal and external vulnerabilities in smartphones. Let's look at them.

In regard to internal vulnerabilities, commercial smartphones (the majority of them manufactured in Asia) contain hardware, firmware and software combined with lots of sensors and radios. The operating systems of smartphones (such as iPhone, Android-phones, Windows phones, Blackberry and the others) are designed to link up the phone's hardware, its sensors, and its radios together. Most of the computer "code" is written to get the job done, but for the most part security plays second or third fiddle on commercial platforms. Indeed, there is so much social networking and connectivity demanded by smartphone users, that the idea of putting in any kind of security perimeter for the smartphone platform is all but verboten. This makes it easy for intruders, thieves, private eyes, lawyers and governments to spy to their heart's content. All these need to do is to exploit some social APP (the technique is called 'Phishing'), plant some malware, or install a spy phone on the mobile device.

What is a Spy Phone

A spy phone is specialized spying software that lives "in the background" on a smartphone. An intruder or hacker controls the smartphone remotely meaning the phone itself can be switched on at any time without the screen lighting up, conversations can be recorded and surreptitiously broadcast, and virtually all the information on the phone can be hijacked. This means contact lists, emails, text messages, photos, videos and files can be grabbed at will.

Spy phones vary in level of sophistication, but if you want to buy one you can find a commercial spy phone for every type of mobile phone and smartphone. It is, of course, illegal to listen to someone's conversations without their permission, but professional spy phone users, and a fair number of amateur sleuths, don't worry about the legal nicety. That's why in the U.K. there is a major phone hacking scandal which has to do with stealing text messages, emails, photos and voice mail messages.

More than 100 major UK firms, not counting a number of newspapers, are said to have engaged in smartphone spying activities, usually working through cutouts (in the main private investigators). This kind of spying either was for economic gain, efforts to compromise a person by learning about their private life, or for salacious reasons. The fact that it was widespread and virtually out of control in the UK should forewarn us that the same is true in the United States.

Chancellor Merkel's Phone

Angela Merkel has a smartphone, and she likely has APPS installed that please her. So one avenue of attack for an intruder is to plant spy phone software on her mobile. Is this what the German counter-intelligence services (probably the BND or Bundesnachrichtendienst) found? While totally speculation, if they did then they probably could "sandbox" Mrs.

Merkel's phone and pretty quickly figure out who was doing the listening. We don't know that this is what happened, but some event certainly triggered Merkel to pick up the phone and complain directly to President Obama. These things, as one knows, just are not done. Gentlemen don't read the mail of other gentlemen or women, to paraphrase Henry L. Stimson, former US Secretary of War (before we decided we should only be for Defense and not for War).

External Spying and Intercepts
The second way to break into a smartphone is external –that is, to intercept conversations. There are a number of ways to do this. One can create a false cell phone tower and intercept calls that way. This method, called IMSI Catching after the International Mobile Subscribe Number that is in every phone, is how you can grab calls from a near proximity to the caller.

In our initial review we thought that "It is unlikely the US used IMSI Catching. " Now De Spiegel is reporting that the spying on the Chancellors phone, which may have gone on for more than 10 years, may have been run out of a US installation in the German capital, a spying operation that was not legally registered with the German government. The location is about one mile from the offices of the Chancellor. This would put it in range for an IMSI catcher. Therefore the use of the IMSI catcher cannot be ruled out.

Another way is to get the cooperation of the Telephone Company or mobile phone company. This works in your home country (as the NSA has proven by downloading all the metadata of the phones of US citizens, and who knows what else) but it is not likely to have worked in Germany because the NSA is not in a position to twist the arms of German cell phone and telephone companies. But it is possible, as an alternative strategy, to tap into trunk lines that carry calls over fiber optic lines. It seems this is a major shared industry between the NSA and their UK counterparts in GCHQ. While they might not get all of Merkel's calls that way, they could get some of them.

Most Likely Spying Method
In short, NSA had plenty of options. We would think the most likely one was to plant a spy phone on Chancellor Merkel's phone, but it could also have been through an IMSI catcher.

In Germany there are many that think Merkel should have taken sterner action when the first Snowden revelations about tapping German phones became public. They say Merkel is, in fact, now also a victim because she did not act.

The plain truth is, of course, that the BND and other German security services were either sleeping at the switch or did not care. Otherwise they would not have let their chancellor's phone get compromised by NSA or by anyone else.

OCT 07 2013

WAS THE NSA BACKDOOR WORTH IT?

[Update: We can now add to our October 7th Reuters' story the following: RSA was paid $10 million by NSA to produce an encryption algorithm in their products with a backdoor. See the Reuters' article "Exclusive: Secret contract tied NSA and security industry pioneer." One wonders about the intent behind the RSA compromise. RSA security products are used primarily by industry, so it would seem the primary purpose would be to have access to industry computers.]

The National Security Agency has three distinct hats –first its job is to collect national security intelligence primarily through signals collection. The second is to support both the government and the private sector by helping in what NSA calls "information assurance." This assignment includes coming up with encryption techniques and codes that can be used by government agencies and by the public. And NSA's third hat, a relatively recent one, is to take action against malefactors who attempt to harm computer networks or pose other national security threats –a cyber attack command to put the bad guys out of business or harm their operations (something like "Stuxnet" against Iraq's nuclear program, for those who follow these things).

Each of NSA's "hats" impinges on the other "hats" so that the job of spying intrudes on the job of information assurance, and the job of attacking malefactors impinges on both other hats. On top of that each of the "hats" has lots of internal risks. If you destroy an adversary's computer network, will that stop the adversary or just cut off your source of information? If you build a better crypto mousetrap will the bad guys use it against you?

No one has yet suggested any good way to disentangle NSA's conflicting responsibilities. Nor do we yet know if there is a practical manner in which spying can be confined only to foreign targets in a highly globalized world.

Just last month one of the nation's most respected security development companies, RSA, decided to remove an important crypto tool from its products. The tool was developed by NSA and there is an interesting history surrounding it.

Called a "Dual_EC_DRBG" for Dual Elliptical Curve Deterministic Random Number Generator, elliptical curve cryptography is a popular public key methodology that improves on earlier generation systems. It was introduced in the middle 1980's and was approved by the National Institute of Standards and Technology (NIST) in 2006. RSA used Dual_EC_DRBG in a wide range of its products, which are sold to governments and to private companies for information security protection.

All modern encryption algorithms requires a mathematical technique called "seeding" to assure no pattern is inadvertently introduced that would make it easy to untangle the encryption. This is achieved by using a pseudo random number generator. In 2006 when the elliptical curve approach was approved, the Dual_EC_DRBG random number generator was pushed by NSA and made part of the library of encryption tools adopted at that time.

In November 2007, Bruce Schneier, an important American cryptographer and computer security specialist, published an article called "The Strange Story of Dual_EC_DRBG." In that article Schneier took a look at the NSA-championed DBRG and quoted from an informal presentation at the Crypto 2007 Conference by two other cryptographers, Dan Shumrow and Niels Ferguson. They showed that the Dual_EC_DRBG had a weakness that could "only be described as a backdoor."

The backdoor is thought to be a kind of skeleton key that makes it easy to break the encryption.

Despite the fact the Schneier, Shumrow and Ferguson (among others) believed there was a back door in the encryption, companies around the world, particularly RSA, went ahead anyway and used the tool.

It was not until this past September, with new revelations as part of the Snowden leaks, that the matter again came up. The documents showed that NSA, acting in concert with the National Institute of Standards and Technology, had inserted a backdoor in its crypto suites. This confirmed exactly what Schneier et al had said six years before. Here was something approaching proof of what Dual_EC_DRBG was all about.

Naturally this is an earthquake in the crypto business world and it makes it clear that NSA "information assurance" program also might be an information spying operation, but aimed at whom?

Foreign governments tend not to use US encryption tools because they don't trust them. But foreign companies do use them because the US "system" (government, banking, health care) require the use of the US crypto. Was the backdoor needed to spy on the private sector?

But there is an even greater risk when a backdoor is put into an encryption system. An adversarial government with significant resources might also figure out how to exploit the backdoor, or if they cannot they will find other ways to get "behind" the encryption engine.

NSA had one interesting, though now transitory, triumph with its backdoor, or at least one can surmise that is the case. Al Qaeda used American encryption libraries to build its own encryption tool for use by its Jihadist terrorists. Their product is called "Mujahedeen Secrets 2" and it is just a repackaging of NSA/NIST approved material. We can all hope Al Qaeda keeps on using the product.

AUG 20 2013

Destroying the Fourth Amendment

Government, The Courts, And Private Industry Are Stealing Our Freedom And Wrecking Democracy

On March 5, 1976 in Baltimore Patricia McDonough was robbed. She was able to give police a description of the robber and also information about a 1975 Monte Carlo automobile standing near where the crime occurred. Thereafter she started getting threatening and obscene phone calls from a man who said he was the robber. The 1975 Monte Carlo belonged to Michael Lee Smith. At police request, a pen register was installed at the phone company central office to record numbers dialed from Smith's home telephone. When the police saw that he was calling Patricia McDonough, they got a warrant to search Smith's residence where they found a page in the phonebook folded down where Ms. McDonough's name was listed. This led to Smith's arrest and subsequent conviction where he was sentenced to six year imprisonment.

The case was appealed on the basis that the pen register was installed on Smith's phone without the police first obtaining a warrant. Smith's attorney argued that the pen register violated Fourth Amendment guarantees of "the right of the people to be secure in their persons, houses, papers and effects, against unreasonable searches and seizures." The appeals court saw this as a critical issue and requested a review by the Supreme Court. This led to a vital decision in a case known as Smith v. Maryland (442 US 736). The Supreme Court decision in 1979, although based on a now nearly extinct technology, not only has resulted in widespread warrantless searching of phone records by law enforcement, but by extension it also allows the National Security Agency and other government organizations to spy on citizen's phone records. The New Jersey case also is important to some Internet businesses that rely on surveillance of their customers to gather information, most notable Google which is using the 1979 Supreme Court decision as a major argument allowing Google to scan customer's emails and extract information "in the normal course" of conducting its business. Google has just filed a Motion to Dismiss in a case pending before the District Court of Northern California against petitioners who are claiming that Google's search of emails is a violation of Federal and State wiretapping laws.

The Supreme Court 1979 decision turned on two issues. The Court asked whether, first of all, the person seeking protection under the Fourth Amendment had a "reasonable expectation" of privacy and, secondly, whether the person's expectation of privacy is recognized as "reasonable" by society.

Put into modern terms, Google says that a user of its Gmail system (there are now nearly half a billion Gmail users) does not have a reasonable expectation of privacy because Gmail is a free service and users are advised that Google can make commercial use of information it gathers from the emails that traverse its system. Google's lawyers also are saying that anyone who sends a message to a Gmail user, even though not directly advised of Google's privacy rules, likewise has no reasonable expectation of privacy.

Similarly the government is saying that it can acquire phone company "meta data" without needing a warrant because users have no reasonable expectation of privacy when they use a public conveyance such as a telephone company –the exact meaning of the 1979 Supreme Court decision. By extension in a current case before the Supreme Court (US v. Brima Wurie), the Justice Department is saying that it can search a person's cellphone without first obtaining a warrant. The Obama administration's brief asserts that there is a risk someone might zero out (or erase) the phone's contents unless it was immediately searched by police. This current case involves an individual involved in a crack cocaine arrest where the mobile phone was among items seized by the police during the arrest.

The 1979 case turned on what is a "justifiable" or "reasonable" expectation of privacy. The court pointed out that since the pen register was installed in the central switching office of the phone company, the person cannot claim that the person's "property" was invaded or that the police "intruded into a 'constitutionally protected area.'" The court pointed out that a "law enforcement official could not even determine from the use of a pen register whether a communication existed. These devices do not hear sound. They disclose only the telephone numbers that have been dialed...." This is precisely the same argument that the US government makes in acquiring billions of phone records ("meta-data"). It means that no one has a reasonable expectation of privacy at least for meta-data and therefore no warrant is needed.

There are many problems with the Court's finding. To begin with, the Government can know everyone you call, when you call, and for how long you call, without seeking any permission to do so. This applies both to international and domestic calls, to every business, organization and to all individuals. Furthermore, the government can obtain this information even though there is no law enforcement rationale or component. Inter alia, this means (based on the 1979 decision) that the government can make whatever use of the information it wants, including disclosing the information collected. In the same manner, Google could (not that it would) disclose to the public that a certain individual, business, or organization is often in contact with X, Y or Z or that it purchases A, B, or C etc. Or Google could turn this information over to the Government, no warrant needed.

In short, the trend in court decisions is leaving individual protection by the wayside. The same holds true for government actions in spying on citizens and for corporate actors doing the same thing. All of this leaves the intent of the Fourth Amendment in the dust, a casualty of modernity and of the misappropriation of our rights and freedoms. The bottom line is that democracy itself is under threat if the right to privacy is disregarded.

AUG 01 2013

SUPPOSE BRADLEY MANNING AND EDWARD SNOWDEN WERE CROOKS?

Neither Bradley Manning nor Edward Snowden are crooks in the sense of stealing information for personal profit. Instead they seem to have been ideologically motivated. Both of them lived "inside" a system that was handling classified and highly secret information. In the case of Manning, he had access to tons of diplomatic cables, military communications, and operational information. In the case of Snowden, he had access to security policies, practices, and the ability to use the system to exploit information collected by the NSA.

Both of these gentlemen are in heaps of trouble. Manning's sentencing hearing has started and, it is likely, the judges will reach a decision by the end of August or early September. Snowden, on the other hand, has been granted asylum in Russia, so he is (for now) safe from prosecution. How long the Russians will protect him depends, among other things, on how cooperative he is with Russia's security authorities and how useful he is to Russia's interests. He could easily be traded back to the United States perhaps in exchange for an important Russian asset in the United States.

The most obvious trade is the case of Victor Anatolyevich Bout, a Russian arms dealer who was arrested in Thailand, extradited to the United States, and sentenced in Federal court to 25 years imprisonment for conspiracy to kill US citizens and officials, deliver anti-aircraft missiles and provide aid to a terrorist organization. The Russians would dearly like to have him back, and they have so-far unsuccessfully pitched their case at very high levels of the US government. Now they have the possibility of a trade, particularly if Snowden is foolish enough to violate the terms of his asylum agreement with the Russian authorities.

Regardless of Snowden's ultimate fate, the more interesting question is whether others in a similar position, could make use of NSA intercepted information for profit.

It is now clear that a good deal of NSA's interceptor work is outsourced. This means that the chain of custody is weaker than it should be, as it relies on whatever security is provided by NSA's contractors. Contractors have an economic incentive not to find problems, since exposing a security breach might backfire and result in the loss of financially important contracts. Furthermore, even if the contractor might want to try and enforce the "rules" (whatever they are), there are two further problems: (1) enforcement takes resources, and supervision resources are costly and lower profitability; (2) private companies don't have extensive links to law enforcement, as a government agency would have; they do not have Inspector Generals and counterintelligence capabilities, as a government agency would have; and they certainly don't welcome extensive security reviews and oversight by law enforcement, counterintelligence, inspector's generals, or anyone else "from the government." Contractors want their sponsors to be happy, to give them high performance ratings, and to trust them. Remember that Snowden worked for Booz Allen, not for the government directly. And while Booz Allen is a well-regarded company with very high standards, Snowden was able to take advantage of the Booz Allen work environment and do heavy damage to NSA and the US government.

Much of the focus of attention these days in on the scope of NSA's activities and the rights of Americans —certainly consequential issues that need airing. No one wants to live in a police state, even if it might be a well-intentioned police state.

But structural issues also need to be addressed. The "system" that we have right now is fraught with danger, and it is not just danger to our national security. It offers an opportunity to crooks of all kinds to steal information and sell to the highest bidder, whether the buyer is a criminal activity itself, a foreign country, or to an industry or organization trying to nail a competitor.

One can argue that if there is a Bradley Manning and an Edward Snowden, it is almost certain there are plenty of criminals making a living on the NSA.

JUL 20 2013

SMARTPHONES AND TABLETS: TWO SUGGESTIONS THAT MAY HELP YOU STAY SECURE

Smartphones and tablets are great! Unlike desktop computers and "schlep-tops" (laptops that you have to haul around), the smartphone can be attached to your waste or wrist or dropped in your coat pocket or bag. It is super-transportable –and powerful.

The average smartphone today has all the computational power of a computer, a slimmed down operating system, rapid loading of countless APPS (the majority of which are free), and connectivity almost anywhere in the world.

What's not to like? And like them we do, as does the world. Even though the pace of adoption is just starting to slow, the number of smartphones passed 1 billion units in the third quarter of 2012. That's a lot of smartphones which have been sold far more rapidly than the PC.

So we should be happy as a lark, or at least as happy as the telecoms who sell us the voice and data services the smartphone needs to function in the wild.

But maybe we should also think a little. We are storing all sorts of personal information on our smartphone such as the names of our friends and business acquaintances, our personal schedule, connections to our social media pages and to our email and SMS messages. Our smartphone knows where we are, where we have been, and if we are using the GPS even where we are going and approximately when we will get there.

In addition, everything we say on a smartphone is being broadcast over radio waves, whether the radio waves are provided by our telecom provider, or through a WIFI (another radio) or Bluetooth (yet another radio) connection. This means that someone interested in our communications has plenty of opportunity to listen in.

Even if our phone is turned off, a hacker or intruder may have the means to turn the phone back on without letting you know. You won't see the screen light up or any other activity on the phone. But ON it is —which means that your most private conversations can be overheard.

How hard is any of this to do? Not very. There are hundreds of companies out there that will sell you the tools —some of them are even free. And the tools are just APPS that you can plant on someone's phone. Sure, there are good spy APPS and cheap junky APPS. But the professionals know where you can find the good ones.

People in America, especially, are very trusting and want to believe people are good, not bad. So they say, no one will be interested in me, so why worry? But people are connected to people, and the target may not be you, but it may be leaders in your company, or the chief technical officer, or the patent attorney, or your tax lawyer. You will have that information on your phone, maybe in your contact folder, maybe in your email, or perhaps in a company supplied APP. In any case, targeting you gets the intruder to the real target —and the result is that the target is compromised and never knows how it happened, since he or she only connects with "trusted" people like you.

Today there is a huge amount of government spying —and we are learning more about it every day. I know that, you say, but I have nothing to hide. Maybe that is true, but are you sure that some civil servant or bureaucrat who has your most personal information will keep it inside the government? Or will he or her make a business out of selling the information —a sort of incidental profit center. No one can say. If your American Express or VISA card or your Capital One card is not in your wallet, but in your phone, look out! What about your social security number? What about your personal identity? It can be stolen, and its theft will be very costly and difficult for you.

The amount of corporate spying and foreign-sponsored espionage is staggering. Ask the Brits who just found out that their favorite evening newspaper was filling its pages by hacking the phones of the famous and not so famous, and anyone else who could give them a good story for their pages. In the British case, the newspaper guys paid private investigators to do the dirty work. And so they did.

Our company, Ziklag Systems, provides a comprehensive solution that is right for the enterprise level — the FortressFone. For personal users who are buying and using their own phones, the guiding word is "be careful –be very careful." Here are two good rules that may help you survive in the smartphone jungle:

(1) When downloading an APP that interests you, pay attention to the "permissions" it is asking for. Don't just tap on "Install." Read what it says and decide if you really want to use the APP if it is taking your location information, connecting to your social media like Facebook and Twitter, or gobbling up your Gmail. If you don't like an APP from someone you don't know connecting to your personal information, don't install the APP.

(2) Keep your WIFI and Bluetooth turned OFF when you don't absolutely need them. If you don't really need them they drain your battery and they may also drain all your personal information. Only connect with WIFI and Bluetooth at truly trusted places. Airlines, trains and coffee shops are NOT trusted places. A lot of con-artists hover around these places and they have intercept equipment ready to grab all your information. You won't "see" them; they will "see" you.

Don't use WIFI or Bluetooth in the airport, on planes or trains unless you have absolutely no choice. And when you must attend an important meeting, lock your phone up in your desk or leave it with the front desk for them to care for it (make sure you have password protection on your phone). This is the best way to keep a spy phone out of your meeting place, your business and your life.

JUN 30 2013

DON'T BLAME NSA ONLY – IT IS BAD GOVERNMENT DECISION MAKING

Every day there are more revelations about NSA-run spying operations. The latest is a story featured in the Sunday, June 30th edition of Der Spiegel, the German magazine with an online edition in English. The story alleges that NSA bugged the EU (European Union) headquarters and spied on EU leaders. With the news blasting in the European press, there is underway a huge reaction about America spying on its "friends."

Of course much of this is crocodile tears coming from Europeans who have been spying on America for years. But that aside, and taking into account that spying on the EU would have to be one of the most boring and stupid assignments for an intelligence agency ever to be given, we can rightly ask is this an example of NSA out of control, or is this an example of poor government decision-making?

To begin foreign spying by the US government is not illegal in the United States. Of course breaking and entering in a foreign country is a crime in that foreign country. So that if the operatives who planted the bugs in EU headquarters were ever caught, they could go to jail in Brussels.

So did NSA cook up this target on its own? Of course not. NSA has about as much interest in the EU as in the tooth fairy.

This is almost certainly an assignment that was generated in the State Department, and may have been undertaken for some vague political or economic reason.

How does it work? NSA is an operational agency, not a policy organization. It carries out assignments that it is given.

Different departments and agencies make requests to NSA through certain channels set up inside the government. NSA then assigns resources to service the request. Deciding what is important and what is not important is not typically something that devolves to NSA. NSA seeks guidance from the leading US agencies and from the National Security Council (e.g., the White House).

So someone decided to request spying on the EU and apparently wanted more than what they were getting in the normal "take" of intercepts NSA collects. Which is what apparently led to an operational team going into EU offices and installing bugs on computer networks and telephone exchanges as alleged by Der Spiegel.

Why would anyone take such a risk given the consequences of discovery and the political ramifications inherent in such an activity?

It looks like making requests for intelligence gathering even from allied countries, is something agencies in the US government do without much thought of consequences.

If this is true, than the real problem is one of judgment and risk assessment, and both of these seem to play little nor no role in tasking to NSA.

The revelations about NSA really are revelations about the US government and its decision making process, or lack thereof, and as regards domestic intelligence gathering, the question of whether the government – more than NSA by itself – has acted within the law and the Constitution.

In front of us there are many extraordinarily serious issues –the collection of billions of phone and internet records, the absurdly wide swatch of information sucked in by NSA computers and systems, or even how this vast information glut (no matter how many supercomputers are deployed) is no substitute for intelligent collection and analysis of real national security information. It is not just that NSA is bloated, it is that our government is out of control and has come unglued from the guarantees in the US Constitution, or thinks it is above all that.

Stripping Americans of their rights and freedoms, trampling on our allies and friends, is something that should concern us and our friends abroad. There is nothing more vital than a truly free America as a beacon of hope. Our government has lost its way.

On the Rise of Cyber Anarchism

A political and ideological movement which I call Cyber Anarchism is impacting governments, corporations and organizations in an unprecedented way because cyber anarchists throw "cyber bombs" instead of conventional bombs. But otherwise their intentions align well with classical violent anarchism of the type that was prevalent particularly in the first 25 years of the last century.

A good analogue is the anarchist Luigi Galleani who operated in the United States from 1901 until 1919. He was a believer in revolutionary violence, and most of the time the violence came in the form of shrapnel-filled bombs that were used against high officials and locations including churches (including St. Patrick's Cathedral), police stations and court houses.

"When we talk about property, State, masters, government, laws, courts, and police, we say only that *we don't want any of them.*" –Luigi Galleani, *The End of Anarchism?*

Galleani was a strong believer in what he called "propaganda by the deed" –namely radical actions that would destroy enemies and bring down governments or other hated entities including the Catholic Church, which the Galleanisti despised.

In many ways Galleani and his followers paralleled the attitude we see among terrorist organizations, where morality is laid aside in favor of "the cause."

"Continue the good war. . .the war that knows neither fear nor scruples, neither pity nor truce." –Luigi Galleani, in *Cronaca Sovversiva*

To be sure there were many variations in how anarchists viewed their mission, on what tactics were appropriate, and where violence was allowed. Anarchist movements were a result of the social stratification of the period, the immigrant experience in America, perceived injustices, and anti-government and anti-regime ideas that sprang up from the middle of the 18th century through 20th century. Unlike fascism which was a statist phenomenon, anarchists rejected the state. Some were anarcho-communists, including Galleani, but they soon fell out with the Communist movement, especially in Russia, because unlike the Soviet Communists, most of the anarchists were not willing to see a dictatorship of anybody, especially any elite.

Which brings us around to the modern version of the Galleanisti – the Cyber Anarchists.

The Cyber Anarchists have not really intellectualized their movement or put across an ideological stand that can stand up analysis. Instead we get the statements of people like Bradley Manning, currently on trial, Julian Assange, currently holed up in the Ecuadorian embassy in London but wanted in Sweden on rape charges, and Edward Snowden, who is on the lamb in Hong Kong.

Of these Julian Assange comes closest to articulating a political philosophy that has strong roots in anarchist thinking. His book (written with Jacob Appelbaum, Andy Muller-Maguhn and Jérémie Zimmermann), "Cypherpunks, Freedom and the Future of the Internet" argues that the Internet has become the tool of the police state, and big corporations are in on the game, heading us toward a totalitarian state and the end of individual liberty. The solution proposed is for everyone to adopt computer security measures, particularly cryptography, to block surveillance by the state. Cypherpunks, of course, go further and promote the idea that their mission is to keep government's accountable as a way of building up public resistance to the attack on privacy.

Reading the statements and interviews given by Assange and many others, it is clear that it is their intention to release information to the public regarding government, corporate, and military behavior and operations. So we have leaks of sensitive diplomatic exchanges, military policy, NSA wiretapping, and information designed to show how many corporate giants are poor guardians of sensitive personal information.

"Cypherpunkism" and Cyber Anarchism are closely related if not the same. But the term Cyber Anarchism is preferred as descriptive of the mission of the Cypherpunks. It raises a key question —is there a point where the Cyber Anarchists mutates into classical Anarchism such as that practiced by Galleani?

Government angst over the compromise of secrets is growing and no one in government knows what could come out next. Will nuclear secrets be compromised, or vital national defense information. As the pressure from Cyber-Anarchists closes in on critical national security functions, surely the government will react strongly.

Meanwhile the causes of Manning, Assange and Snowden continue to attract a growing following. How they and their followers will behave under stressful conditions is unknown.

Will the Palmer raids come again?

JUN 6 2013

WILL CHINA STOP CYBER-ESPIONAGE? ABSOLUTELY NOT

With Rebecca Abrahams

No matter what President Obama and China's President Xi Jinping agree this week, China will not stop cyber espionage.

China may decide, as a result of the upcoming summit meeting, to crack down on hackers who operate independently, or who moonlight for profit in the hours they are not working for either China's government or China's military. That will be a bone to try and lower the tension that has been building between China and the US on the issue of cyber theft. But it won't really make a big difference.

There are, roughly speaking, five kinds of cyber crime.

The first is based on vicarious hacking by groups of computer geeks who want to show off their prowess and gain bragging rights for successfully attacking important institutions and organizations. The "thrill" involved is to show how smart they are, how brilliantly they can defeat the CIA or the Pentagon.

The second group grows out of the first but it has become ideological. Ideological hacking is hacking for a political purpose. Many of the ideological hackers are really anarchists in modern dress. This kind of hacking has been growing and is illustrated by phenomena such as Wikileaks and its leader Julian Asange, currently holed up in the Ecuadorian Embassy in London while wanted by Sweden where he has been charged with rape.

The third type of hacking is "For Profit." Information is stolen, bank accounts and money machines are pilfered, and sometimes blackmail is used. For Profit hacking is not always separable from ideological hacking or from vicarious hacking.

Fourth is cyber crime against individuals and political groups carried out by governments. Sometimes this is pursuant to law and follows a legal process, but not always (even in the US where phones can be tapped and computers can be invaded without a warrant or clearance by a court).

Fifth is cyber crime for national security reasons. This is a specialty of China. Recent information says that China is annually stealing $300 billion worth of national security information, much of which is weapons designs.

Why? There are essentially three reasons why China is doing this.

The first is that stealing the information is easy to do. There are hardly any credible barriers to scooping up defense information, government data, and the proprietary information of private companies.

The second reason is that there are not any consequences. This is crime without punishment. And because China owns a large part of the US Treasury, the enthusiasm by US government leaders to crack down is tempered by concern that our own economy would unravel if we push too hard. On top of that, a lot of our top industry people are making money on China.

And the third reason is that China cannot be a superpower without US technology. There is very little innovation in China, despite large investments, the presence of foreign companies, a strong electronics industry, and a huge number of Chinese nationals educated abroad (subsidizing plenty of American graduate schools of engineering, science and cyber studies).

Taken together this put the US in a bind. Lacking a credible strategy to confront the losses, the US defense posture is at risk thanks to the China thieves. And more and more companies will also feel the heat as China's clones of their products swamp the US market.

Meanwhile, one thing Xi Jinping will not do is allow China to be anything less than a superpower, so he must continue robbing the US blind. And he will.

May 28 2013

Finding a Cure for China's Technology Theft

With Rebecca Abrahams

The news is out –semi-officially– thanks to a report by the Defense Science Board. The Board, which was established in 1956, is made up of civilians who advise the Pentagon on a variety of technology-related subjects. It has released a report, Resilient Military Systems and the Advanced Cyber Threat, which makes it clear that the Pentagon's cyber "hygiene" is weak and US defense technology has been effectively targeted by foreign governments. The result is that most advanced US weapons systems, from the F-35 stealth fighter to the most advanced underwater torpedoes, and everything in-between, has been stolen. While the word "China" is not mentioned, everyone knows that it is China that is systematically purloining our technology.

The fact is, we can say we have two defense budgets –one for us and one for them. Indeed, as things stand today, the technology pipeline to China is wide open, and we are losing billions and billions of dollars of investment and seriously compromising our security.

While the Report of the DSB is serious and important, unfortunately it is not "news." The fact of the matter is that China's rip off of America's defense technology assets has been going on for a number of years. There are numerous public reports about it, and the intelligence community has been watching this happen for an even longer period.

It is fair to ask a straightforward question. Why have we let this go on?

We believe the answer is that we have approached the problem with a fundamentally flawed concept on how to stop Chinese cyber theft.

The Pentagon's idea, which is more or less shared across the government, is that the answer is to build better cyber defenses. While cyber defenses are certainly important, so far implementation of effective cyber defenses remains incomplete and, to some degree, elusive. Technology is moving so fast, and hacking has become so extreme, that keeping up is nearly impossible. The DSB is pushing for more and better cyber defense measures, but the jury remains out whether this tactic can succeed.

Defense technology is shared between government organizations and the military on one side, and industry on the other. Millions upon millions of pages of documentation are associated with every defense program, and much of this documentation is not classified.

The reason for this is operational. It is probably impossible to classify all defense department documents since doing so would limit the number of engineers and technicians who can work on defense programs, make sharing with allies and friends extremely difficult, and create a massive supervisory burden that today's system cannot manage.

If information is not classified, typically it is stored on computers that also are not classified. What does this mean? It means that the information is not encrypted or scrambled. In turn that means that if the information is stolen, it is readily accessible by the thieves.

What has to change is the ground rule on encrypting sensitive, but not classified information.

Most government information is poorly protected because it is not encrypted –information such as tax forms, social security data, health and human services documents to name a few. The bulk of defense system information is not encrypted.

The classical division between classified information and unclassified information is no longer functional. We need to implement encryption, not classification, for all government materials that are not accessed by the public, and particularly for defense information. Defense contractors should be directed to do the same.

Good encryption will block the Chinese from using stolen information. While it won't prevent cyber attacks (we still need good cyber defense for that), it will blow up China's effort to use our defense systems against us.

May 19 2013

The Spy & the Mobile Phone

An American, Ryan Christopher Fogle, working as a third secretary in the US Embassy in Moscow was arrested by Russian security police and subsequently deported. The arrest, featuring photos of the man pushed to the ground and wearing a bizarre wig, and other snapshots of his interrogation, along with other wigs, cash in envelopes, a compass, a flashlight, three different sunglasses, a Moscow map atlas, a letter in Russian, an RFID shield, and a knife have raised numerous questions. The Washington Post said there was something "fishy" about the case, and CBS News and others commented that the mobile phone Fogle was ostensibly carrying was very old and did not have any smart phone features.

We have no idea if this is the usual kit of CIA spies. One can argue that all of it was planted on Fogle and because he was a CIA operative, it did not really matter. Certainly the CIA was not going to comment, one way or the other. Secret services neither confirm nor deny.

While we have no inside knowledge on Fogle and the case the Russians are making, two items caught our attention.

The first was the RFID "sleeve." This is a metallic sleeve into which you can put a passport, an ID badge and credit cards. Once inside, external snooping devices cannot read the passport, driver's license, ID or credit cards because the sleeve shields them from electromagnetic waves. You can buy these online and they are recommended for protecting your

ID and your credit card information. It would make sense for a spy to have a sleeve like this.

The second was a mobile phone, a very simple phone without the data channels and fancy screens of modern smart phones. Why would a spy use a simple phone?

The reason is that a simple phone is harder to track than a smart phone. Such a phone would lack the WIFI, Bluetooth and GPS features of a smart phone, it would contain very little information, and it is likely the SIM card (that authorizes the phone) was under some fake name. So the agent or spy would be able to operate without being easily tracked. In fact, it seems the Russians were able to grab him because he set up a meeting with his Russian target, and when he went to him he was grabbed by the Russian FSB security police.

Even so, the Russian security people were able to record a phone conversation with the target, because the target tipped them off. The offer of up to $1 million to spy for the United States did not turn the target into a cooperating resource.

Fogle also supposedly offered the source a way to communicate through Gmail but to do so either with a "clean" mobile phone or a "clean" laptop computer, which according to news reports, the CIA was willing to pay for if not purchase. He recommended using an Internet cafe as a way of improving on anonymity. While such cafes may be useful in places such as Pakistan (where terrorists use them), in Moscow one can be reasonably sure that anyone entering such a place is photographed and ID'd. So this proposal should go into the category of "stupid."

In any case, we still can't be sure that Fogle wasn't set up and that there isn't "something fishy" about the whole thing. But what the Russians have put on the table so far also makes sense. Be careful with your smart phone.

May 10 2013

ATM Heist — Who Is Behind It?

The big story this week is the work of sophisticated thieves who were able to take cash from ATM machines in the United States and in at least 23 other countries. The amount stolen is estimated at $46 million. While about a dozen have been arrested for the crimes, there are no doubt plenty of others who so far have eluded the police, and the amount stolen could be much higher than so-far reported.

How was it done? Two Middle East banks were hacked by professionals. One of the banks, Rakbank is located in the UAE, the other, the Bank of Muscat is in Oman. In addition, an as yet unnamed Indian credit card processing company was also hacked. The scam was to create "pre-paid" money cards (VISA, MasterCard) ostensibly issued by the banks. The scammers created the pre-paid accounts and they removed the fail-safe dollar ceiling on withdrawals, so that one card could potentially empty an ATM. The cards themselves are typical magnetic strip cards commonly used in ATM machines.

Looking at the crime itself, there are two striking facts.

The first is that the hacking must have been an inside job, because the hackers understood the banks' set up, how the accounts were organized, and had the know how to manipulate the supervisory software. They were able to create the accounts within the bank and credit processing facility, including authentication, disable the cash limits normally applied on accounts, and operate the scam on a global basis through a network of associates. So far there have not been arrests of any insiders, but it is only a matter of time before they are apprehended.

Years ago a huge bank heist was pulled off through cyber attacks on Citibank accounts. It was also a multinational operation, and it required insiders to help in the theft. Essentially that scam involved moving money from one account to another. Like the ATM case, it was a multinational operation affecting accounts and transactions in many countries. Once money was transferred, the owner of the now cash-rich account would go to the bank and withdraw the cash or transfer the cash elsewhere or convert it to another instrument, such as bonds.

There were some arrests and convictions, but the hidden hand in the Citibank case were Russians in an organization the FBI called "The Russian Business Network." It is well to keep in mind that the Citibank case also involved stealing ATM pins.

We don't yet know the masterminds behind the $46 million ATM crime, and it remains for law enforcement to try and ferret out the real source of the scheme. It would have to be an organization with global connections and with strong organizational capabilities and links to an underground of criminals willing to rob individual ATMs for a share of the loot. A Russian Mafia linked organization cannot be ruled out.

Another potential source for the operation are terrorist groups with the capability to carry out such operations, perhaps linked to Iran. This needs to be explored. The targets, after all, were Middle Eastern Banks that represent the establishment in the UAE and Oman. While $46 million is not an especially large hit on these banks, given the resources of these banks, we need to keep in mind that the amount so far reported may only be part of the actual crime. An insider group may also have taken very large sums from these banks, and used the ATM scam to draw attention away from pilfering large accounts at the banks.

The other striking issue about these theft operations targeting banks is how poor the banking security system actually is, and how the system lacks simple protection such as strong authentication and encrypted accounts. One of the reasons is, of course, a desire by banks to exploit modern electronic transactions to the fullest, because they require very little labor or overhead, making it easy for banks to load them with transaction fees and credit charges. Small losses are covered by the Bank's and credit card company's insurance. In fact, as we move rapidly to a cashless society, or one that accepts electronic tokens instead of paper dollars or checks, banking security issues loom large. <u>Bitcoin</u>, for example, has already been hacked and is proving utterly unreliable and suspect. In fact, the entire banking and credit system is vulnerable and poses a considerable economic and security danger to modern nations.

AUG 13 2012

WHO IS BEHIND THE GAUSS VIRUS?

The Kaspersky Labs, based in Moscow and well regarded says that it has uncovered a computer virus that targeted banks in Lebanon, the Palestinian territories and in Israel. While not saying "who" invented the Gauss virus, Kaspersky makes the case that the new virus, called Gauss, is closely linked to the Stuxnet and Flame virus. Presumed leaks to the <u>New York Times</u> finger the CIA and Israel as the sponsors of Stuxnet.

There is always a little more than suspicion that should accompany any, and all, such declarations.

Stuxnet, as is now understood, focused on the controller systems of Iranian centrifuges. The Stuxnet infection caused the centrifuges to operate erratically defeating their ability to extract bomb-grade uranium from uranium hexafluoride gas. (An interesting sidelight is that the Iranian centrifuges are derived from a European design, and the controllers and other electronics, as well as the special materials, come from Europe and appear to be in ample supply.)

But is Gauss really a "son of Sam" type virus?

Kaspersky Labs, through its Secure List Blog says:

We believe the theory that Gauss is used to steal money which are [sic] used to finance other projects such as Flame and Stuxnet is not compatible with the idea of nation-state sponsored attacks.

If the Secure List Blog is right, and if we accept that the Gauss is similar to Stuxnet and Flame as the Lab insists, then suspicion is thrown on the original claimed sourcing of Stuxnet and Flame –e.g., that these viruses were a CIA-Israeli deal.

For what it is worth, cooperation between the US and Israel on Iran has been poor, if not worse. The CIA for the past decade has insisted the Iranians are not close to having a nuclear weapon, and even in the most recent admission that the Iranians are closer than the previous CIA estimate, the CIA is still very far apart from the public Israeli assessment. Furthermore, the administration has very strongly opposed not only physical intervention against Iran, but the administration has taken a strictly hands off approach, and has not supported the Iranian opposition or encouraged regime change (something they were glad to do in Egypt, Libya and Syria and strongly hinted at in other countries like Yemen, Jordan and Bahrain).

So believing the CIA and Israel actually cooperated on Stuxnet or anything else seems hard to believe. And the so-called leaks had plenty of political motive for President Obama, who has been trying to tell the American Jewish community that he is the best friend Israel ever had.

We also note that Russian cyber-thieves have been looting banks around the world for years. Clearly the cyber thieves had at their disposal the resources to carry out these thefts.

Could it be that all these viruses come from Russia instead of Israel or the CIA, or alternatively that there is an under-the-table deal between Israel and Russia to secretly block Iran's nuclear programs instead of collaboration between Israel and the CIA?

Israel's relationship with Russia sometimes looks better than the relationship with the US After all, President Putin found time to visit Israel and his visit was positive, even in the midst of the Syrian civil war. President Obama has not gone to Israel during his presidency.

Oddly, given that Kaspersky operates in Russia and no doubt has a positive relationship with the Russian government, it is very strange they would take the lead in exposing the Gauss virus if Gauss had any conceivable link to the Russian government. But politics is always a process and things change rapidly. Maybe the Russians are starting to worry that Israel really will hit Iran and they are sending them a message?

So while the Gauss virus origins remain unknown, the suggestion that it is linked to Israel and the CIA can probably be ruled out. The rest we really don't know.

JUN 07 2012

ON VACATION CONSIDER A QR CODE FOR YOUR KIDS

Last November I made a modest proposal for putting QR Codes on a person's body –something I called an R-Too (from the Star War's robot). With vacation-time approaching, considering removable QR Codes on children could be a life saver.

Many years ago, when I was seven years old and my brother Bob was five, we went to Atlantic City for a week's vacation. I don't know how it happened but my little brother wandered off. In those days (we are talking over 50 years ago) there were no cell phones, or call forwarding. So when my brother was found by some life guards about a mile up the beach, Bob could tell them where he lived, but that was not of much help since we were all away at the sea shore. There were no message machines then, and Bob did not have any information to offer. After about five hours of frantic searching, we finally reached the inlet in North Atlantic city and found my brother, happily supplied with ice cream by the Life Guards. He was happy –my mother was frantic and near collapse by then.

A QR code can contain lots of information so in case of a child wandering off or getting lost, his parents can be quickly found.

Since I wrote my article last November, you can now buy decal paper for an inkjet or laser printer for a few dollars, and there are a number of free QR Code generating services on the Web where you can quickly churn out a bar code that can contain your kid's name, your mobile phone number, your email and anything else you want to put there. You generate the code, print it on the special decal paper and transfer the design to your kid's arm or leg. It will last a few days and you can bring extra copies with you to replace one that faded too much.

Maybe it will seem silly, but today's world is a lot more complicated than when I grew up. In those days we trusted people and we did not lock our house. No one worried about kids being out on the street at night. Today everything is faster, more uncertain, and –yes- dangerous.

So do yourself and your young children a favor, particularly in the vacation period when you are away from home. Consider sticking a QR code (an R-Too) on them.

My article from last November is below.

Have a WONDERFUL and SAFE vacation.

NOVEMBER 2011

IT IS TIME FOR R-TOOS™

QR CODES – square barcodes that store information – are all around us. Scanned by equally ubiquitous smart phones, you find QR CODES on bus advertising, t-shirts, business cards, catalogues and grocery store shelves. The data links and Internet connections are fast and easy, linking consumers to consumer information.

That makes this a great time for R-Toos™.

Not an actual tattoo or a small "Star Wars" robot, an R-Too™ is a wearable, semi-permanent tattoo of a QR CODE that would link to a cloud connection with information you want to share. Your R-Too™ could be linked to your company's homepage, your social networking page, your phone number, e-mail address or other information. You choose what you put on the cloud – meaning, as with all exposed information, that you have to choose wisely.

An R-Too™ can be applied to your head, arm or other body part using a machine or transfer for semi-permanent ink or henna. If the right definition can be achieved, an R-Too™ can be a real tattoo – the design would then be permanent, only the information on the cloud would change. The medium doesn't matter; what matters is that people will have a quick way to communicate the way people like to do now – by playing with their smart phones.

R-Toos™ are a great idea because in modern society, sharing information in useable bits is what we do – social, business, educational.

If you want a practical application, consider child security. There are parents who implant chips in their children as an identification measure – if the child is lost or kidnapped, the chip provides definitive information. It seems a little bit radical, however, and the chip can only be read by the limited number of people with special equipment – and that's only if the child remembers to tell someone that its there. On the other hand, if a family on vacation is concerned that a child might wander off at the beach, a henna R-Too™ connected to the parents' cell phone number would be useful. Any person with a smart phone could scan the R-Too™ and reunite child and parent.

Many cultures have worn "scan-able" codes for centuries. Consider the Tilaka of India. The Tilaka is a mark or marks worn on the forehead or other parts of the body, composed of different colors, providing information about a person's religion, caste, marital status, etc. Tilaka marks can be removed or changed, and they have this in common with the R-Too™.

What the Tilaka and other cultural body art cannot do is provide information beyond what an observer can see. You cannot get someone's email address, personal web page, or opinion about the state of the world from the equivalent of a Tilaka*. The R-Too™ provides a nearly infinite resource.

---

* In Hinduism the Tilaka is a mark worn on the forehead and other parts of the body.

MAY 15 2012

THE SPY ON YOUR CELL PHONE IS A PROFESSIONAL

Vladimir Vetrov, Agent Farewell
From American Thinker

Every day in the United States, professional cyber-spies are stealing tremendous amounts of information. Mainly from Russia and China, these spies target computer networks and increasingly seek entryways through mobile phones. Modern mobile phones — Smartphones — are powerful, networked computers, but they lack the firewalls and safeguards typically installed on PCs. What protection is commercially available is weak and unsatisfactory.

America's cyber-systems are under attack because what they hold is extremely valuable. Everything from the design of a stealth fighter-bomber to the investment portfolio of a powerful entrepreneur is open to professional cyber-spies and, thus, to the governments that sponsor them.

For political reasons, the United States has done very little finger-pointing at the culprits. While there has been talk about getting tough with cyber-spies, so far, at least, there is little evidence of strong action against the governments that train and send them. That leaves the advantage with the intruder.

But who are the intruders? Examples from the past can help us form a picture of the people recruited and how they work.

The Russians developed an elaborate technology-spying operation starting in the 1960s. Directorate T was created from the former Department 10 in 1963 to intensify the acquisition of Western strategic, military, and industrial technology. By 1972, Directorate T had a headquarters staff of several hundred officers subdivided into four departments, in addition to specialists stationed at major Soviet embassies around the world. The Directorate's operations were coordinated with the scientific and technical collection activities of other KGB elements, and with the State Scientific and Technical Committee (GNTK).

The job of Directorate T was to collect technical information needed to support the Soviet Union's infrastructure. Much of the focus was on computers and microelectronic technology and know-how. By the early 1980s, the Soviets found themselves in head-to-head military competition with the United States, needing to make up deficits in critical areas — primarily in microelectronics. This meant an active program to get access to the technology, smuggle examples back to the Soviet Union, and collect information from US government sources. Parallel to Directorate T was Soviet military intelligence, which worked to obtain Western weapons and weapons designs.

In all, it was a very large bureaucracy made up of well-trained professionals. Many were multilingual; each was directed to his or her target by an elaborate acquisition plan. Promotions and rewards were based on successful operations against targets in the plan.

Directorate T was an elite outfit, and it had the attention of top Soviet leaders, as it did their Western counterparts. One of the most remarkable successes of French intelligence in the 1970s and 1980s was recruiting a senior Directorate T agent, given the codename Farewell. Farewell supplied the French, and ultimately the United States, with an inside view of Soviet technology collection efforts. Farewell's real name was Vladimir Vetrov, and he worked for Line X, the operational arm of Directorate T. Eventually Vetrov was arrested, according to the official story, for murdering his mistress and an off-duty police officer who happened on the scene. In jail, Vetrov's boasting alerted Soviet counterintelligence officials to a bigger story, namely spying for the West. Sometime in 1985 he was tried as a traitor and spy and executed.

As a model, Vetrov was a very talented, highly trained person who spoke excellent French and some English. He had a mathematics and engineering background, and he was well-paid, was allowed to travel, and enjoyed many of the perks afforded the Soviet *nomenklatura*.

Today's cyber-spies, whether Russian or Chinese, would need to be trained like Vetrov. That is to say, they would have a strong technical background and be capable of handling English (reading and comprehension, since mobile phone intrusions require language skills). This means that these are highly professional people who would need to have good government salaries and perks, and who would constantly be evaluated on the value of the acquisitions they brought in.

Probably, like Vetrov, they would be recruited while still in university. In many cases, the best of them would be sent abroad, especially to the United States, for graduate education and to improve their knowledge of the target country. The number of Chinese undergraduates on US campuses in 2010 increased 43 percent from the previous year, according to the annual Institute of International Education Open Doors. Chinese students form the largest number of foreign students in the US, with 157,558 enrolled in 2010. The nearest rival was India with 103,895.

Not all Chinese students go home to be spies, of course, but for China there is a double-benefit — there are the spies they send to enlarge their American vocabulary and scientific background, and there are students who can be recruited in future.

No one knows how many Chinese cyber-spies there are, but estimates in the tens of thousands are probably close to right.

The Russian situation is different. China is trying to suck up most of America's technology and know-how and wants to control key individuals in decision-making positions. The Chinese need to know with day-to-day precision what is going on, accounting for the large number in the US on an ongoing basis.

The number of Russians studying in the US is quite small, because Russia is in cyber-spying mostly for the money, targeting mainly financial institutions, banks, trading companies, and probably some government agencies and organizations. Russian military intelligence, of course, still targets America's weapons systems and command-and-control networks. While we don't know for sure, a large part of Russian spying is probably done with human agents instead of electronically.

The modern cyber-spy — sponsored by his government; well-trained; proficient in English; capable of understanding, assessing, and managing his target — represents a formidable national security challenge for the United States. In the 1980s, thanks to Farewell and a remarkable relationship between President Ronald Reagan and French President Francois Mitterrand (Farewell was their agent), the United States and its allies launched a major program to shut down Soviet techno-spies. The project ultimately was successful.

Today we need a major program led from the top, with our allies and friends on board, to confront the growing vulnerability of all Western systems and the entire security umbrella. The basic elements would be:

- Enhance counter-intelligence. The FBI needs to figure out who is being trained in the US and, wherever possible, boot out Chinese agents. If we put pressure on their "rising stars," the Chinese will quickly figure out we are on to their game.
- Start recruiting their guys. Farewell is the perfect example of how and what to do. A strongly proactive recruiting program, starting with Chinese studying here, would send a message — one that the Russians understood, and one that China won't miss.
- Reduce access to American industry and scientific institutions. This was done to the Russians, and it paid off. It would be a big warning to Chinese scientists and engineers who prize their access to our scientific and engineering communities.
- Put our allies and friends to work hitting Chinese scientific and industrial targets, especially state-owned targets. A "hit-back" policy is important to establish some "ground rules" for how the game is played. If there is a Chinese attack on one of our Air Force computer systems, or on a top Army leader through his Smartphone, then hit-back attacks on similar targets are not only legitimate, but politically necessary.

These are "starter" suggestions, and to make them work, we need leaders to step forward now as they did in the past.

MAY 07 2012

THE NATIONAL SECURITY RISK OF MOBILE PHONES

Thanks to modern computer technology, privacy has been taking a beating. Nowhere is this more the case than with the mobile phone, particularly mobile phones that are also powerful computers – Smartphones.

- In 2011 the number of Smartphones sold exceeded the number of PC's sold.
- In a few years the number of mobile devices will dwarf the number of PC's.

In 2011 there were 5.9 billion mobile subscribers – one each for 87% of the world population. There presently are 1.2 billion mobile web users worldwide. In 2011 there were 8 trillion text messages. In the last three years 300,000 mobile APPS were downloaded 10.9 billion times. Paying by mobile was worth US $240 billion in 2011 and will be US $1 trillion by 2015. Between 500 million and 1 billion people will access financial services by mobile by 2015.

Like PC's, Smartphones are vulnerable to hackers and intruders, but the problem is more serious. In order to be useful, Smartphones always have to be open to networks and, if compromised, can even be switched on when they are supposedly inactive. In fact, the only way to effectively kill a Smartphone is to remove its battery, but in some products the battery is integrated and average users cannot pull the battery out.

The Smartphone is a hacker's dream. Not only can he see and exploit what is on the phone, but the phone itself is an open window on the user's activity. It can hear his voice and the voices of others even when the user is unaware, it can turn on the phone's camera and it can provide an exact location so the user's location is known. This gives possible terrorists and criminals knowledge they should never be allowed to have. A 21st century assassin may be tapping the Smartphone of his victim.

Attacking Smartphones is so popular that there are hundreds, if not thousands of companies in the United States and around the world producing spy phone software. Watch the advertising – you can find out what your wife or girlfriend is up to, listen in on competitor's conversations, find out where your children are and where they have been, and much, much more. Not only, you can read their emails and "texts", look at their calendar, and hear what they say.

People have come to think of their Smartphones (and sister tablet devices) as indispensible, leading some to rationalize away the known threat of hacking by saying, "well I have nothing to hide" or "there is nothing in my emails that is in the least interesting to anybody." But it isn't true.

Today's smart phones use social media just like computers, so Facebook, LinkedIn. Google+ and other social "apps" are providing important information that can be used to "get to" the target, for example through his children, friends or colleagues.

Government agencies and military organization are at considerable risk. While departments handling sensitive information may require to be locked up on certain occasions or in certain sensitive locations, most of the rest of the time the Smartphone is "on.". Consider a typical Pentagon employee who wants to stay in touch with a child or a spouse or an elderly parent. Today it is hardly practical to isolate people or get them to support a policy that isolates them during the working day.

The same is true in industry, in the financial services sector, in health care, and in energy and transportation. We are talking about huge numbers of people, all of whom can be a target of an intruder or hacker.

Given the immensity of the potential sources of data, it follows that aside from individuals hacking their wives, kids, friends and co-workers, the real beneficiaries of the smart phone revolution are foreign governments who can be plugged into top decision-makers and military leaders and hosts of other decision makers in targeted countries.

For the United States the attack on smart phones and tablets represents a national security threat. As a reservoir of technology, know how, finance, and military prowess, the US is, to say the least, the world's number one most tempting target. It should come as no surprise the smart phones in the United States are under constant attack, just as are computer networks. The difference is that the mobile platform is delivering critical information in real time.

US laws and export controls do not block the sale or export of spyware or the underlying technological know-how. Law makers need to look into the absence of export controls and push the administration to urgently address the issue.

Can we stop spyware and spy phones? Is there a technical solution?

One proposal being looked at is that government senior-level personnel use specially designed, and very expensive, secure mobile phones. According to news reports, Boeing has been commissioned to build a secure smart phone for top government officials.

Custom-designed products compete poorly against commercial smart phones. The US government has, from time to time, sponsored efforts to build special solutions. Most of them fail because they rapidly become obsolescent.

Another approach is to use anti-virus software and anti-malware software on Smartphones. Up to a point these work against known targets, although they often lack the horsepower to actually clean the phone without wiping it completely. The problem with a complete wipe is that backups of data and APPS cannot be used because the old infection is still inside.

A new start up company, Ziklag Systems (now rebadged as FortressFone Technologies) has a solution that can actually clean off both known and unknown spyware. The technology to do this is complex, but the clean-up can happen without losing vital data from the phone while saving all non-malicious "APPS." Ziklag's technical team has been working with Israeli government and defense officials, where the threat of spy phones is very real and could imperil the country's security. Ziklag is now in the process of moving its technology to the United States and should soon be in a position to help American governmental agencies, critical infrastructure clients and the financial community.

As decision-makers in government and industry realize the risks involved, the market for effective solutions for mobile Smartphone and tablet security is likely to grow very quickly. So too will the risk to national security markedly increase. It is important to think urgently about shutting down the supply of tampering and intrusion products targeting Smartphones and tablets, and to support solutions to block the most dangerous spy phone attacks.

MAR 25 2012

KING DAVID AND THE SUPERCOMPUTERS

In the Book of Samuel we read: "Now there was no smith to be found throughout all the land of Israel; for the Philistines said, 'lest the Hebrews make themselves swords or spears,' but every one of the Israelites went down to the Philistines to sharpen his plowshare, his mattock, his ax, or his sickle."

The emergence of a united Israel under King David is difficult to explain, particularly given the backwardness of the Israelite economy and what seems a lack of incentives for integration. While we do not know all the reasons, it seems the military emergence of Saul first and David after can be explained by the transfer of critical iron making technology to the Hebrew tribes in Judah.

Saul and David emerge as the first national leaders after Israel adopted the Kingship model to consolidate power and to defeat its enemies. But the Kingship model, while centralizing power and creating an administrative system for taxation and military organization, is not enough to explain the great change that swept over ancient Israel.

The southern part, Judah, was mountainous and hilly with little in the way of exploitable resources. In the context of the times, it was agriculturally poor, lacking in settled cultivation, and supported itself through animal herding and aggressive raids on its neighbors. Saul and David are both formidable adversaries against their primarily non-Hebrew neighbors.

But the biblical text makes clear that some of their neighbors had superior military capability, particularly the Philistines who controlled the coastal lowlands. In Judges 1:19 we read: "And the LORD was with Judah; and he drove out the inhabitants of the mountain; but could not drive out the inhabitants of the valley, because they had chariots of iron."

The chariots seem to have been able to operate even in relatively rough terrain because their wheels were strengthened and improved with iron, scythes were attached to the chariot to cut down opposing foot soldiers, and the charioteers were protected by iron armor covering the "basket" from which they operated the chariot and fired or threw weapons (arrows and spears, javelins and axes respectively). We know from the Bible that once David became King, one of his major military preoccupations was the acquisition of "iron chariots" in order to dominate his enemies. References to the manufacture of large quantities of iron nails and fittings used in construction in Jerusalem also make clear the importance of iron in the period by linking the production directly to King David.

Until then, the Philistines* controlled iron production – both the forging of iron and the smiths who worked the iron either into weapons or for agriculture (plowshares, axes) and construction (nails, fastenings, brackets, pins). Archaeological evidence shows that the technology was found in Philistine border towns and the Biblical text points us to David's presence in there.

David had been pushed out of the Hebrew-controlled areas by a jealous Saul. When he heard that Achimelech, a leading priest, had sheltered David and given him food, Saul had Achimelech and some 85 priests at Nob killed. He then destroyed the town, slaying the women, children and infants and with them the oxen, donkeys and sheep. David and his men were in a dangerous and exposed position as they fled into Philistine territory, outnumbered by and inferior to Saul's forces. David and his men stayed under Philistine protection and David was hired out to the Philistine King, Achish.

It seems likely that the transfer of iron technology took place during this time.

Iron technology had immediate military significance, since the dominant weapons and armor protection then in Hebrew hands were bronze and copper, and replacement supplies were very hard to come by because of raw material supply problems. The Biblical commentary notes the lack of weapons in the hands of David and his men. The entire region, wherever possible, was learning to substitute iron for copper and bronze.

Iron spears and iron tipped javelins, and iron swords as well as iron armor layered onto shields, conferred almost immediate military superiority. One can recall that it was the huge, iron-tipped spear of Goliath, and his iron sword, as well as his huge size, that frightened off all challengers, except David.

Iron production in the ancient period was a combination of technology for properly operating the furnaces and the manner in which the furnaces were heated but not over-heated (which would result in brittle wrought iron or an iron that was too soft to be of use), and how the materials was worked (through a hammering and quenching process).** Learning the technique would have taken time. According to the texts, David and his men were with the Philistines for sixteen months – sufficient time to learn.

Supercomputers
If iron production and the technology and know-how helped ensure the first united Kingdom of Israel, a fact still celebrated today, what can we say about supercomputers 3,000 years later? Why is the linkage of any conceivable relevance?

US military superiority, what has been called the Revolution in Military Affairs (RMA), comes from microelectronics and computers. America's ability to not only field "smart weapons" but also to design advanced equipment, means a strong base of dedicated high speed computers.

An important reason why the United States "won" the Cold War was superiority in electronics and computers. Massive investments by the Soviet Union were unable to compensate for the growth of American military superiority based on a "qualitative edge," of which a good part was due to computers and electronics.

Another key benefit of computers and electronics is that fast computers can crack enemy codes. The supercomputer was largely an American invention pioneered by major companies such as IBM and by scientists such as Seymour Cray, Gene Amdahl and Steve Chen (born in Taiwan).

The United States, therefore, has spent uncountable sums on a massive infrastructure of supercomputers to crack encryption codes and for related intelligence tasks. On top of what already has been invested, next year the US will open NSA's new Utah Data Center in Bluffdale. According to *Wired News*, "This is more than just a data center," says one senior intelligence official ... [which is] critical, he says, for breaking codes. And code-breaking is crucial, because much of the data that the center will handle—financial information, stock transactions, business deals, foreign military and diplomatic secrets, legal documents, confidential personal communications—will be heavily encrypted. According to another top official also involved with the program, the NSA made an enormous breakthrough several years ago in its ability to crypt analyze, or break, unfathomably complex encryption systems employed by not only governments around the world but also many average computer users in the US.

The US, therefore, depends on supercomputers for designing and building military equipment, for code breaking, and also for designing and "testing" nuclear weapons.

And for years US supercomputers have been the target of potential adversaries, particularly the Soviet Union (now Russia) and China. So far as is known, Russia does not have supercomputers. But China does, and the number and capability is growing. How did this come about?

Like King David's sojourn to Gaza and his time with King Achish, the United States decided to allow China to purchase from the US increasingly sophisticated supercomputers, and permitted the transfer of the underlying know how and the algorithms essential for modern supercomputers.

The transfer of supercomputer technology to China from the United States started in the 1990's and continues to this day. Apace with it is the access Chinese scientists have to America's supercomputing industry and scientific community. While Chinese scientists are not invited to visit NSA, they do visit US supercomputer centers and visits are reciprocated by top US scientists going to China, such as the Lawrence Livermore Laboratory visits to their supercomputer counterparts in China. Today China claims to have the world's fastest supercomputer, and has a very large installed base of supercomputer machines now used for both scientific, commercial, military and intelligence work.

A recent article in *The Wall Street Journal* ("China's Not-So-Super Computers", March 23, 2012) tries to argue that China is not getting much value out of its supercomputers and that the country lags behind the US

The article is based on wishful thinking; on the order of King Achish believing that David's stay in Philistine territory and the help David gave to the Philistine Army in battling their enemies was benign. David had a strategic objective and so do the Chinese.

The truth is the majority of China's supercomputer program, which is probably analog to the US, is not in plain view to outside observers. What we do see is growing Chinese aggressiveness represented in part by highly successful computer hacking against highly secret US programs (such as the Joint Strike Fighter), with the supercomputers behind the effort in allowing the Chinese to hack encrypted as well as open networks and systems.

We know the result. King David, with access to iron-making, took control over the Hebrew tribes, created a singular state, and pushed back the Philistines. His success was based on trust given him by King Achish.

The US Government, over multiple administrations, must have a unique trust relationship with China, since the effusive transfers of technology, especially the case of supercomputers, is hard to explain otherwise.

So it seems there is a linkage between King David and Supercomputers. The question that still remains is whether the net result for the United States will be to end up as did the Philistines.

---

*The Philistines are thought to have acquired Iron-making technology from Cyprus and/or Greece. The notion of an "iron chariot" is not a chariot composed of iron, but a chariot with key parts using iron for strengthening. This may include parts of the axle, particularly the hubs, wheel struts and the wheel "tire" which may have been strapped with iron. Some experts also speculate that the term "iron chariot" the Bible also concerns the iron military equipment in the hands of the Philistines. Egypt, it appears, got its chariot technology from the Canaanites, and chariots first appear in Egypt in the Hyksos period. Roughly 1600 B.C. Hyksos were probably of Canaanite origin and Egyptian technical terms of the chariot and its components are all borrowed Canaanite words. Along with the chariot the Hyksos introduced the composite bow, greatly improving the range and lethality of archers. The Egyptian chariots precede the Iron-age period and did not use iron in their construction. (King David died around 970 B.C.). Iron making developed because of severe shortages of copper and tin, a crumbling geopolitical situation that made trade and commerce in this particular period extremely hazardous, meaning copper and tin could not be imported reliably. Recent discoveries in Tel Beth Shemesh in Israel (probably then a Philistine controlled town) of an iron smithy, and in Jordan at Tel Hammeh of an iron foundry dating from around the time of the death of King David (both using almost identical technology), demonstrates the accuracy of the Biblical claims in the Book of Samuel regarding iron making.

FEB 07 2012

THE REVOLUTION IN TRANSPORTATION AFFAIRS

It got started on the wrong foot, the program has been delayed, the costs of the program have grown, and at moments the United States correctly saw it as a potential threat, but the European GPS program, called Galileo, now looks like it will go ahead.

Galileo is a European version of the US GPS system. It was initially offered to the European public as an alternative to the US program on the grounds that the US GPS satellites are operated by the US Air Force while the European consortium would essentially be under the authority of the civilian-led European Space Agency. Euro-leaders touted the idea that the US could not turn off the GPS signals at a time of emergency and that civilian leadership was better than military. For a time US policy makers tried their best to kill the Galileo project but more recently agreements have been reached allowing Galileo to be compatible with the US GPS constellation.

Even the US GPS project has turned out to be something far different than originally envisaged. At its start in the 1970's, the US GPS was a taxpayer-financed military project. GPS would support military systems and only incidentally be of commercial interest.

The problem with the idea is that the development of the GPS satellite network took place at the same time as the revolution in microelectronics and microprocessors. What might have previously required a large, rack mounted electronics box could now be concentrated on a handful of microchips. Today, for a dollar you can buy GPS chips in small quantities, and pay even less if you buy in the thousands. The microprocessor revolution has made it possible to put a GPS unit in a car for $50 and in a cellphone for virtually no added cost to the consumer.

Consequently, the dominant users of GPS today are every-man and every-woman. If you want to, and your kids cooperate, you can know where you kids are at any moment, where the nearest hospital is, or the location of a famous monument. Thanks to digital maps, you can navigate to any place you can find on the map within 25 feet, sometimes better. This can be improved (but not for low cost applications) with various augmentation systems. The US has a nationwide National Differential GPS system which combines ground and ocean stations with satellites to achieve higher accuracy. (There is also a special augmentation system for aircraft.)

Galileo offers accuracy equal to the augmentation systems but without the high cost, maintenance, and support.

The European GPS system's accuracy is achieved by a special atomic clock that was developed for space applications by a small team in Italy working for Selex Galileo, part of the Finmeccanica group. The special clock has been successfully tested on board the Giove-B test satellite, a systems demonstrator platform for the Galileo satellite network. The device is called a Hydrogen MASER Atomic Clock. MASER stands for Microwave Amplification by Stimulated Emission of Radiation.

The clock inside the US GPS uses a rubidium clock which loses around 3 seconds in 1 million years. By contrast, the Hydrogen MASER clock will lose 1 second in 3 million years, or around 10 nanoseconds per day. In Galileo there are four clocks in each satellite (2 active, 2 backup)– 2 Hydrogen MASER and 2 Rubidium.

So why do we need a clock accurate to 1 second in 3 million years? Because the clock, along with other improvements, allows the satellite to provide accuracy to cheap hand held or mounted GPS/Galileo receivers at less than 12 inches (11.8 inches or 30 cm).

When Galileo technology is linked to a new generation of mapping technology there are very significant benefits. To begin with, it is now possible to automate and control highway traffic because traffic spacing can accurately be managed and speeds adjusted and regulated to permit highway to operate far more efficiently. Sequencing of traffic has been tried before, but has been based on very simple parameters and only in limited environments, such as "holding" and "dispatching" vehicles entering roadways. Galileo's clock opens up a new field of regulation that by making highways more efficient will save billions in road construction and allow entrances and exits to have smart management.

A second technology that will compliment the new generation of GPS receiver is the accurate mapping of roadway beds using synthetic aperture radar-based maps (SAR). Most of the US has already been mapped using SAR-equipped aircraft. The idea is to find the actual height from sea level of road beds and to communicate that information to a vehicle's computer. In this way the engine and transmission of the vehicle can automatically and seamlessly adjust fuel burn and transmission gearing to optimize the use of fuel. Independently, cars with the maps "inside" the vehicles GPS and computer could save 5% fuel or more. Combined with GPS traffic management, the savings in fuel and in time will be even more dramatic.

While it got off on the wrong foot, the European Galileo system and SAR-based maps offer to significantly improve highway traffic and reduce wasting fuel and time. In turn this will improve the productivity time of workers, which is lost when vehicles are tied up in traffic, and expedite the delivery of goods and materials at lower cost thanks to less lost time.

In emergencies, one can easily imagine more efficient management of vehicles in crisis situations, since these systems reside in vehicles and do not need to depend on the power grid.

Progress has been made between Europe and the US to the dicey security questions risen by GPS and the misuse of GPS technology by potential adversaries and terrorists. Clearly we are on the brink of a revolution in transportation affairs.

July 05 2012

GPS Hijacking: Team of US Faculty, Students Take Control of Drone

Commercial airliners rely on GPS as well as military aircraft
Courtesy PJ Media

Faculty and students at the University of Texas at Austin have proven that a sophisticated surveillance drone can be hacked mid-flight via its GPS. The same could be done with virtually any type of drone, or even with a commercial airliner.

Drones, or UAVs (unmanned aerial vehicles), are used both domestically — particularly along our southern border — and by the military and the CIA abroad, especially in Afghanistan, Pakistan, and elsewhere. Last week, a small team of faculty and students was able to take control of a Department of Homeland Security drone by "spoofing" its GPS. They did what the Iranians appear to have done last December when they gained control over a US Air Force RQ-170 stealth UAV and landed it in Kashmar, Iran. The Iranians then put the RQ-170 aircraft, with a damaged underside and repaired wing, on display. It seems that the Iranian pilot/operators were less than familiar with the airplane's flight envelope and landing procedures than the UTA group, but still they managed to take control of it and to get it down on the ground relatively intact.

On May 9, a Russian Sukhoi Superjet 100 slammed into Mount Salak in Indonesia, killing all 45 people on board. The plane, a demonstration version of the Superjet series, was on a promotion tour, carrying journalists and VIPs for a planned 30-minute flight. Alexander Yablonstev, an experienced pilot, was said to be familiar with local terrain. According to Travel Daily News, the air traffic control tower (ATC) did not realize that the plane was missing until at least 20 minutes after the crash. Recordings show that a flight request made by pilot Yablonstev was neither acknowledged nor answered by the ATC.

While the Indonesian and Russian governments have drawn no official conclusions, Russian media is promoting the idea that the Superjet 100 was brought down by "electronic jamming" by Americans at the Indonesian airport. It is, they opine, a case of Western "industrial espionage." Komsolskaya Pravda, once the voice of the Communist youth movement and now Russia's top tabloid, quoted an unnamed general of the GRU (Russian military intelligence) on the subject and reinforced the "theory" with comments from Sukhoi officials.

Realistically, it is hard to argue that the Superjet posed a competitive threat to the United States. There is only one American commercial aircraft manufacturer, Boeing, and it helped Sukhoi with the Superjet design. More likely, Sukhoi feared its first venture in commercial aviation would collapse if a flaw in the aircraft caused the crash.

NOV 28 2011

OUR FAULT: CHINA, SUPERCOMPUTERS AND NATIONAL SECURITY

Newsweek is carrying an important article on China and supercomputers, written by Dan Lyon. The thrust of the article is that China is ahead of the United States in supercomputers and this development is causing great concern. China's rapid development of supercomputers does not come as any surprise. In fact, China's success comes from the transfer of American technology at least since the end of the Cold War. Far from developing its supercomputers in isolation, China had available to it all the American expertise, know how, hardware and software it needed to launch its ambitious supercomputer development program.

This is exactly what I warned about fifteen years ago in numerous articles and in Congressional testimony. These warnings did no good. In fact, the transfer of technology got worse, not better.

It is true that, today, modern supercomputers are readily available on a global basis, as massively parallel supercomputer networks can be accessed by scientists and engineers from just about any global location. But in this sort of environment it is also complicated to try and hide research objectives or use supercomputers to crack encryption codes.

The growth of supercomputing in China will have grave consequences for the United States. It will negatively impact America's high technology economy because supercomputers offer rapid design of machinery and equipment and the ability to run advanced simulations reducing time and cost in developing technology applications.

It will impair American intelligence because it will enable China to crack computer and encryption codes and launch ever-more sophisticated attacks on cyber-based systems.

It will help China leapfrog in military technology, as in the rapid development of stealth-enabled weapons, automated and advanced recognition algorithms, space weapons and advanced nuclear warheads.

America's freedom of action to turn off the technology spigot to China is compromised over our dependence on China for monetary support and the overall poor condition of America's economy.

There is a total lack of commitment to technology security to protect our country. This needs to change, and fast.

Below is what I said in 1997 about supercomputers and China.

TEXT OF REMARKS OF DR. STEPHEN D. BRYEN PREPARED FOR DELIVERY ON THURSDAY, NOVEMBER 13, 1997 TO THE NATIONAL SECURITY COMMITTEE OF THE HOUSE OF REPRESENTATIVES

Supercomputer Export Control Policy
I appreciate the opportunity to testify today. Let me take this opportunity to congratulate the Committee for its successful effort to put in place restraints on the sale of supercomputers. The Committee's action and its leadership in this area are an important accomplishment.

Over the past four or more years the administration has pursued a reckless policy on technology transfer, and it has shown a total disregard for prudent technology security measures. The administration is pushing sales at the expense of security.

The failure of the administration's policy is reflected in the fact that numerous supercomputers have disappeared and cannot be found. In addition, experts in our government believe that many computers sold to China have been upgraded to supercomputer status without proper notification given to the Department of Commerce. While there is no firm number, it is not implausible to believe that China may have already acquired between 100 and 150 supercomputers. In any net assessment, it has to be assumed that many, if not all, these machines are being used, or can be used to design weapons.

Technology security policies and procedures are an important part of our national defense strategy and programs. Without a coherent technology security program, the threat to the United States and to its friends and allies will increase perhaps to unacceptable levels.

The administration appears to understand this when thinking about Iran acquiring nuclear capability, or Iraq producing chemical and biological weapons. But, except for these two points of light and clarity, the administration fails to understand what it means to transfer sensitive technology to other countries.

China is a case in point. Our objectives in respect to China are to see China play a responsible role in world and regional affairs and to have China participate in general security arrangements that will benefit peace and stability. But, while we pursue these goals, we also are pushing the contrary policy of transferring advanced technologies, such as supercomputers, that are going right into China's weapons programs, including nuclear weapons developments.

So far as I can determine, the Defense Department has prepared no evaluation of the impact these technology transfers will have on our overall national defense posture. There is no assessment of what the transfer of supercomputers will do to China's timetable of deploying Tomahawk-type cruise missiles; nor is there any understanding of what would happen if such weapons were sold to countries such as Iran or Iraq. It is truly unfortunate that the Defense Department has remained silent on such an important strategic issue.

Some say, why should we care? After all China already has nuclear weapons. So what difference do some supercomputers make?

This argument obscures what China hopes to achieve in enhancing and modernizing its nuclear arsenal. Today a superior US nuclear arsenal can counter China's nuclear delivery systems. Consequently, China has to operate in the shadow of US nuclear superiority.

However, if China can develop long range weapons, which are difficult to locate and destroy, China will be able to credibly threaten US assets. This will embolden the Chinese military and political leadership to believe it can act more aggressively on a regional or global basis. For example, China will be far better positioned to threaten neighbors such as Taiwan or, even, Japan; and the US will find it more difficult than ever to respond.

I believe that an effective technology security program can slow down any leap forward by China's military. Moreover, a technology security program is particularly important during a period where we continue to cut the defense budget and slow down important initiatives, such as ballistic missile defense.

Supercomputers are one of the important tools China needs to build small and efficient nuclear weapons and to be able to "test" these weapons in simulations where our intelligence agencies cannot detect their progress.

Other complimentary technologies -such as advanced machine tools, hot section engine manufacturing know-how, the global positioning system- are being sold to China and will be used by China to build the ballistic and cruise missiles that will be a threat early in the next century. In fact, while the United States has, from time to time, complained about other countries transferring weapons technology to China, the truth is we are the worst offender because we are providing the know how that enables state of the art weapons development, particularly WMD systems.

Understanding Recent Events & Cosmic Forces

PART 3

MAR 26 2014

Noah -Hollywood Missed the Big Story

Hollywood missed a great opportunity to make a powerful movie about Noah and the deluge. Instead they made a flashy film with little real substance. The Noah story is actually part of a puzzle that has been with us as long as has the Bible. Thinking through the puzzle can help us understand our ancestors. I am strongly of the view that when we understand our past (as opposed to having idealized notions that are abstracts devoid of reality) we help define our future and gain a chance to influence what happens to us and our descendants.

There are a number of ways to visualize the Noah story. One way is to simply consider the story of Noah and the deluge as folklore. But how to explain the folklore?

The key passage in Genesis reads: "And the Lord said, I will destroy man whom I have created from the face of the earth; both man, and beast, and the creeping thing, and the fowls of the air; for it repenteth me that I have made them." If this passage means exactly what it says, then it is very difficult to explain. While man's sins can be understood to have angered God, the destruction of all the animals on earth is not understandable from a moral point of view.

By Photographer: Donna Foster Roizen. Copyright holder: Frederic Jueneman [CC BY-SA 3.0 (http://creativecommons.org/licenses/by-sa/3.0)], via Wikimedia Commons

This leads to the thought that the story of the deluge or flood is not a folk tale. It is something that happened. Noah is in the story to help explain how some survived and the rest did not. And it manages the thought for man; but not for the animals that died. "Noah found grace in the eyes of the Lord. ... Noah was a just man and perfect in his generations, and Noah walked with God." There is a presumption that animals don't count in God's eyes, something that offends our modern sensibilities.

If the story of the deluge has historical truth, how can we be sure? As Immanuel Velikovsky explains to us, the story of the deluge is found in traditions all over the earth, and many of the cultures that have this memory have had no contact with western religion. There is so much evidence behind the story of the deluge, both from historical memory preserved in religions and in cultural traditions, and physical evidence, is it possible that the world was inundated by rainfall sufficient to cover all of the earth except some high mountain peaks?

Before answering the questions, we need to consider the condition of mankind before the deluge, accepting that a deluge did in fact occur.

Generally speaking, most contemporary science and archaeology thinks of man as slowly evolving technologically, starting out living in caves and opportunistically hunting, eventually moving to a more settled life, cultivating trees and vegetables and managing herds of animals. Along with these developments, man starts using stone impalements, then learns to fashion copper, then bronze and eventually iron.

There are some significant problems with this comfortable analytic view of man's "progress." To begin with, the changes in technology, in animal husbandry, in cultivation and farming did not occur evenly in all places. There were clusters where development was rapid; in other places there was hardly any change. Embedded in the Biblical texts, in writings from ancient Sumer and Babylonia and elsewhere, there is a suggestion that something dramatic happened, essentially changing mankind and vesting him with considerable technological tools that he hitherto lacked. Perhaps this is what is meant in Genesis which declares, "There were giants in the earth in those days; and also after that, when the sons of God (bnei Elim) came in unto the daughters of men, and they bare children to them, the same became mighty men which were of old, men of renown."

Plenty of people have been looking for evidence of these giants, called Nefilim in Hebrew. Nefilim are the sons of Gods and man. The idea that they were actual giants is either accepted for what it is, or hotly disputed even by rabbinic authorities. In particular Rabbi Akiva (Rabbi Shimon bar Yochai, 100-160 AD) would actually curse anyone who made this translation. But one way to view it that bridges both the literal translation and the various interpretations offered by authorities on the matter is that Nefilim certainly means very wise men who came from afar, an image that carries on down into Christianity's three wise men. Velikovsky thinks that it was an encounter with beings from another planet that transferred a block of knowledge that transformed mankind. As he says, "But if we are today on the eve of interplanetary travel, we must not declare as absolutely impossible the thought that this Earth was visited, ages ago, by some people from another planet. "

There is one feature in the Bible that may be an actual give away. It has to do with the life span of man. In Genesis God says, "My spirit shall not always strive with man, for that he also is flesh: yet his days shall be an hundred and twenty years." Noah on the other hand is given a life span of over 900 years. As one author writes: "the Bible teaches quite plainly that the early patriarchs often lived to be nearly 1,000 years old and even had children when they were several hundred years old! Similar claims of long life spans are found in the secular literature of several ancient cultures (including the Babylonians, Greeks, Romans, Indians, and Chinese)."

A year is measured today as 365 days. In ancient times it was variously measured as 360 or 365 days. It would be obvious to anyone in ancient times, that attaining even a life span of 120 years would be something of a miracle. So what is going on here? Is it possible that others living on the earth (those with wisdom and power) had different biological clocks than we? And can be think that assigning extremely long lives to the founders of the Hebrew religion and many others was intended to directly associate them with the Nefilim?

Most cultures report that the period before the deluge was one of great prosperity. There was more than enough food to supply mankind's needs, and the climate was reported as excellent. Before the deluge there was no environmental disaster.

So was the deluge some kind of climate change? Maybe, but not the way environmentalists would lead you to believe.

As many scientists have pointed out, even if it rained and rained, there is simply not enough water, hydrogen or oxygen on earth that if it all spilled down at once could cover the earth more than a foot or two.

Thus if the deluge happened, something extraordinary occurred.

It is Velikovsky's contention, which I accept, that what happened as a startling interplanetary event that impacted the earth. Vastly simplified the story is that Saturn and Jupiter essentially were twin stars that formed a kind of super nova. In ancient times Saturn was an extremely bright planet. Over a number of encounters the nova exploded. As Velikovsky explains: "The prevalent view is that a nova results from the interaction of two stars in a binary system when the two members disrupt one another on close approach. In such a case filaments of the disrupted star are torn out of its body and hurled in great spurts, to be absorbed by the companion star. The sudden transfer of matter is thought to set off the star's cataclysmic explosion."

From the earth looking out, the prelude to the vast explosion went on for some seven days, marked by a immensely bright light in the sky. When the explosion happened, the earth was thrown into disarray, its orbit was disrupted, and the fallout from the planetary collision was immense amounts of hydrogen and water coming from the nova raining down on earth. This caused massive flooding, changed the boundaries and size of the sea, and may also affected nearby planetary objects including the moon. For Saturn it meant a result in a greatly diminished size, a further out orbit from the sun, and it was seen as much dimmer.

It is possible during the ancient time when Saturn was in orbit much closer to the earth, its rings were observed by astronomers, because (as far as we know) the ancients did not have the optical technology needed to see Saturn's rings in its present-day orbit. However we do know that most ancient cultures relied heavily on astronomical observations, and what they recorded was generally highly accurate. Saturn's rings, or "chains," are depicted on many ancient sculptures. Saturn was also worshiped by many cultures, including Middle Eastern. Names for Saturn included Kronos, Osiris and Tammuz; also Kevan and Adonis. Speaking of both Saturn and Jupiter as binary stars they were referred to as Adonoi ("my lords").

Hollywood missed the big story.

MAR 18 2014

My Theory of What Happened to MH-370

[As of the date of publication MH-370 has yet to be found.]

[**Editor's Note:** June 23, 2014. The London Guardian reports today that "Investigators searching for flight MH-370 consider a catastrophic event leading to oxygen starvation the most likely scenario in the disappearance of the Malaysian Airlines Boeing 777." Thereafter according to the experts the plane flew on for many hours under autopilot control. The experts and investigators have come to this conclusion based on satellite derived information and other data. You can read what I believe happened in the scenario outlined below, written on March 18, 2014. I have not changed or updated the original story in any way. When the plane is finally found, evidence of an explosion on the aircraft will be found, which to me is the most likely cause of the catastrophe. I think the Malaysian government, among others, has done an incredibly poor job in handling the search and in releasing faulty information about the flight path, about the crew, and the passengers. I suspect strongly there is a cover up of information, although I am not sure of the reason for the cover up. There is a possibility they know a terrorist was on the plane.]

It is the middle of the night. The cabin lights are dimmed, most of the passengers have dozed off. A large "bang" is heard, rousing the passengers. Within a second or two, oxygen masks drop from above. Eerily, there is no message. The flight attendants say nothing. All the lights are now out, the temperature has dropped, and the oxygen is not flowing through the tubes. The plane at first ascends a few thousand feet from its established pathway; in fact well above its safe altitude. Then it begins to turn and almost doubles back on its original course. But now it is descending slowly so that by the time it crosses back over the Malaysian mainland, it is down to around 10 to 15,000 feet above sea level. It now seems to stabilize and hold its altitude, as it flies on.

Observers on oil rigs at first saw the plane, a great distance away and there seemed to have been a fire. But after some 15 seconds, the fire was out, probably blown out by the jet stream.

The plane can fly like this for many hours. But the passengers all were made unconscious by the depressurization. Some of them might remain alive, but none of them, including the flight crew staff, can function.

The pilots are both dead. The transponder went off when the explosion in the cabin area happened. We now know that the story that the transponder was off when the pilots made their last call to ATC (Air Traffic Control) was false. The transponder went off after the call.

Photo by Laurent ERRERA from L'Union, France [CC BY-SA 2.0 (http://creativecommons.org/licenses/by-sa/2.0)], via Wikimedia Commons

There were no cell phone calls. This tells us unequivocally that everyone was unconscious or dead. Otherwise calls could have been made at any time as the plane flew on. At the plane's altitude over Malaysia, there is no doubt calls could be received. But there weren't any.

Years ago when I was learning to be a pilot my IP (Instructor Pilot) told me to take my hands off the stick and my feet off the rudder. "Just watch what happens," he said, as I reluctantly let go of the yoke. The plane flew on; in fact it was more level and stable than my piloting allowed it to be. "An airplane wants to fly," said the IP, "and it will fly if there is sufficient air speed."

A wounded airplane, where the controls are mainly destroyed by a bomb, can still fly and can even seem to be on course. Now when the plane was wounded, it could have turned sharply as the blast hit and the pilots grabbed or pulled at the controls. But once the explosion was over and the pilots unable to do anything, the plane could go on for some time. The evidence tells us the plane flew for some number of hours.

How far would it have gone? If there was a rupture in the plane's skin, as was probably the case, over time it would get bigger and incoming wind would eventually further damage the plane's systems.

My guess is that there was a bomb on the plane. Probably in one of the forward cabins. Remember that the 9/11 hijackers and some of the wannabe hijackers, booked first or business class seats. Whether there was any attempt to hijack the plane remains uncertain. It does not seem too likely, because some commotion in the plane's cabin probably would have been detected. The idea that sophisticated hijackers, or the pilot and copilot together, somehow flew the plane to a secret runway seems far fetched and unproven.

Eventually the plane will be located. Probably it is deeply embedded in the ocean bottom. It could have "landed" itself on the water and slowly drifted to the bottom, without breaking up. That will make it hard to find.

By Greg L [CC BY 2.0 (http://creativecommons.org/licenses/by/2.0)], via Wikimedia Commons

Is such a self-landing possible? With empty fuel tanks (no oil slicks) and gently descending, the plane could have put down safely, much like US Airways Flight 1549 that was brilliantly piloted to a safe landing on the Hudson river. Readers will recall that the plane stayed afloat for some time as it drifted down the Hudson river. There was no debris. Eventually it was stopped and salvaged. Malaysian Airlines Flight MH-370, with no one conscious on board, could have laid on top of the waves and eventually filled with water and sank.

Without finding the airplane, it is impossible to demonstrate any theory. No one so far is claiming to have blown up the plane or attempted to hijack it. Military "primary" radars have not reported "seeing" the plane where it could have entered someone's airspace. That does not prove it did not anyway happen. A number of experts in Israel think it was an Iranian operation. And Israeli air defense systems are on alert if in fact the plan is to use the plane as in a suicide attack on Israel, a replicate of 9/11. But right now there isn't any convincing evidence for this kind of hijack. And from the few facts we know —a plane at a very high altitude, calm pilots, and no cellular phone calls, points in a different direction.

There have been reports that some shoe bombs have been designed to blow up the cabin door of an aircraft. Such a bomb might do a lot more damage, such as blowing out the windshields of the cockpit and depressurizing the aircraft.

Perhaps we will soon find out the answer to the mystery of the missing plane and lost passengers and crew.

NOV 23 2013

AMERICAN FOOTBALL: HELMETS, CRACKED EGGS, AND A RED CARD

With Shoshana Bryen

Reprinted from American Thinker

American football is a violent game and it is rare that one ends without injury. A dislocated shoulder, broken ribs, cracked collarbones, or a torn ACL — this and more is what we watch on the weekends.

Aiming for the quarterback is axiomatic. If defenders can hurry, shake, or hurt the quarterback, he can lose his rhythm or be driven from the game, leaving the offense in the hands of a second or even third-string player. The worst of these hits is helmet-to-helmet contact, which is just what it sounds like. A defensive player, sometimes a lineman or a free safety, attacks at speed and slams his helmet into the opposing player's helmet. If he does his job, the offensive player, whether quarterback, receiver or lineman, can end up with a concussion.

For the National Football League (NFL) addressing on-the-field brutality is as much matter of business practice as conscience. The loss of a top quarterback or other star player translates into a loss of millions of dollars. Furthermore, players and their union are successfully filing suit against the league for concussion and memory-related injuries. And finally, horrific stories about brain-damaged players are flooding the news, and owners worry that the government will begin to investigate football violence as it did drugs in baseball.

Focusing primarily on "defenseless" players — those who are off the ground or otherwise unable to move away from an oncoming hit — the NFL has: (1) made helmet-to-helmet hits a 15-yard penalty; (2) levied personal fines against players whose actions appear especially egregious; (3) instituted new procedures to better check players for concussions; and (4) begun researching better helmets.

Outlawing helmet-to-helmet hits makes sense, but officials miss a lot of hits and the 15-yard penalty does not fit the crime. A defender can cripple a quarterback or receiver and send him to the hospital, and the on-field consequence is only 15 yards.

Fines on players, some of them seemingly substantial, also do not stop foul play. They are a disincentive to an individual player, but not necessarily to a team — accounting for the New Orleans Saints' team decision to deliberately hurt opposing players. The money can be taken care of in new contracts, endorsements, or some other means of compensation.

The new rules to check players are certainly good. Head injuries, however, are not always easy to detect and even the best sideline or locker room diagnostics will miss cumulative injuries. The brain is still a mysterious organ, and the kind of injury that led former NFL linebacker Junior Seau to take his own life probably would not have been picked up early enough, even with the best diagnostics.

This leaves helmets. A modern football helmet is very hard plastic with interior shock-absorbing pads. Look at the condition of a player's helmet during a game and you will see lots of scratches but no dents. Football helmets don't dent and the pads don't really protect against the internal damage of a traumatic head-to-head shock. The brain is essentially torqued inside the player's skull, slapping against the bone. If you ever banged your head and "saw stars" you have some idea what happens. The brain, suspended in fluid and flexibly attached, isn't designed to rattle around in there. These injuries, furthermore, are cumulative: impaired vision, memory loss, foggy decision-making, slurred speech, and imagery so twisted that people sometimes want to kill themselves, and sometimes do. "Improving" the survivability of a helmet by making it harder may actually increase the likelihood that a player will see the helmet as a weapon, and no improvement can stop the g-forces and shock that twist and damage the brain.

Which brings us to two solutions that might work better and make the game more a game of skill than a game of kill — one by improving the crucial equipment, and one by taking a page from football's cousin, soccer, where players are almost entirely unprotected.

The Cracked Egg
A helmet could be designed to begin to fail when certain types of impact takes place. Your car bumper, for example, is good for an impact at 5 miles per hour but not one at 60 mph.

If helmets had an outer skin designed to crack when too much force is used, a player with a cracked helmet could be suspended from the game — a direct and immediate disincentive for leading with the helmet. Teams would focus on skill and safe tackling because even the poorest official would see a cracked helmet and remove the offending player.

Red Card
In addition to the cracked helmet, college and professional football needs a Red Card, which is what soccer referees use to punish players for egregious and unprofessional attacks on others. A Red Card on the soccer field has two consequences. First, the offending player is ejected and then barred from the next game. But more important from the team's point of view, the ejected player cannot be replaced on the field, meaning the team has to play one down. The team and the coaches have great incentive to teach players to use their skills rather than brute force to achieve their ends. And the player's loyalty to his team will help ensure that he curbs his more violent

hits in order to stay in the game. The same would be true in football — when a team has an incentive to play skillfully, thuggery will disappear.

A "cracked egg" helmet and the Red Card could help restore football as a game of skill, and would over time significantly reduce brain injuries to players. The NFL is trying to go in the right direction, but the League has to do more to restore the honor of the game.

OCT 14 2013

WHAT ASTEROID 1950 DA MAY MEAN

It is called 1950 DA because it was first seen in February, 1950 and then it disappeared. It was not seen again until December 31st, 2000, and it was also picked up on radar in March, 2001. Scientists believe that 1950 DA, which is a 1.1 kilometer-wide asteroid, spinning through space, will come close to or in fact crash into the earth on March 16th, 2880 –that is, 867 years from now.

What does this mean?

Last February a meteorite traveling at over 33,000 miles per hour crashed into Russia's Ural region. The result was an explosion equal to about 300 kilotons. It created a huge fireball, damaged some 3,000 buildings, and caused many injuries. The meteorite weighed around 10 tons and it probably broke up as it entered the atmosphere, resulting in three ground hits. Compared to 1950 DA, the Ural's meteorite was tiny.

In 1908 at Tunguska there was an airburst of a small asteroid or comet with a size between 200 to 630 feet. Some estimates put the blast as high as 300 megatons of TNT, about the same size as the MX nuclear warhead. While the blast happened largely in a wilderness area, it is estimated it destroyed some 80 million trees. Scientists are still studying the Tunguska event –but it is all but certain it was a near-earth collision either by an asteroid or comet.

There is a school of scientific opinion that the Tunguska comet or asteroid will return. Some experts think its return can occur as soon as 2045, or in only 32 years.

Vitaly Romeiko, the director of the Department of Astrophysics at Zvenigorod Observatory, said in an interview in Moscow that the 1908 event was caused by a fragment of the Encke Comet's tail that entered the Earth's atmosphere as a ball of ice with small interplanetary fragments (dust particles) and, upon entrance, exploded due to the negative ions in the comet and the positive ions found on Earth. He pointed out that the Encke Comet also revolves around the sun and comes near Earth every 3.3 years.

Romeiko has participated in 23 expeditions into the Tunguska region.

Olga Gladysheva, a senior fellow at the A.F. Ioffe Physics and Technical Institute in St. Petersburg, supported Romeiko's theory in a separate interview with RIA Novosti, adding that the part of the comet's tail separated and created a giant ice ball that was created in a vacuum, and, therefore, made several explosions as the particles inside expanded and the ball disintegrated.

The Russian scientists base their theory on the fact on the absence of any meteorite material in the area, no rock fragments, or no impact areas that would create a crater.

Gladysheva said part of the comet's tail entered the Earth's ionosphere at more than 80 kilometers above ground, which is an intense area of atmospheric electricity. She said a major blast occurred over the epicenter at an altitude of 7-10 kilometers above the Earth's surface. The significance of the blast was due to the overly charged ions and differences in the positive and negative poles in the comet and Earth.

Romeiko said the ice ball that formed around the comet's dust particles before striking Earth would explain the absence of a crater or meteorite particles. The particles from the comet would be very minute and could most likely be found in the lower layers of peat moss in the area, which is frozen in permafrost.

These recent events, and events projected to happen in the future based on current-day science, indicate that there are powerful forces at work which we barely understand.

In an earlier essay, we commented on the work of Immanuel Velikovsky. His most famous book, World's in Collision was published in 1950, around the same time that 1950 DA was observed.

The Velikovsky thesis is that human history was deeply affected by planetary events which occurred in modern history, not billions of years ago. Velikovsky looks at what happened when, based on the evidence he gathered, a comet passed near the earth causing a massive upheaval, a change in the earth's orbit and its polarity, and nearly brought an end of history.

Velikovsky's methodology is mostly based on the analysis of historical records of different cultures, but with the strongest emphasis on Middle Eastern, Egyptian and ancient Greek sources including Biblical sources. Descriptions of the upheaval, images of the heavens recorded by ancient astronomers, and data from other cultures that are parallel to the major sources, create a powerful record. And the historical record is reinforced by strong evidence that such events can again repeat themselves in future, should 1950 DA have a near encounter with the earth.

So why is it that most scientists and most historians either treat Velikovsky's work with contempt, or simply reject his thesis?

Velikovsky, who lived in the eye of the storm he either created or exposed, tried to understand the nature of the visceral reaction against his work. He thought about it in psychoanalytical terms and saw it as a form of mankind's denial or the great suffering and pain caused by past events, pain that had to be sublimated.

Maybe. But a significant part of the story is told in the Bible in the events leading to and resulting in the exodus of the Hebrews from Egypt and of events that follow. And the Exodus is an event that is celebrated in the Jewish religion and is a core part of the Christian and Muslim traditions. It is the idea of the rebirth of mankind.

Modern science, and secular history, probably has blindness, a profound one, in grasping that nature may be more complex and rich in the sense of possibility than merely what can be measured and recorded.

As we learn more about the future that is yet to unfold, we need to see both the dangers and the possibilities.

SEP 23 2013

LIFE OUT OF COMETS AND OUR FUTURE

Lawrence Livermore scientist Nir Goldman has been predicting that comets may have carried pre-biotic materials to earth which, in collision, formed amino acids which form the basis of life. The comet materials include water (in the form of ice), ammonia, methanol and carbon monoxide. Now an international team of scientists in the United Kingdom tested the Goldman hypothesis by firing a high speed projectile into comet-like materials. The shock of the impact created amino acid materials.

As this is written a huge comet, named ISON, has emerged from behind the sun. It is still not known what will become of this comet – it can break up coming too close to the sun, or it can continue its travel. Scientists say that the comet will miss the earth by millions of miles.

Comet ISON by TRAPPIST/E. Jehin/ESO (http://www.eso.org/public/images/potw1346a/) [CC BY 4.0 (http://creativecommons.org/licenses/by/4.0)], via Wikimedia Commons

But ISON and the Goldman experiments bring home a concept about the vagaries of outer space and the role comets have in creating life.

Consider, for example, that life can be created from the shock of an impact of a comet. It means, among other things, that if the planetary conditions to support life exist, then life can be created and recreated by disturbances in the universe, and not only on earth but literally in any solar system.

Most modern science is built around the notion that it takes billions of years and a slow process for life to develop and for species to evolve. This may yet hold true, but it is also possible that life can be reinvented and restarted, and even if there is evolution there is also shock and awe.

Beginning before World War II, Immanuel Velikovsky came to the conclusion that our earth was hit by at least one, and probably more than one comet which had huge consequences, almost wiping out life on earth and setting in motion a period of instability, orbital change, and vast upheavals on earth. He reached this conclusion by reading ancient source materials where the events were recorded –including the Bible which records the escape of the Hebrews from Egypt and momentous events, some described as plagues, and others as miracles such as the parting of the Red Sea and manna from heaven. Velikovsky believes that manna was, in fact, organic material thrown off by the comet that collided or nearly collided with the earth. The shock came from both the near collision, which disturbed earth's orbit and polar orientation, and from huge electrical discharges between the comet and earth –shock and awe.

Velikovsky was targeted by scientists in the United States who attacked his findings without putting any of them to the test. Velikovsky was a close friend of Albert Einstein, and in the last weeks of Einstein's life the great scientist began to see how Velikovsky's theories were being proved out by scientific data gathered by space probes. A few other scientists were willing to take a look at Velikovsky's findings and discoveries, but the level of hostility to him and to his work was so great that he was treated as a heretic and, had burning at the stake been available in 1950, Velikovsky would surely have been burned.

This sort of brutal gang psychosis by scientists is not anything new. We see a lot of it at work today in discussions over climate change. Velikovsky, himself a psychiatrist, understood the phenomena even though he was never prepared for the intensity of the attacks on his work. Velikovsky was one of the world's most original thinkers, but he was also human and vulnerable.

If we link together what Goldman and others are finding, reconsider Velikovsky, and start to ask the right questions, a great deal can be learned. We might begin to visualize alternative futures as well as re-understand our past. This is an adventure of great importance, and scientists should embrace the opportunity and not wage war against the messengers.

May 14 2013

The 3-D Plastic Gun and Airport Screening

There is growing alarm about 3-D guns, essentially plastic guns that are produced through a process called 3-D Printing. 3-D guns produce two issues —the possibility of manufacturing guns by individuals and groups that are not gun manufacturers and are not licensed in any way. In this way, guns proliferation morphs into a staggering problem, even bigger than we have today with illegal firearms. While government can outlaw the 3-D printing of guns, how to enforce such a ban is vexing. Governments have not been able to control the illegal flow of guns, which account for most crimes. That is why no one really wants to talk about controlling illegal guns. 3-D plastic guns makes the problem worse.

The second problem is security, especially at airports, in public buildings, and other places where there is screening for weapons.

3-D guns do not, for the most part, show up on X-Rays, or on other types of scanners.

Many years ago this problem reared its head with the Glock hand gun, which was plastic and was made in Austria. I know a lot about the problem because my staff at the Defense Department worked with the Glock people so that their guns would not slip through X-Ray scanners and magnetometers.

Today we have far more sophisticated scanning equipment than we had 25 years ago. But whether it can catch a plastic gun is open to question.

The Transportation Security Administration in the United States has spent hundreds of millions of dollars, perhaps more, on trying to secure airports. It has improved scanners, and introduced new millimeter wave scanners that virtually undress a person. But the vulnerability is less the person, shoe bombers excepted, than it is with carry on bags where scanning is known to have multiple weak points and failures.

Today's terrorists are well informed and sophisticated enough to know about these weak points, or to test what they think are vulnerabilities, sending so-called "mules" through security screening lines to see if they can beat the system. Not only this, but because rogue states such as Iran, and troubled countries like Pakistan, Syria and Yemen, already have security scanning equipment, terrorists can work out ways to trial their bomb and gun smuggling strategies "locally" thanks to permissive regimes or healthy bribes. It is not surprising, for example, that sophisticated bombs were smuggled on board flights originating in Yemen and heading either through Dubai or London to the United States, with the intention of exploding over Chicago and causing mass casualties.

Aircraft themselves are bombs, as the 9/11 hijackers demonstrated.

It seems, therefore, that the current technology we have may not be up to the job of screening for 3-D-printed plastic guns and we should be concerned.

For many years there has been a strong debate between American security experts and Israeli ones on the question of how to go about screening aircraft passengers. The Israelis opted for a human method, namely carefully interviewing people to try and find any potential risk. Baggage is also scanned (just as in the US), but instead of relying on "get-naked" technology, the Israelis rely on smart people who are very well trained to find a dangerous person.

In the US this approach was rejected, partly because the US has so many airports that putting in place a mature and capable interviewing method was a daunting challenge; and partly because the method is very slow. If you take a plane to or from Israel you are advised to be at the airport for check in at least 3 hours before the flight.

Is there a middle ground that might help achieve some of the results the Israeli's get, and could help solve the hard-to-identify 3-D plastic gun?

In February of this year, the magazine HSToday_published a front page article that explained a system that could detect a passenger's intentions with a fair degree of accuracy, and do that quickly and without the target knowing it. The technology, which was developed in Israel, uses a type of scanner, but it is remote from the passengers in the security line. A number of countries have tested the system and are now installing it at airports, rail stations and on border crossing points.

I was surprised that neither TSA nor the Department of Homeland Security responded to the article or inquired about the technology. They would have learned something, and if someone gets through with a plastic gun and does some damage, it would be a tragedy because perhaps the disaster could have been avoided.

Tributes
PART 4

FEB 20 2014

A Nice Story in a Sea of Pain and Distress

A few years ago I had the privilege to meet with Dr. Rafi Beyar, Director, Rambam* Health Care Campus and Professor, Biomedical Engineering and Medicine, at the Technion. The Rambam Health Care Campus and the Technion are both located in Israel. The meeting, arranged by my wife, included Hal Koster, the head of the Aleethia Foundation, a group working with wounded soldiers in the United States. The topic of conversation was how to "compare notes" between what the Israelis have done dealing with traumatic injuries caused by war and what has been done in the United States.

For more than ten years my wife Shoshana and I have been working with Hal Koster who today heads the Aleethia Foundation. We first met Hal through a friend of ours, Maarten Singelenberg. Maarten has been one of the leading marketing experts in the food trade in Washington DC. One of his clients was a restaurant located a few blocks from the White House, called Fran O'Brien's. Fran O'Brien was a Cleveland Browns and later a Washington Redskins football player (he was an offensive tackle). His son Marty and Hal Koster operated the restaurant. They were friends with "the milkshake man," 'aka' Jim Meyer, who was visiting wounded soldiers at the then Walter Reed Army Medical Center, then located further up 16th street. Jim would bring trays of frozen milkshakes to the wounded guys. Inevitably they would ask why he was doing that, and what he knew about war and the trauma of being wounded and losing limbs. Meyer, in reply, would lift both his pant legs showing two prosthetic limbs. Jim was wounded in Vietnam. He realized that you can recover and live a full and complete life****, but you need help and care, and most of all a feeling that you still have an important role to play in the world. It was this idea that got Jim to speak to Hal and Marty. They concocted the notion that they would bring the wounded soldiers, somehow and someway, to their restaurant and give them an amazing evening away from the hospital wards and therapy rooms. A steak dinner. A beer or two. Maybe some young ladies?

That is what got the Fran O'Brien dinners going. What Maarten learned on his visit to Hal and Marty, that it was hard for them to keep their restaurant profitable and support 30 or more free guests every Friday night. So my wife and I, and later many others, started raising money because we saw the huge benefit of the dinners.

Hal Koster

It was attending many of the Friday night dinners that I got to see some of the medical miracles performed to help our guys (and later a few military gals too) return to a normal life. The caregivers were extraordinary, and the new technology, at least what I could see of it, was amazing. Even more amazing was what we saw from the wounded warriors themselves: grit, determination, huge spirit, and a desire to return to their units as soon as they could (the Army, Marines or other service permitting). The dinners also attracted leaders from the Pentagon such as the Chairman of the Joint Chiefs of Staff, Peter Pace, and the Deputy Secretary of Defense Paul Wolfowitz and his successor Gordon England. Not only did these high level visits raise spirits and provide a connection "right to the top," but it paved the way for the Pentagon to start employing wounded warriors and encouraging others to do the same.

Dr. Beyar and Hal had a lot to talk about the day we met for lunch.

Rambam does for Israeli soldiers and for others affected by war what Walter Reed Army Medical Center (now co-located at the Bethesda Naval Medical Center) does for our troops.

The Jerusalem Post and other news outlets feature compelling stories about a Syrian child with a severe head injury being rushed across the border with his 11 year old brother and his father. His mother and sister were killed in the same blast that wounded the two boys. Crossing the border and on the road to Rambam, the 11 year old also passed. This left the father and his barely surviving son. The boy was comatose, and his father was asking the hospital to do whatever they could to save his son, telling them "he is all I have left."

The boy required emergency brain surgery to relieve pressure on the brain caused by swelling. Without the surgery he could not live. The extensive surgery was carried out, the boy was kept in an induced coma, and then, as he recovered, more surgery was needed to replace the parts of the skull that were removed and then to start therapy, including physical recovery and speech retraining. Some weeks after he entered the hospital, he walked out with his father.

Dr. Rafael ("Rafi") Beyar

The story is very moving, very sincere, but not unusual. For decades Israeli hospitals have been open to treat the dire medical needs of their neighbors. Israel has been terrific in emergency medicine and trauma care. That is why, whether it is the Philippines or Haiti, the Israeli teams have performed so well in saving lives and restoring hope.

Can we take a lesson from this? Dr. Beyar and Hal Koster understood immediately what they have in common --the mission.

---

*"Rambam" is an acronym of the Hebrew name of Moses Maimonides (1135-1204). Rambam was a rabbi, a philosopher and a renowned physician.
****Jim Meyer holds an "Alive Day" every year, a well attended event where funds raised go to support wounded soldiers.

Disabled Army veteran Paul Miosek (left) reunites with Jim Meyer, a Department of Veterans Affairs employee and long-time volunteer at Walter Reed Army Medical Center, at the 20th Annual Disabled Veterans Winter Sports Clinic, in Snowmass Village, Colo. Miosek credits Mayer with opening his eyes to new possibilities while living with a disability. Photo by Donna Miles Department of Defense

OCT 28 2011

A TRIBUTE TO AN AMERICAN HERO

An American hero passed away in September; on December 30th he will be laid to rest at Arlington Cemetery. It takes time these days to arrange interment at Arlington.

Captain Harry J. Price, US Navy (ret.) died at his home in Bluffton, South Carolina at the age of only 68. Harry served seven tours in Vietnam, spanning four years. In 1970, he led 94 combat patrols while in command of River Division Five Fifty Four at Song Ong Doc, during which he earned both the Silver Star and Bronze Star for gallantry and heroism in combat. Later the same year, while leading River Division Five Nine Four, he added the Navy Commendation Medal and Vietnamese Staff Service Medal for operations during the final re-supply of Phnom Penh, Cambodia.

Harry moved on to naval intelligence where his work contributed greatly to American understanding of the emerging Soviet threat and enabled the US to mount strategies to deal with the Soviet military build up. Along with a handful of experts at the CIA, Harry's discoveries, insights and findings contributed greatly to the winning of the Cold War and the collapse of the Soviet Union.

He did it in two ways. First, Harry was one of the first to recognize the importance of reverse-engineering weapons from our adversaries. Reverse engineering is often done just to learn design secrets so that a weapon or system can be copied. Today we are experiencing that sort of attack – primarily from China – targeting our national security resources, defense industries and military computers from their computers.

Harry's collection was not intended to replicate the items but to understand how they worked, the frequencies on which they operated, and what they were made of. In fact, what they were made of – direct copies of American microchips in many cases – emerged as one of his most important discoveries.

In Harry's day, collecting information on the weapons of an adversary was complicated, and that was his second skill. He was a master at finding Russian and Warsaw Pact equipment for exploitation. Sometimes he used contacts with friendly countries, but he also set off on various "adventures" – very secret and sometimes very risky – making deals to get his hands on Russian equipment. Harry was after the most modern items he could get hold of in his exploits.

Sometimes it was sold on the black market by a Russian airman or sailor, but sometimes it was just luck, as it was when equipment was lost at sea. In one case, a Boy Scout troop near Bangor, Washington discovered a Soviet sonobuoy on the beach. The sonobuoy was designed to record the sounds of passing US nuclear submarines. The recorded hum of the propellers could be fed into Soviet torpedoes so that they could track and kill American submarines without any active sonar, which would have alerted the Americans to their presence. Harry was a key beneficiary of the Boy Scout's find, and from it he produced important information that helped the Navy understand the threat and helped the Defense Department understand the "state of the art" of the Russian's technology.

The sonobuoy contained a multi-track open-reel tape recorder much like the tape decks people used in the 1980's to record music. Notwithstanding the mechanical issues of a tape deck in a sonobuoy bobbing around in rough seas, it worked.

Replaying the tapes, Harry started to hear something strange in the background. As he isolated the background sound from the sound of the submarines, he discovered that the tape had previously held a recording of Russian opera. It seems that, lacking adequate supplies at sea, the ship's captain provided a tape of his own and pressed it into service.

Some of the electronics also were haphazardly installed. The circuit board that converted the sounds recorded into a digital format and commanded a pop up antenna, was tied down by shoelaces. The circuit board had apparently been rushed out to the Russian ship, and installed on board by sailors eager to drop off the buoy in time to listen for the latest model US ballistic missile submarines headed out to sea, probably SSBN/SSGN 726, the USS Ohio.

In the 1980s, the USSR was investing more than 25 percent of its gross domestic product into an unprecedented defense buildup. Reversing the electronics used by the Soviet Union helped tell about the network the Soviets had assembled, led by Directorate T of the KGB, to acquire American technology. Microelectronics and computers held the key. If the United States could counter the military build-up effort by using electronics and computers as a force multiplier, the gargantuan Soviet challenge would go down the drain.

Harry's work was critical because if we knew what they had, DOD could also get a pretty good idea of where they were getting the pilfered material, and could work to shut down their sources of supply. And that is what the US did.

Thanks to Harry and many others in DOD and the CIA and a network of like-minded experts in industry, the effort did pay off and the Russians never reached the technological capacity they needed to protect their huge investment. They were unable to exercise their strategic master plan which would have forced the US out of the Middle East and Asia. And the Soviet Union disintegrated.

The collapse of the Soviet Empire was not a thunderbolt from the blue – it was the result of people, including Harry Price, understanding the shaky underpinning of the communist system and pulling out the supports until the structure fell. Not very many Americans know of Captain Harry Price, but they should. He is a true American hero

FEB 22 2012

A War Memory - The Band Plays On

Kalhausen is a small village in France, in the Alsace-Lorraine, near the German border. In 1940 this area was annexed to Germany by Hitler.

In 2004, traces of American troops who liberated France were discovered at the local school. They left some graffiti and their names engraved on the attic walls.

The 104th regiment of the 26th Patton Third Army division came for the first time in the village on the 6th December 1944 in the morning. A few days later they were followed by the 87th Golden Acorn division and at Christmas time by the 44th infantry division of the Seventh Army – which was involved in Nordwind in the 17th SS Panzergrenadierdivision counteroffensive.

My uncle, Norman Sataloff was among them, from the 44th. He was in the 44th Band and he also served in GR (graves registration).

Norman "Sadie" Sataloff on drums (1942)

The graffiti's were found in the school underneath wallpaper that was being removed to be replaced with new. One of the drawings (which you will see in the article below) was done by my uncle Norman. His wartime nickname was "Sadie", and the graffiti says Sadie Sataloff. He lists himself as a "bassologist." In fact he was extremely talented and could play everything from the violin to the clarinet to the trumpet to the bass. He often performed with my mother -she still is, at 94, a pretty good pianist.

*Photo courtesy of the Kalhausen Historical Association

I discovered all this by accident because I found a war-time photo of my uncle and I was wondering about the name of the unit he served in.

I knew all the stories about his time in the Army band and in GR. This was no easy service, because the bodies were often booby-trapped by the Germans and he got stuck with his foot on a live grenade just under a body he was lifting to remove for burial. He stood in place for many hours as his fellow soldiers figured out a way to liberate him without the grenade going off.

Unfortunately, Norman died too young of a heart attack in 1960. He was, above everything else, my favorite uncle and I was very close to him.

It is amazing, after all this time, to find a memory of him in a French village school from 1944. I owe a great deal to Bernard Zins and the Kalhausen Historical Association who took the trouble and care to find this historical memory and bring back fond memories of my uncle. For those who would like to learn more, Bernard's article "LES GI DE LA 44e DIVISION D'INFANTERIE" can be found on the Internet.

For me, the band plays on.

Apr 23 2012

The Tim Tebow of the Army: A Memorial Salute to Maj. Gen. Orde Wingate

On April 22nd a touching ceremony was held at Arlington Cemetery for Major General Orde Wingate. Though a British Army officer, he was buried at Arlington in 1950. Wingate died when his aircraft crashed in India, returning from Burma. The bodies of the nine men lost in the B-25H Mitchell Bomber were first interred in India, but in 1950 moved to the United States. The reason was a UK-US agreement regarding the remains of unidentified troops -if the majority were American they were buried in the US, and if the majority British, burial was to be in the UK. In this case the crew and passengers was made up of five Americans and four British. The remains were, by the technology of the time, unidentifiable so they were moved to Arlington Cemetery where there is a memorial to them in Section 12 at site 288.

Orde Wingate (1938) Public Domain

Orde Wingate was the Tim Tebow of the British, American and future Israeli army. Why? Because like Tim Tebow he was a devout Christian who found his inspiration in the Bible, and like Tim Tebow he was able to innovate and find ways to succeed even when he lacked equipment and mass.

Wingate got many of his ideas from the Bible and he applied them in Ethiopia, where he was sent to confront Italian forces occupying the country. Wingate formed what we would call a "special force" consisting of British, Sudanese and Ethiopian troops, to which were added Palestinian (later Israeli) Haganah SNS units. The group's size was, at its largest, some 1,700 men –but it succeeded in forcing the surrender of over 20,000 Italian front line troops, largely by deceiving the Italian Expeditionary Force on the size of the Wingate operation. Wingate's unit was called the Gideon Force, named after the Bible's Gideon. The name Gideon comes from the Hebrew Gidon, and means Destroyer or Mighty Warrior.

Before his operation in Ethiopia, Wingate played a critical role in training and leading the Haganah, the Jewish self-defense force with responsibility for the Special Night Squads. While subsequent British post World War II actions in Palestine, under a British mandate, found the British Army at loggerheads with the Haganah, before World War II the Haganah proved itself to be helpful to British interests. In fact, one of the important objectives of Haganah forces, supported by Wingate and the British, was to prevent Arab sabotage of the petroleum pipelines belonging to the Iraq Petroleum Company and to confront the Arab Revolt, then in progress. Most importantly, Wingate devised unique battle tactics, particularly night operations, and provided extensive training for Haganah forces. The ideas put forward by Wingate eventually formed the basis of ideas about how to run a military force, strongly at variance with traditional attitudes.

Wingate's last venture was operating in Burma behind enemy (Japanese) lines. Japan had a much superior force, but Wingate's leadership of his small force of "Chindits" which was 77th Indian Infantry

Brigade and in 1944 3rd Indian Infantry Division caused the Japanese many problems. The name Chindit is a corrupted form of the name Chinthe, which is a Burmese mythical beast that guards the doors of Buddhist temples. While there are different views about the overall success of the Chindit operation, some military historians claim -based on Japanese Army wartime assessments found in captured documents- that the Chindit penetration of Japanese Army forces forestalled the will of Japan's military leaders to invade India. Had the war moved to India, it would certainly have stirred nationalistic sentiments there, and could have significantly affected the Pacific War operation and its final outcome. Even potentially worse, it could have forced the redeployment of UK forces from the European theater, delaying D-Day and giving Hitler more time to mount a defense against the Allies.

Wingate's original thinking, both in confronting regular armies and in dealing with insurgencies, is, of course, greatly relevant to the issues the US and its allies face today.

Orde Wingate was befriended by Winston Churchill and Franklin Roosevelt. In Israel he trained Yigal Allon and Moshe Dayan among others.

Was Wingate the Tim Tebow of the military forces he so gallantly led? He was because he always took the initiative, used the tools he had available, and demonstrated leadership and made his entire team responsible for victory. Wingate's core idea of leadership was "Follow Me."

Most of all, Orde Wingate looked to the Bible for ideas and solutions, and it seems he found there what he sought. Perhaps the next time Tim Tebow is on the field, it will cause us to think about Orde Wingate and his amazing accomplishments.

DEC 07 2011

REMEMBERING BERNIE

On Sunday, December 4, three days before the 70th anniversary of Pearl Harbor, we came to bury Bernie Silver. He was 95 years old.

I, as his son-in-law, was honored to be able to say a few words. Since the funeral, Bernie is still very much on my mind. Bernie was married twice (his first wife Shirlee died of cancer). He had three children who adore him, Barbara, Shoshana (my wife), and Mark. He lived to enjoy his grandchildren and great grandchildren. Ina, his second wife, cared for him and helped him as he grew older even though she also had to fight cancer, a major heart attack and operation, and other medical ills.

Bernard Silver was born in 1916. He was a highly intelligent, creative, but quiet person. As a young man, he delivered milk in Trenton, New Jersey in a horse-drawn truck. A little later, figuring out how to service and repair typewriters, he fixed the Underwood's, Remington's and Royal's for businesses in Trenton. He also repaired typewriters at the State Prison. Later in life he always loved to start off a conversation with, "When I was in Trenton State Prison…"

When the war came he enlisted, like tens of thousands of other young men. So, too, his brother Ray. His other brother, who had physical problems, could not serve.

Bernard Silver in his M-10 Tank Destroyer

He served in North Africa, in Italy, in France and into Germany. In the last phase of the war, he was commander of a tank destroyer, an M-10. The M-10, based on an older Sherman tank chassis, had a 76mm (3 inch) gun with special shells capable of stopping German Panzer tanks.

He was at the landing at Anzio, a particularly bloody and messy affair. On the Allied side there were 43,000 combat casualties (7,000 killed, 36,000 wounded or missing). On his war record you will see that he had the European, Middle Eastern and North African medal with the bronze arrow device, signifying the Anzio landing.

Along the way, Bernie received a Purple Heart and an Oak Leaf cluster, meaning he was wounded twice. He never told his family.

In France, he made a single handed capture of three German officers in a small village. Exactly how he did it we do not know. What we know is he was awarded a Bronze Star for this action on July 26, 1944. He rarely talked about the Bronze Star.

Somewhere in France he was able to find his brother Ray, who was with Patton. How he found his brother we never learned.

In Paris he somehow commandeered a truck full of cigarettes. Don't Ask Don't Tell had already started.

His top rank was Sergeant, although the few pictures we have of him in uniform show him with corporal insignia. He was with Company D, 25th. Tank Battalion which was part of the 14th Armored Division, known as the Liberators.

He was discharged from the Army in September, 1945. His sister Ruth, who was working at Fort Dix in New Jersey, was waiting for the bus to come and bring her brother back. Ruth was with us on Sunday. Bernie had sent her his Purple Heart decoration, but asked that his mother not be told that he had been wounded.

The Jewish War veterans participated in the ceremony for Bernie, saluted, played taps, and presented the flag placed over the coffin to his widow, Ina.

When Bernie came home he worked as a butcher for his parents who owned a small store in one of the declining neighborhoods of Camden, New Jersey. Later on, Bernie bought a tap room (a bar), as they were called in New Jersey, and worked extraordinarily long hours. The neighborhood got more and more dangerous -truly Camden was, by then, an urban war zone. Bernie stayed at it -it was how he, along with Shirlee, worked to make sure their three children could be successful, have a good education, and do better than they did.

Because the kids were already in bed when Bernie came home at night, he put aside Sunday for the family day. He and the family always did something on Sunday, even if it was a simple drive in the car and an ice cream sundae or milkshake. Inexplicably, Bernie did not like chocolate. Butterscotch was his favorite.

Bernie did not wear any of this on his sleeve. He was like many, many others of America's Greatest Generation.

There was a very strong affection that sons like Bernie had for their parents. What they did and saw in World War II stayed away from their parents, their wives and their children. To tell of the terror, the fear and the horror was, for them, impossible.

Bernie, as I said, was a quiet man. He lived a quiet life. He was always on the side of his family, and did what was in his power to do, which is why they loved him so much. He had a long life, and a good one as he would measure it. He served his country well.

There are many like Bernie, I am sure. We will miss Bernie and all the others. I hope we won't forget what they did for us.

AUTHORS

Stephen D. Bryen received his PhD at Tulane University and became an Assistant Professor of Government at Lehigh University. In 1971 he became Executive Assistant to Senator Clifford P. Case (R-NJ) and in 1975 a Professional Staff Member of the Senate Foreign Relations Committee. He served as Deputy under Secretary of Defense in both Reagan administrations and was the founder and first Director of the Defense Technology Security Administration. After leaving government Dr. Bryen was appointed a Commissioner on the US-China Economic Security Review Commission. Later he became the President of Finmeccanica North America. Today he heads SDB Partners LLC and is Chairman of FortressFone Technologies.

Rebecca Abrahams is an award winning veteran network news producer. At ABC News she was the recipient of the Peabody and Edward R. Murrow awards for Excellence in Journalism. She is an experience television producer most notably for her HBO program "Section 60: Arlington National Cemetery." She was a producer for the BBC and Smithsonian Channel of "The Hunt for Bin Laden" and she is the co-creator of the Washington Post's "Live Online."

 **Shoshana Bryen** has more than 30 years of experience as an analyst of US defense policy and Middle East affairs, and has run programs and conferences with American military personnel in various countries. The former Senior Director for Security Policy at the Jewish Institute for National security Affairs (JINSA), Mrs. Bryen was for 17 years author of the widely read and republished JINSA Reports. After serving as JINSA's Executive Director during the 1980s, she focused on planning and running national security related programs and conferences in the US, Israel, Jordan, Taiwan and elsewhere. She has worked with the Strategic Studies Institute of the US Army War College and the Institute for National Security Studies in Tel Aviv, and lectured at the National Defense University in Washington. Her work has appeared in *The Wall Street Journal*, the *New York Sun* and *Defense News*, among other outlets, as well as in JINSA Reports. Currently she is at the Senior Director at the Jewish Policy Center in Washington DC.

Printed in Great Britain
by Amazon.co.uk, Ltd.,
Marston Gate.